TRANSGRESSIVE SEX

Fertility, Reproduction and Sexuality

GENERAL EDITORS:

David Parkin, Director of the Institute of Social & Cultural Anthropology, University of Oxford
Soraya Tremayne, Co-ordinating Director of the Fertility and Reproduction Studies Group and Research Associate at the Institute of Social and Cultural Anthropology, University of Oxford, and a Vice-President of the Royal Anthropological Institute
Marcia Inhorn, William K. Lanman Jr. Professor of Anthropology & International Affairs, & Chair of the Council on Middle East Studies, Yale University

TRANSGRESSIVE SEX

SUBVERSION AND CONTROL IN EROTIC ENCOUNTERS

Edited by

Hastings Donnan and Fiona Magowan

Berghahn Books
New York • Oxford

First published in 2009 by

Berghahn Books

www.BerghahnBooks.com

©2009 Hastings Donnan and Fiona Magowan

Library of Congress Cataloging-in-Publication Data

Transgressive sex : subversion and control in erotic encounters / edited
by Hastings Donnan and Fiona Magowan.
    p. cm. -- (Fertility, reproduction and sexuality ; v. 13)
  Includes bibliographical references and index.
  ISBN 978-1-84545-539-2 (hardback : alk. paper)
  1. Sex customs--Cross-cultural studies. 2. Sex. I. Donnan, Hastings. II.
Magowan, Fiona.

  HQ16.T73 2008
  306.77089--dc22

                              2008046654

British Library Cataloguing in Publication Data

A catalogue record for this book is available
from the British Library.

Printed in the United States on acid-free paper

ISBN: 978-1-84545-539-2 (hardback)

Contents

PREFACE

It is perhaps worth beginning with a short note on how this book came about as both editors have come to the topic from different perspectives. One of us has been working on boundaries and boundary crossing and the other on the performative power of gender through embodiment and body politics. It seemed to us that these two areas might productively be brought together and be illuminating in various ways that appear to be under explored, particularly in relation to the mixing and crossing of gender boundaries and the politics and practices of sexual subversion. The book is the result of our aim to contribute to this small but growing field and each of the chapters tries to draw out several aspects of the many diverse and sometimes fiercely contested perspectives on sexual practices at different times and in different parts of the globe.

We have also tried to capture this multiplicity of perspectives on the crossing of sexual boundaries and their embodiments in the title of the book as well as by its cover which, we hope, encapsulates many of the ironies, preoccupations and contradictions associated with sexual transgression. For instance, it is clear that the cover photograph plays with humour and irony by distorting the objectification of women and the male gaze through exposing various modes of transgression. There are many ways of gazing, and transgression depends upon whose view you consider, in terms of who is looking at whom and in what way. The woman in the photograph is in a dominant pose, even though it may appear that she is being looked at. Yet, the man has had to go undercover in order to gaze, and his attempts at transgression have been exposed in the process. Transgression, then, may not be viewed solely in the male gaze but in the way in which the dynamic between the pair occurs. The exposure of the transgressive act through the man's submissive position at the woman's feet and her dominant stance distort the objectifying power of the man's gaze as both become willing participants in the act of looking at each other and posing for the photograph. This play on humour and irony is just one aspect of the many dimensions of sexual transgression that are explored in this volume.

Hastings Donnan and Fiona Magowan
Belfast, November 2008

CHAPTER 1

SEXUAL TRANSGRESSION,
SOCIAL ORDER AND THE SELF

Hastings Donnan and Fiona Magowan

This book is about sex that crosses or threatens to cross boundaries and about sex acts that flout social, moral and cultural convention. The topic is timely. Never before have we been so exposed to, knowledgeable about and seemingly accepting of the range of sexual practices and activities once known only to professional sexologists or contained in the erotic exotica of anthropologists. Sexual variety and experimentation have now become the everyday fare of teen magazines, television soaps and Internet chat rooms as a titillating tattle that stimulates sales and perhaps much else besides. Anything goes, and the self-gratification of what was yesterday perceived as sexual perversity has been replaced by what today is understood as the self-fulfilment that follows from the practice of sexual diversity.

These developments concern many, particularly those who see in them declining moral standards, and we examine later in the book how moral boundaries are mapped in space, regulated and policed, generating widespread alarm when they are breached and giving rise to strategies of subterfuge, evasion and subversion. But the chapters also variously explore other boundaries: those of sexual imagination and 'good taste' as well as those of the self and the social order, focusing on everything from sex across culture, class, gender and age to sex at the borders between human and animal species. Such sexually transgressive acts arouse passions in more ways than one and the boundaries that are violated or upheld become flashpoints of violent contest and dispute whose study, this book contends, reveals much about how social life is ordered and perceived. These acts are consequently notoriously difficult to investigate and as some of our contributors show their study raises profound methodological and ethical issues for the researcher who observes and records them and who may even become directly involved. Often they can be studied only through long-term, intense engagement with those who practise them, for they are frequently marginalised, hidden or denied, a research focus to which the ethnographic methods of the anthropologists who make up the contributors to this collection are especially well adapted.[1]

The work that follows, then, is the result of close association with those whose practices are described, often over many years of detailed fieldwork and careful elucidation of the broader cultural context within which certain acts take place or particular beliefs are held. Accounts from contemporary Oceania, the Pacific, South Africa and South-east Asia as well as from Euro-America clarify the forms that transgressive sex can take beyond the more usual popular emphasis on the latter and generate the potential for comparative insight into sexual diversity. This can be especially important for public health workers and clinical practitioners, who are primarily concerned with the practical health risks and emotional consequences of some kinds of sexual activity, particularly in relation to the transmission of HIV/AIDS, as well as for those whose sexual practices may put them at risk because of the cultural context in which they occur, as several of the chapters illustrate in the negotiation of gay sexuality in the Cook Islands, France and Poland. So too with the issue of young people and sex that is the central focus of three chapters (on Northern Ireland, England and South Africa), and where an anthropology that is at once localised, comparative and global sheds light on how young people's apparent escalation of sexual involvement at an ever-younger age constitutes a practical challenge not only for youth workers and parents but also for the young people themselves, albeit for different reasons and in different ways. And similarly in the chapters that examine child prostitution in Thailand and sexual violence among Australian Aborigines, forms of sexual transgression that are particularly problematic to address when they straddle the boundary between competing legal and political regimes. In each case explored in this book, the potential for over-pathologising transgressive sex is curbed by paying careful attention to all of the voices involved, including that of the anthropologist (one chapter reflects upon issues for women researchers in encountering sexual transgression during fieldwork). However, before elaborating further on the substantive themes of the chapters, we first consider the kinds of analytical approach and perspective used to study and conceptualise sexual transgression.

Perspectives on transgression

Transgression has been increasingly recognised by social scientists as a key frame of analysis through which to view social and sexual transformations of the world. Sex is a powerful mediator in transgressive contexts, since sexual encounters invoke uneasy tensions between consent, demand, resistance and reciprocity, in which elements of domination, vulnerability, risk and safety all play a part. Transgressive acts, principles and institutions highlight the cultural specificities of sexual intercourse, as the liminal position of transgressors and transgressed challenges possible and desirable sexual interactions. Sex, at first glance, might appear to be a natural bodily phenomenon, but it has been clearly argued that the experience of sexuality is produced through structures of power, knowledge and performance (see Foucault 1980; Butler 1990). Transgressive sexual acts and practices impact upon each other through ludic plays of mirroring. These mirrors of transgressive nonconformity allow us to see through issues of power and control that are variously public and private, implicit and explicit, verbalised and embodied across a range of diverse social structures and cultural forms. Sexual transgression is an enticing and hazardous proposition for reorganising human agency, perception and action as its inherent sense of crossing limits, amplifying margins and repositioning power can extend and transform the boundaries of the social body, social order and the self.

Central to the book's argument is an exploration of how sexual transgression operates at these edges of social boundary maintenance as well as how the ambiguities of the transgressive sexual body lead to processes that may dissolve, transform and reconstitute senses of self, moral action and body politics. By unravelling this nexus the contributors reveal how agents negotiate, deploy, redefine and subvert the performative possibilities of sexual bodies at their transgressive limits. They raise issues of propriety and impropriety around the visible control of sexual acts and interrogate the slipperiness of sexual transgression as an elusive and fluid concept, shimmering precariously at the peripheries of social existence, evoking uncertainty and danger.

Anthropology has long studied sexual acts that cross boundaries and that have the potential to challenge or confirm the moral, legal, social, economic, political, ethnic, racial and other limits in any particular cultural context, even if in the past such acts were not always referred to by the now fashionable term 'transgressive'. So too in sociology a 'weak-kneed version' of transgression (Jenks 2003: 3) was once the focus of a 'sociology of deviance' that in the latter half of the last century spawned numerous qualitative studies of 'deviant subcultures' which violated societal norms and values, such as the subcultures associated with prostitution, promiscuity and pornography (see Gagnon and Simon 1967; Douglas 1970; Bryant 1977). But in anthropology probably the most obvious example is the incest taboo, a prohibition on sexual relations with close kin that was regarded by generations of scholars to be the very basis of a stable social order and the breach of which was thought to entail apocalyptic outcomes for society and humanity. Only the very powerful could flout such sexual prohibitions, as in the classic textbook example of Ptolemaic Egypt, where for thousands of years brother–sister marriages were famously contracted by the ruling dynasties to demonstrate and preserve their wealth and power. Different forms of power and their violation clearly come into play in related kinds of familial sexual transgression, as in parent–child incest, and in other forms of child sexual abuse, including the so-called ritual and satanic abuse in late 1980s Britain. These have also been a focus for anthropological debate, which raised questions about the practice, structure and organisation of power within the family and the household that had a public policy as well as an academic impact (La Fontaine 1990, 1994).

Of course historically anthropologists have studied many other kinds of sexual transgression in addition to incest. Often linked to the exercise and performance of power, such acts could be coercive or consensual, and could define, maintain, blur or transcend the boundaries that they crossed, which were often conceived as the structural boundaries of class or caste, or the racial boundaries across which miscegenation was proscribed, or the boundaries between Europeans and the non-Europeans they colonised and where sexual control was both an instrument and a metaphor of domination (see Stoler 1992). Sexually transgressive roles too have long attracted the anthropological gaze, from early studies of the Plains Indians berdache (or two-spirit) to research on the *travestis*, hijra and *xanith* of Brazil, India and Oman respectively, where the boundaries crossed were not just those of structure but more often those of self. In fact, the transgressive and boundary-transforming potential of so many ways of sexual being from transvestite to transgender to transsexual is now so frequently invoked that the prefix 'trans' is seriously in danger of being overworked.

Drawing on this long-standing interest in anthropology in what now would probably be called 'transgressive sex', the contributors to this book provide new cross-cultural insights into the experiences, practices and moral dilemmas raised by different kinds of sexual transgression, the categorisation of which emerges from the peculiarities of cultural and historical conditioning in each of the places where they undertook fieldwork. Johnson illustrates how the rise of 'perversions' in the West is a product of shifting moral codes variously based upon medical, psychological and pathological explanations. In addition, the global spread of tourism and sex commodification has meant that governments have had to address the deleterious effects of foreign sex trade on children such as in Thailand (Montgomery), while, in Britain, summer funfairs aimed at tourists have become sexual playgrounds for teenagers, who are seen to threaten the moral well-being of the nation (Clisby). Two contributions show how contravening the moral order of public spaces marks the bodies within them as respectable or vulgar (see Roche and Lindegaard and Henriksen), while one analyses how places invite bodily transformations via sexually transgressive encounters (Gaissad). What is considered transgressive may be hotly contested and Cassidy documents how responses in the USA and UK to sex with animals seem to vacillate between legislating against this minority sexual act and apparently condoning it through giving it airtime in the media. Even among those who share sexual orientation and preferences, like the Polish gay and lesbian activists described by Baer, there may be no agreement over what counts as transgressive. In other parts of the world, religion has been instrumental in shaping the concept of transgression and in the Cook Islands, Vanuatu and northern Australia, for example, traditional sexual mores have been variously influenced by modernity and Christianity, ironically inviting sexual licence as much as sexual restriction (Alexeyeff, Kristiansen, Magowan). Finally, one author takes up the challenge of reflecting upon the sexual practices of the anthropologist by considering sexual experiences between transgressors and the transgressed

(Kristiansen). Each of these contributors addresses theoretical concerns in the anthropological literature on transgression whilst also critiquing and extending current perspectives on the relationship between social structure, sexual agency and erotic intersubjectivity.

Theorising transgressive sex

The theoretical possibilities of transgression, in general, and sexual transgression, in particular, have been variously interpreted by anthropologists through breaches of personal and group norms. Transgression has been marked by 'dirt avoidance' and 'sex pollution' (Douglas 1966); 'symbolic inversions' that highlight contradictions in cultural codes (Babcock 1978); and the excesses of classical and grotesque bodies that reveal the mediatory role of the 'carnivalesque'.[2] 'Doubleness' is inherent in this latter instance of bodily transgression as 'there is no unofficial expression without a prior official one or its possibility' (Stallybrass and White 1986: 16).

Since the early Renaissance, transgression has most commonly been analysed as a structural mode of inversion referring to 'a turning upside down' and 'reversal of position, order, sequence, or relation' (OED n.d.: 1477, cited in Babcock 1978: 15). Davis (1978: 177, 182) has argued that, in France and England in the sixteenth and seventeenth centuries, sexual inversion offered positive licence for unruly women to flourish 'on top' through challenging hierarchical structures and playing upon uncertainties in the distribution of power in politics and family life. Such role reversals bring into focus those who have the authority to determine what constitutes the 'inherent dominative mode' (Raymond Williams cited in Stallybrass and White 1986: 4) by unwittingly ensuring that the conditions are set for those who perceive themselves to be inferior to challenge the orthodoxy. Role reversals also operate as a 'means of social control, of social protest, of social change, and of social deviance' (Babcock 1978: 30). Babcock (1978: 22) has noted that studies which draw upon inversion generally imply perversion and primarily homosexuality and that they consider 'role reversals' and '*not* actual sexual practices'. These kinds of structural inequalities move away from performative analyses of transgressors to focus instead upon transgressive schemata in which social class and politics may be seen as mutually reinforcing elements in structural stability or instability.

The study of such structural reversals has a long pedigree in social anthropology, where they were often seen as a social safety valve that functions to contain conflict, and they stretch back to classic accounts of becoming king for a day through to Gluckman's (1970) analyses of 'rituals of rebellion'. Thus Gluckman describes how in certain ritual contexts Zulu women could behave like men, commit public obscenities, go naked and sing lewd songs in a licensed vulgarity that far from subverting the social order confirmed and legitimated it. Although to some early observers such role reversals appeared to challenge the structures of power, Gluckman argued that this behaviour was rarely revolutionary but rather constituted one way in which the social order could be maintained by harnessing the potentially divisive forces of society within a ritual context that permitted their contained expression. The licensed relaxation of the usual constraints thereby merely served to emphasise them, although Gluckman stressed that these reversals were closely regulated by the rituals of which they formed a part and were permitted only when the social order was considered sufficiently resilient not to be endangered by them.

For Gluckman, then, sexual licence in the ritual context was rarely transformative in any more than the sense that it incorporated potential conflict as a functional element of a social order's cohesion and thus reproduced the balanced equilibrium that he considered lay at the heart of the societies he studied. According to many ethnographers, other aspects of popular culture that include role reversals and inversions, such as carnivals and festivals, can similarly be seen as forces of conservatism that reconfirm the existing order, although they may contain within them a utopian and egalitarian radicalism that endures beyond the event itself. The ludic enactments and heightened vulgarities that typify carnival and that are usually conceptualised as a subaltern critique of the dominant structures may be more than mere 'play', and may reflect an agenda with real social and political objectives, but the social order of the day is likely to resume as normal following carnival's temporary transgressions and indignities (and may even be discernible within the carnival itself; see Clisby, this volume). So too with the transgressive behaviours associated with carnival that are transformative of the self. Among the different elements of carnival that anthropologists have emphasised (see Gilmore 1988 for an overview) is the use of masquerade as a licensed cover for ordinarily proscribed bodily acts, whereby participants transformed by mask and costume engage in outlandish sensual and bodily pleasures and obscenities that are otherwise denied, and through which they are 'reborn for new, purely human relations' in a context where all hierarchies and quotidian selves are temporarily suspended (Bakhtin 1984: 10). After the carnival, however, it is very much business as usual, and in the end these transformations of the self are limited as a force for change by virtue of the fact that, located within the structure of carnival, they arise from a conventionalised repertoire of predictable and standardised behavioural violations (Hauser 2006: 141).

In contrast to these structural modes of inversion, theorists of sexual experience, such as Leiris and Bataille, have focused their attention on the emotion and aesthetics of erotic desire in sexual relations by exploring a 'world of play' that leads to the dissolution of the self (Bataille 1986: 275). For Bataille, transgression is not just about breaking rules, but about their completion, since every rule has contained within it the possibility of its violation, and every crossing constitutes its affirmation. As he puts it, 'The transgression does not deny the taboo but transcends it and completes it' (Bataille 1986: 63). In other words, a rule and its transgression are mutually defining. The implications of transgression here are clearly rather different from the 'structural' notion that we have outlined so far, for here transgression is 'not simply a reversal, a mechanical inversion of an existing order it opposes' but entails a mixing of categories and an interrogation of the boundaries that separate them in a process unlikely merely to return us to the status quo (Jervis 1999: 4). According to Bataille, the relationship between taboo and transgression is thus both contingent and dynamic, enabling change while simultaneously ensuring stability, in a process that once again might look as if transgression is necessary to maintain the system, although in this case 'certainly not in functionalist terms' (Jenks 2003: 95, 107).

This volume attempts to engage both these approaches to transgression by exploring inversions and role reversals not only as part of the social, political and cultural conditions of production but also through the erotic nature of transgressive sexual practices and experiences of actors. In other words, the book is concerned with transgressions that focus on structure and those that focus on the self, and with the relations between these. The anthropologist is also implicated in transgressive structures and their agency by reflecting upon thoughts and cultural practices that are located betwixt and between normative and transgressive life worlds of the subjects, both real and imagined. Köpping (2002: 253, 278, italics in original) understands the multiple movements between these mental states as ruptures of self-consciousness that represent '*transcendence beyond transgression*'. He illustrates how the anthropologist may be both 'tricked' and 'seduced' in an effort to know the Other without actually being able to achieve total union with those among whom she or he works, a point to which we return below. He shows how such plays of seduction operate not only in intersubjective relations but in the entanglement of 'intertextuality and intersubjectivity' within fieldwork that can 'shatter' anthropological frames (Köpping 2002: 24).

Sexual transgression in historical perspective

What people consider to be sexually transgressive has always differed in degrees of tolerance within and between societies in spite of the codes of sexual propriety sanctioned by official scientific or state discourse. In the history of the West, the word 'sexuality' and the meanings we attribute to it today appeared in the late nineteenth century when self-gratifying sex was seen as a pejorative act and labelled perverse or deviant, explained through the psychopathology of the patient (Krafft-Ebbing 1965). It has been argued that as perversion emerged as a concept, so, too, did the concept of the pervert when doctors and psychologists moved away from medical explanations of the sexual body to psychiatry in order to articulate and explain the pervert's tastes, impulses, desires and corporeal dispositions (Davidson 1987: 37).

Just as the actor and the act were self-perpetuating in that each reflected the transgressive potential of the other, so categories could be redefined as the rules of the moral order changed. In early scientific accounts, the categories of masochism and sadomasochism were quite unknown to medics and scientists and such sexual acts were viewed as perversions of the social order. In 1629 (or 1639 according to some accounts) John Henry Meibom, a physician of Lubeck, documented a number of cases in which flogging was viewed as a way of generating lust. He notes:

> A citizen of Lubeck, a cheesemonger by trade, was cited before the magistrates, among other crimes, for adultery and the fact being proved, he was banished. A courtesan, with whom this fellow had often an affair, confessed before the Deputies of the State, that he could never have a forcible erection, and perform the duty of a man, till she

had whipped him on the back with rods; and that when
the business was over, that he could not be brought to a
repetition unless excited by a second flogging. (Meibom
1961: 20–21, cited in Davidson 1987: 42)

Yet, where sexual pain and excessive sexual self-pleasure were
once outlawed as religious abomination, physiological
abnormality and psychological debility, in modern times they
have been reconceived in sadomasochistic domains as an
individual's right to transcend more conventional modes of sexual
pleasure and eroticism.

Conflicting discourses of social and moral impropriety around
sexual pleasure and the right to personal satisfaction have proved
problematic throughout history. Johnson (chapter 9) shows how
categories or labels such as 'homosexuality' and 'transgenderism'
that were once viewed as 'perverse' have gradually come to be
seen as essential characteristics of being human, and, as a result,
these reconfigurations have rendered all subjectivities inherently
problematic. While both nineteenth-century sexology and twenty-
first century queer anthropology attempted to overcome
moralising discourses of exclusion, Johnson points out that,
paradoxically, both have highlighted sexual transgression as 'a key
site for' and an 'index of cultural and moral hierarchies' thus
reinscribing the transgendered body as part of a wider moral
framework. Moral discourses have variously construed
transgenderism '*either* as the site of and index for moral degeneracy
and/or sexual pathology *or* as the site of and index for the universal
variability and/or indeterminacy of the sexual subject'.

As we shall see in the chapters throughout this book, the
cultural conditions that shape sexual practices lead to diverse and
contrasting notions of transgression, which the contributors
engage through a consideration of the themes outlined below.

Controlling sexual bodies

Moral boundaries and categories of sexual transgression both
come into being and are made visible through performance.
Transgression takes place in the body and should be recognised as
an effect of bodily experience. All of the chapters in this volume
address the agency of the body as generative of transgressive
feeling, action and attitude. As Köpping (2002: 23) argues: 'the
transformation of ideas cannot occur without the surrender to
practice which is inscribed in our bodies and only expressible or

re-traceable through the sensual encounter with the environment and thus through performative praxis.' Contrary to viewing bodily transgression solely as a symbolic marker of sexual misdemeanour that encodes social principles (Douglas 1966), or as a site upon which the social order works to constrain and discipline social action through the exercise of power (Bourdieu 1977: 14; Foucault 1977a), the contributors to this collection illustrate how transgressive sex is a modality of action in which the body responds through sensory and emotive experiences of interpersonal relations to produce transformative attitudes with the potential to affect social structures.

In transformative bodily processes, actors recognise the existence of taboos that limit their worlds and yet, in violating sexual laws, they bring sexual taboos more vividly into perspective by creating conditions of mental tension and anxiety that give credence to the taboo. It has been argued that as gendered agents, the experience of transgression occurs differently for men and women in heterosexual relationships but a number of writings on transgression assume a male subject as the initiator of transgression who is dependent upon women's self-loss in order that the man may engage in transgression (Foucault 1977b; Bataille 1986). Bataille (1986: 17) notes that:

> The transition from the normal state to that of erotic desire presupposes a partial dissolution of the person as he exists in the realm of discontinuity ... In the process of dissolution, the masculine partner ... has generally an active role, while the feminine partner ... is passive. The passive, female side is essentially the one that is dissolved as a separate entity. But for the male partner the dissolution of the passive partner means one thing only: it is paving the way for a fusion where both are mingled, attaining at length the same degree of dissolution.

Bataille's (1986) theory of eroticism revolves around the ability of one partner to view the other's image as dissolved in the act of transgression. However, as Clisby (chapter 3) demonstrates, this is only one aspect of what makes erotic encounters transgressive for the teenage girls whose feminine being is rendered limitless in the 'seasonal' lover (see also Surkis 1996: 21) when they are seduced by 'summer lads' at the seaside. The age, class and gender of these young, white working-class girls, combined with the hedonistic possibilities of the liminal seaside setting, are central elements in the construction of these acts as defying the limits of 'public

middle-class morality'. The girls themselves proclaim that they
are out to have a good time, and as willing agents put themselves
into the hands of the seasonal visitors to achieve this end. As they
themselves say, 'It's that old notches on the bedpost business ...
let's see how many lads we can get off with this summer.' The
result is widespread moral panic at the rising rates of teenage
pregnancy, thus generating very public ramifications from what is
seen as more than just a private act. Here, the image of
transgressive eroticism is largely shaped by public stereotypes of
what Clisby refers to as the 'abjected working class white girl who
is expected to be promiscuous and simultaneously condemned
for being so'. The result is that some economically deprived areas
of the United Kingdom with high rates of teenage pregnancy
among such women are regarded as 'sink holes' and 'black spots'
in a 'geography of blame' (Russell 2001: 227).

Disclosing sexual behaviour within a restricted group in which
a range of sexually transgressive behaviours is practised may give
rise to negative evaluations but may not result in any prohibitions
being enforced. Lindegaard and Henriksen (chapter 2) illustrate
how young coloured South African women push the boundaries
of sexual respectability with their friends in terms of dress and
deportment whilst upholding a virtuous image for their parents in
order to avoid punishment. The pursuit of 'respectability' is a
central goal for all young women who live in Cape Flats, since
only by being considered respectable is it possible to be part of the
networks of familial support that are critical to everyday life in
this poor coloured township of Cape Town and that ameliorate
the kinds of reproductive vulnerability which Tremayne (2001:
16) suggests are often found where poverty, gender and sexuality
intersect. Respectability is above all a question of behaving
according to the moral norms of the neighbourhood and these
not only forbid sex before marriage, but frown on any act that
draws attention to a young woman's sexuality. Stallybrass and
White (1986: 10) have remarked that 'body-images "speak" social
relations and values with particular force' (see also Köpping 2002:
168) and in the moral context of Cape Flats, where 'every
adolescent sexual act is transgressive', girls must be cautious not
only about where they go and whom they meet, but also about
how they dress, walk and sit. Breasts, buttocks and bearing are all
bodily signs that can be manipulated to indicate sexual abstinence
or availability, and all the young women, but especially those
who are sexually active, must maintain a careful balance between
the two as the situation dictates. Thus, while 'sexually active
virgins' divulge their experiences to a small group of friends, they

sustain a fiction of sexual inactivity before everyone else, creating spaces of sexual visibility and invisibility, disclosure and secrecy in the process, a strategy which in the context of poverty and gender inequality puts them at high risk of practising unsafe sex (see Price and Hawkins 2001).

Similarly, Roche (chapter 4) illustrates how some young women in Derry, Northern Ireland's second largest city, engage in sexual experimentation in 'free houses', away from the gaze and sanction of their parents and a wider public that as in the Clisby case has been gripped by successive moral panics at the increase in teenage sexual activity. Parental homes vacated for a day or weekend and left in the charge of teenage offspring are highly prized by Derry young people as places to host parties that transgress public morality (and in some cases the law) by engaging in underage drinking, drug-taking and sex. However, Roche argues, the boundary between free house and wider society is not as clear-cut as the young people themselves often suggest, since in the free house too rules of appropriateness apply and the behaviour of partygoers is evaluated, tolerated or criticised according to the acceptable 'norms' of teenage sexual practice amongst their peers. Thus it is unacceptable to be seen to be having sex by one's younger siblings, and it is unacceptable to sleep with someone who is in a 'steady relationship' with someone else. While at one level 'public' convention may be flouted through participation in teenage sex 'hidden' in the free house, at another level the 'private' sexual acts that take place there are no less subject to moral codes, though these are made visible only as the boundary between public and private shifts. In the following section we examine this relationship between secrecy, space and visibility more explicitly.

Secrecy, disclosure and spatial transgression

Openness implies visibility but transgressive sex risks public disapproval. Thus, visibility brings into focus the issue of whether increasing openness in sexual experimentation means that practitioners must exercise greater restriction over 'private sexual acts'. As the visibility of transgression creates problems of consensus over acceptable sexual practices, it can cause groups to be mobilised along sexual, religious, ethnic and political lines. For the members of the gay and lesbian movements who have been activists in seeking social and legal recognition, it is the 'public witness' of their sexual preference that arouses anger from those hostile to the movement (see Mason 2001).

As Baer (chapter 7) demonstrates, efforts to raise tolerance for homosexual people in the Polish university town of Wrocław fuelled disagreements about what constituted a common sexual identity amongst gay and lesbian groups. The sexual visibility of these groups, many of whose members felt excluded from public political space, has been viewed as a threat to the established order of academia and government. Spectacular public demonstrations were organised that brought together a broad range of activists with very different perspectives and interests, but participants often remained divided over what constituted appropriate action for Polish gays to take. While some sought a 'safe space' to express their views and sexuality in private, others tried to politicise the sexual act as a radical critique of the wider social, political and economic order. Baer argues that a key problem for gay and lesbian activists is the need to establish a common identity, though their major issue is a lack of public visibility, with most Polish lesbians preferring to stay in the closet. The issue of how homosexuality is perceived is complex, shifting and context-dependent as it variously articulates individual, local and national politics.

'Coming out' raises different issues cross-culturally in part because sexual identity has long been subject to verbal confession as integral to social acceptance. Privacy and its disclosure, then, is an issue of changing others' perceptions about one's sexual preference. Once a declaration has been made about homosexuality, it is difficult to control how others will interpret or perceive that statement (Cohen 1991). A reluctance to disclose sexual preference due to fear of social pressure or rejection has characterised both being in and coming out of the closet of homosexual oppression (Sedgwick 1990: 71–7). Alexeyeff (chapter 6) considers how it is a serious breach of taboo to speak of homosexuality with *laelae* in the Cook Islands despite the fact that homosexuality is hyper-visible and integrated into public, mainstream performance spaces. Flagrant displays of homosexual sex are permitted in such contexts but proscribed in everyday life, which demands subordinating expressions of individual desire to familial and community obligations and responsibilities that are rooted in a conception of personhood based on hereditary and occupational status rather than individualistic sexual orientation. As long as homosexuality is silenced in this way, and even though it is an 'open secret' in situations of 'play', *laelae* can be 'constructed through other aspects of their identity'. In the Cook Islands, transgressive talk is thus the issue rather than transgressive sex, and for *laelae* it is acceptable to show one knows what sexual identity is being performed provided one is quiet about it. Silence is a realm of power that plays a crucial mediating role in endorsing transgressive acts and principles, as silence implies tolerance.

Gaissad (chapter 8) further shows how secrecy and silence around the homosexual body is produced in relation to place through night-time cruising in parks in Toulouse and Marseille. Even though cruising is highly visible, it is shrouded in secrecy by the privacy and darkness of park bushes, and also turns these public spaces into volatile, risky and unsafe places that become restricted to homosexual activities, and that contrast with the comparative safety that characterises gay clubs and bars (Hindle 1994: 11). In determining cruising opportunities and negotiating their safety, these homosexuals become 'body maps' of topographic sexual possibilities: 'a cartographic matrix of practices for surveying, screening and supervising the times, places and ways in which one is manifest as homosexual' (Mason 2001: 32).[3] While these men are continually defying municipal planners by finding new bushes away from newly installed street lighting, or by appropriating derelict buildings, they are also involved in self-surveillance in order to continue their secret homosexuality. Despite intervention efforts by AIDS organisations to educate them on aspects of sexual risk, their avoidance of NGO activities constitutes an 'intentional transgression as a form of resistance' (Cresswell 1996: 23).

Resistance is often expressed in terms of claiming territory through visible demarcation or rewriting such as in the use of sexual graffiti in toilets. Gay men cruising for sex are recreating spaces and places through their sexuality and it is partly the silence and secrecy around their practices that lead to the sense of trespass as they reverse the normative use of public spaces for private acts. Even when social sanctions occur, and spaces of transgression such as car parks or bushes are reclaimed for public use, other areas offer the potential for transgressive action instead. As Cresswell (1996: 175) notes, 'Transgression's efficacy lies in the power of the established boundaries and spaces that it so heretically subverts. It is also limited by this established geography; it is always in reaction to topographies of power.' Even though these particular transgressions are transient, the cyclical, repetitive nature of night-time cruising is seen as permanent, attracting the attention of policymakers and health workers, who demand social transformation or sanction, and whose own actions are seen as transgressing the rules of secrecy and consensual silence adhered to by those engaged in acts of anonymous homosexual sex. Human bodies and the social body then are simultaneously written into the topographic map determining trajectories of possible social elevation or demise. Whether it is hiding the truth of one's sexuality or making sexual identities visible, bodies are culturally ordered according to evaluative measures (Mason 2001: 26, 35). In this process, the spaces in which transgressions occur, like those who are categorised within them, are subject to change.

In the West, the fact that heterosexual marriage has been viewed traditionally as the norm means that heteroerotic desires have proved to be unproblematic forms of sexuality (see Mason 2001: 26). Yet 'common' perceptions of heterosexual, one-on-one consensual, private sexual intercourse as the dominant mode of sexuality are contradicted by the possibilities afforded by a range of alternative sexual identities such as 'porn queens', 'dominatrix', 'swingers', and so forth. What constitutes transgression for some is regarded as insufficiently transgressive for others, and there is little agreement over what are the relevant boundaries to challenge. Changes in the way practices are categorised are as much due to the kinds of sexual experimentation involved as they are to the sexual identities of the people who occupy those categories. In a process that Hacking (1984: 122) has called 'dynamic nominalism', the human sciences 'bring into being new categories which, in part, bring into being new kinds of people'. One such category is 'zoosex', in which the boundaries have been stretched to include not only inter- and intra-sex intercourse but interspecies intercourse. As Cassidy (chapter 5) argues, the 'zoosex' that became publicly visible in the 1990s constitutes just one of many possible relationships with animals in a continuum of human–animal engagements that have been prohibited or endorsed across a range of cultural contexts depending upon specific historical conjunctures. For example, she narrates how, in sixth- and seventh-century Europe, bestiality was thought to be comparable to masturbation, whilst in 2005 in Missouri a 1685 law was enforced to prohibit bestiality and efforts were made throughout the US to discourage its increasing presence on the Web and in the media. That interspecies sex can coexist alongside outraged reaction to such acts reflects the absence of an agreed distinction between humans and animals and the wide variety of often conflicting and contradictory attitudes to animals that characterises Euro-America. This is the context, then, within which the parallel and opposing trends of secrecy and disclosure to which such acts are subject must be understood, and which makes, as Cassidy says, human–animal sex a 'peculiarly productive space' within which to explore the relationships between humans and animals and between morality and sexuality more broadly. Even in these newly recognised arenas of sexual experimentation, cultures only permit certain levels of change to occur to the social body, and even these must be vetted and verified in a public form. Just as interspecies sex expands boundaries of sexual experimentation, so certain kinds of licence that challenge established boundaries of acceptable and unacceptable sexual behaviours may be permitted in ritual contexts, as we consider next.

Double inversions: non-transgressive transgressions

The notion of the festive is one that highlights bodily excess, whether in extravagant celebration, lavish ritual or displays of debauchery, and in doing so brings into focus the pollution in the holy (Douglas 1966) and the interconnectedness of what have often been seen as opposing forces. However, festivals and rituals are highly ambivalent domains in which reversals of social norms do not always or necessarily contradict each other but may reinforce one another. Thus, ritual allows social boundaries to be dissolved at the same time as it highlights the integral nature of boundaries to the process of their dissolution (Babcock-Abrahams 1975).

Discursive norms exist for the control of sexual transgression as much as for normative sexuality and thus there is a 'complementarity of symbols in a given classificatory scheme' rather than a set of opposing characteristics (Köpping 2002: 167). Each is entailed in the other and so it is not surprising that what was once transgressive may become normative and vice versa. In some cultures, transgressive rituals serve to enforce normative sexual laws so that not to engage in ritual sex acts would be transgressive. For example, amongst the Sambia of Papua New Guinea, transgressive ritual sex is the norm where male fellatio is required as part of initiation into manhood. If young boys resist ritual fellatio it is seen as transgressive and 'men threaten castration and murder if they break these taboos' (Herdt 1987: 233). These ritual periods of transgression are ephemeral and their 'excesses are curbed by a framework: it consists of ceremonialism and form, or etiquette, or again of different kinds of preparations, from ascetic, physical and spiritual exercises to sexual abstinence' (Köpping 2002: 122). Consequently, the transgressive sexual body cannot exist permanently at the limits of transgression since it is always paradoxically entrapped by 'excess and enclosure which constitute it simultaneously' (Libertson 1977: 1005).

Similarly, Australian Aboriginal communities traditionally have set stringent controls over sexuality taught and imposed throughout life via a series of rituals that included circumcision for boys and puberty rites for girls. Magowan (chapter 11) argues that, with the demise of youth involvement in ritual and increasing exposure to Western influences, it has become harder for Aboriginal families to discipline youth and manage sexuality. Where ritual once required women to have sex with men other than their husbands – so that refusal to transgress in this way was regarded as transgressive – this is no longer practised. The impact of Australian sexual values has meant that 'love marriages' between couples are fairly common, although men still hold the right to take an underage wife by arranged marriage. Where resistance to this by teenagers has led to domestic violence, they have sought alternative forms of protection under Australian jurisdiction. Conflicts between Indigenous customary law and Western judicial rulings pose major dilemmas around the meaning of sexual transgression. Rape is difficult to establish because traditional notions of honour and respectability for kin are such that women are made responsible for the possibility of inviting shame upon a family, even when sexual violence has occurred. Thus, closure is not always possible between two laws, since the repercussions for families which step outside the remit of customary law may have ongoing effects beyond the jurisdiction of the courts. As in Australia, conflicts between international law and local judicial processes in Thailand have posed major dilemmas around the meaning of sexual transgression.

International surveillance has meant that not only are local audiences formulating opinions about how sexual transgression should be dealt with but, in some cases, international pressure has been brought to bear upon countries which do not enforce strict enough controls over sexual exploitation, especially where structural and power inequalities mark the relationship between transgressor and transgressed. Montgomery (chapter 10) details how an explosion in the commercial exploitation of Thai children for sex by Western men abroad has meant that these men may be prosecuted within their own home countries. She argues that the focus on the unacceptable behaviour of Western men meant that Thailand was 'absolved of any guilt for allowing or encouraging certain forms of prostitution' and at the same time it played upon 'Western fears about paedophilia and child abuse'. The campaign against child prostitution became a symbol for all that was 'wrong' with contemporary Thailand, and a metaphor for what were seen as the many other negative effects of Western influence. Yet, while the commercial sexual exploitation of children by foreign men became the 'defining image of transgressive sex in Thailand', and a banner under which many different national and international interests could rally, other forms of sexual abuse involving children were largely overlooked. Thus, at the same time as Asian countries clamped down on international sex tourists to assuage foreign feelings of revulsion, Thai officials were complicit in condoning underage prostitution along their country's border with Burma where they allowed young Burmese girls to work on the Thai side so that Burmese men would not frequent Thai prostitutes, the possibility of which they regarded as inappropriate and culturally repugnant. As Montgomery clearly shows, not all forms of commercial sex with children were 'transgressive', and what in Thailand counted as transgression was shaped by a mix of moral, political and economic imperatives both within and beyond the country itself.

The anthropologist tricked, trickster or Peeping Tom?

By engaging the issues posed by sexual transgression, the anthropologist may be implicated in moral judgements about transgressive practices. Such engagements operate along a continuum from advocating in international legal contexts to engaging in intimate relationships in local field research, inviting potentially conflicting roles. The roles of the anthropologist as trickster, as strategist and as reflexive field analyst have been delineated in a number of studies, from Clifford and Marcus's *Writing Culture* (1986) to Rao and Hutnyk's *Celebrating Transgression* (2006), although anthropologists' involvement in sexual transgression is one area that has received relatively little attention despite calls for a more self-conscious anthropology of the erotic dimension of fieldwork (Newton 1993). One exception is *Taboo*, a collection of essays that sets out to examine 'sex, identity and erotic subjectivity' in the field (Kulick and Willson 1995). However, based on his reading of *Taboo*, Köpping (1998) remains sceptical of the value of reflecting on sexual transgression in the field and of the intellectual insights to be gained from sexual intimacy between ethnographer and native. Such accounts, he argues, are far too likely to focus on the self than to produce novel understandings of the people studied or of the ethnographer's own cultural world, and in *Taboo*, he suggests, we learn more about the authors' own sexuality than we do about the sexuality of those with whom they became sexually involved. In fact, Köpping continues, sexual relationships in the field may be counterproductive for the anthropologist, and make the research more difficult than might otherwise have been the case, thereby underlining the benefits of the 'original' fieldwork strategy of celibacy.

Of course, unlike Morton and Dubisch, upon whose chapters in *Taboo* Köpping chiefly focuses, not all fieldworkers have a choice about their sexual engagement in the field, so that analysis of the reasons such involvement comes about can be revealing, particularly when the views of all the parties concerned can be included. Deceit and trickery have been highlighted as deliberate strategies of pretence and duplicity in some instances (see Köpping 2002), although transgressors and anthropologists may also be duped or delude themselves about the nature of their actions. Kristiansen (chapter 12) shows how sexual invitation and 'positioning' may be misrecognised between the anthropologist and her male informants in Vanuatu, leading to cross-cultural ambiguities and anomalies in interpretations of sexual consent and force. Kristiansen demonstrates how an understanding of the performative and practical dimensions of transgression – rather than its purely discursive possibilities – is critical to the analysis of deceit, trickery or delusion between the anthropologist and her informants. In a series of unsolicited sexual encounters, she shows how her actions were read as sexual invitations leading her to rethink notions of intersubjectivity and friendship in the fieldwork process. Writing elsewhere about anthropological transformations of understanding in the field, Köpping (2002: 21) notes how 'an interweaving of intertextuality in the head and intersubjectivity in field practices ... leads to a transformation of one through the other in a never-ending process of the performative switch from action to reflection and back'.

In this 'switch from action to reflection' we are led back to Bataille, for whom transgressive sexuality was as central to his life as it was to his writing, and whose theories of eroticism and transgression drew extensively on the libidinous pleasures and desires of his personal experience. As Jenks (2003: 95) points out, this can be 'quite shocking or playfully transgressive according to whether the reader wishes to turn away or engage', and some passages in Bataille do indeed provide disturbing examples of darkly transgressive composition that encourage us to reflect on what we write and publish. Malinowski's diaries certainly raised eyebrows when they first appeared and we have already noted how publication of *Taboo* led some to wonder if writing about 'one of the most intimate encounters possible in the field serves any useful purpose beyond the titillation for a salacious audience which laps up such stories' (Köpping 1998: 10). Those who read work about sexual transgression (in the field or anywhere else) may also come to feel or be regarded as themselves transgressive, as if the very act of reading made them complicit in the deed itself by offering it an audience. Something of this is apparent in Crapanzano's (2004) essay on 'The Transgressive and the Erotic' where he describes in explicit detail the autoerotic acts of Billy-George, a cross-dresser crippled by polio and suffering from a rare skin disease. Reading Crapanzano's (2004: 130–32) account, we are put 'into the position of an intruder, a peeping-tom' as we 'watch' Billy-George enact his sexual fantasies in his home surrounded by sadomasochistic drawings and a collection of Barbie dolls used as props in his violent and pornographic stories. 'Caught in his performance', our reading about it (and Crapanzano's writing of it) may amplify and mirror its transgressive effect.

Conclusion

In some ways, sexual transgression is like a series of mirrors as the extension of one transgression leads to other transgressions, which are then reflected back onto and through public opinion, as well as through social practice and understanding. Information technologies have been instrumental in this transformation, reconfiguring perceptions of transgressive sex by providing access to highly eroticised sexual imagery and consumer demand for a wide range of sex products. Technological innovations have opened up exponential possibilities for sexual communication via Internet chat sites, porn sites, mobile phones and dating sites. As a consequence, the boundaries of transgressive behaviour, emotions and sensualities are continually being challenged and extended. What was once considered taboo and sexually inappropriate is becoming normalised and normalising as 'transgressive sex' enters conventional cultural discourses. Ascriptions of 'perverse' sex acts or eroticised perceptions of the body are also continually evolving in societies that lean towards increasing openness. Openness, in turn, is transformative of the sexual and intersubjective body that must continually re-establish itself within conflictual spaces of sexual negotiation.

While there is a transformative power in sexual openness that can reorganise perceptions of boundary maintenance and bodily porosity, there are also exceptions to the rule where the possibility of increasing openness leads to a 'double inversion' as people seek more conventional ways of expressing sexual desire. A proliferation of transgressive acts can, in fact, lead to a reversal of openness and, despite ongoing access to transgressive possibilities, people and governments may push for policies to control sexual practices either because of pressures upon how they are perceived or because of deleterious effects of sexual transgressions upon society. All the chapters in this volume comment on the relationship between public and private in relatively more open or closed modes of sexual permissiveness and show that sexual selves are in some cases extended and changed, while in others they are constrained and subjugated to the rules of social action in new forms.

Notes

1. Six of the chapters in this collection were first presented as conference papers at a panel on 'Transgressive Sex, Transforming Bodies' at the European Association of Social Anthropologists' Eighth Biennial Conference in Vienna in September 2004. The remaining chapters were specially commissioned to extend the geographical scope and thematic range of the volume. We would like to thank Marion Berghahn, Soraya Tremayne and the anonymous referees for their comments and suggestions when preparing the papers for publication.
2. See, for example, Stallybrass and White's (1986) deconstruction of Bakhtinian notions of 'high' and 'low' culture.
3. Mason (2001: 32) argues that homosexuals deal with the specific problem of homophobic violence through the concept of the body map.

References

Babcock, B. 1978. *'The Reversible World: Symbolic Inversion in Art and Society.* London and Ithaca: Cornell University Press.

Babcock-Abrahams, B. 1975. 'A Tolerated Margin of Mess', *Journal of the Folklore Institute* 11: 147–86.

Bakhtin, M.M. 1984. *Rabelais and His World*. Bloomington: Indiana University Press.

Bataille, G. 1986. *Eroticism: Death and Sensuality*, trans. M. Dalwood. San Francisco: City Lights.

Bourdieu, P. 1977. *Outline of a Theory of Practice*. Cambridge: Cambridge University Press.

Bryant, C.D. (ed.). 1977. *Sexual Deviancy in Social Context*. New York: New Viewpoints.

Butler, J. 1990. *Gender Trouble: Feminism and the Subversion of Identity*. London: Routledge.

Clifford, J. and G. Marcus. 1986. *Writing Culture: the Politics and Poetics of Ethnography*. Berkeley: University of California Press.

Cohen, E. 1991. 'Who Are "We"? Gay "Identity" as Political (E)motion (A Theoretical Rumination)', in D. Fuss (ed.) *Inside/Out: Lesbian Theories, Gay Theories.* New York: Routledge, pp. 71–92.

Crapanzano, V. 2004. *Imaginative Horizons: an Essay in Literary–Philosophical Anthropology.* Chicago: Chicago University Press.

Cresswell, T. 1996. *In Place/Out of Place: Geography, Ideology, and Transgression.* London and Minneapolis: University of Minnesota Press.

Davidson, A.I. 1987. 'Sex and the Emergence of Sexuality', *Critical Inquiry* 14 (Autumn): 16–48.

Davis, N.Z. 1978. 'Women on Top: Symbolic Sexual Inversion and Political Disorder in Early Modern Europe', in B. Babcock (ed.) *The Reversible World: Symbolic Inversion in Art and Society.* London and Ithaca: Cornell University Press, pp. 147–89.

Douglas, J.D. (ed.). 1970. *Observations of Deviance.* New York: Random House.

Douglas, M. 1966 [1980]. *Purity and Danger: an Analysis of the Concepts of Pollution and Taboo.* London: Routledge and Kegan Paul.

Foucault, M. 1977a. *Discipline and Punish: the Birth of the Prison*, trans. A. Sheridan. New York: Vintage Books.

———. 1977b. 'A Preface to Transgression', trans. D.F. Bouchard and S. Simon, in D.F. Bouchard (ed.) *Michel Foucault: Language, Counter-memory, Practice: Selected Essays and Interviews.* Ithaca, NY: Cornell University Press, pp. 751–69.

———. 1980. *Power/Knowledge: Selected Interviews and Other Writings, 1972–1977*, ed. C. Gordon, trans. C. Gordon, L. Marshall, J. Mepham, K. Soper. New York: Pantheon.

Gagnon, J.H. and W. Simon (ed.). 1967. *Sexual Deviance.* New York: Harper and Row.

Gilmore, D. 1988. *Carnival and Culture: Sex, Symbol and Status in Spain.* New Haven, CT: Yale University Press.

Gluckman, M. 1970 [1956]. *Custom and Conflict in Africa.* Oxford: Basil Blackwell.

Hacking, I. 1984. 'Five Parables', in R. Rorty, J.B. Schneewind and Q. Skinner (eds) *Philosophy in History: Essays on the Historiography of Philosophy.* Cambridge: Cambridge University Press, pp. 103–24.

Hauser, B. 2006. 'Divine Play or Subversive Comedy? Reflections on Costuming and Gender at a Hindu Festival', in U. Rao and J. Hutnyk (eds) *Celebrating Transgression: Method and Politics in Anthropological Studies of Culture. A Book in Honour of Klaus Peter Köpping.* Oxford: Berghahn, pp. 129–44.

Herdt, G. 1987. *Guardians of the Flutes: Idioms of Masculinity.* New York: Columbia University Press.

Hindle, P. 1994. 'Gay Communities and Gay Space in the City', in S. Whittle (ed.) *The Margins of the City: Gay Men's Urban Lives.* Aldershot: Ashgate Publishing, pp. 7–25.

Jenks, C. 2003. *Transgression.* London: Routledge.

Jervis, J. 1999. *Transgressing the Modern: Explorations in the Western Experience of Otherness.* Oxford: Blackwell.

Köpping, K.P. 1998. 'Bodies in the Field: Sexual Taboos, Self-revelation and the Limits of Reflexivity in Anthropological Fieldwork (and Writing)', *Anthropological Journal of European Cultures* 7 (1): 7–26.
———. 2002. *Shattering Frames: Transgression and Transformations in Anthropological Discourse and Practice.* Berlin: Dietrich Reimer Verlag.
Krafft-Ebbing, R. 1965. *Psychopathia Sexualis, with Especial Reference to the Antipathic Sexual Instinct: a Medico-forensic Study,* trans. F.S. Klaf. New York: Stein & Day.
Kulick, D. and M. Willson (eds). 1995. *Taboo: Sex, Identity and Erotic Subjectivity in Anthropological Fieldwork.* London: Routledge.
La Fontaine, J.S. 1990. *Child Sexual Abuse.* Cambridge: Polity Press.
———. 1994. *The Extent and Nature of Organised and Ritual Abuse: Research Findings.* London: HMSO.
Libertson, J. 1977. 'Excess and Imminence: Transgression in Bataille', *Comparative Literature* 92 (5): 1001–23.
Mason, G. 2001. 'Body Maps: Envisaging Homophobia, Violence and Safety', *Social and Legal Studies* 10 (1): 23–44.
Meibom, J.H. 1961. *On the Use of Flogging in Venereal Affairs.* Chester, PA.
Newton, E. 1993. 'My Best Informant's Dress: the Erotic Equation in Fieldwork', *Cultural Anthropology* 8 (1): 2–23.
Price, N. and K. Hawkins. 2001. 'Young People's Sexual and Reproductive Health: Towards a Framework for Action', in S. Tremayne (ed.) *Managing Reproductive Life: Cross-cultural Themes in Sexuality and Fertility.* Oxford: Berghahn Books, pp. 194–220.
Rao, U. and J. Hutnyk (eds). 2006. *Celebrating Transgression: Method and Politics in Anthropological Studies of Culture. A Book in Honour of Klaus Peter Köpping.* Oxford: Berghahn.
Russell, A. 2001. 'Teenage Pregnancy and the Moral Geography of Teesside, UK', in S. Tremayne (ed.) *Managing Reproductive Life: Cross-cultural Themes in Sexuality and Fertility.* Oxford: Berghahn Books, pp. 221–34.
Sedgwick, E. 1990. *Epistemology of the Closet.* Berkeley: University of California Press.
Stallybrass, P. and A. White. 1986. *The Politics and Poetics of Transgression.* Ithaca, NY: Cornell University Press.
Stoler, A. 1992. 'Sexual Affronts and Racial Frontiers: European Identities and the Cultural Politics of Exclusion in Colonial Southeast Asia', *Comparative Studies in Society and History* 34 (3): 514–51.
Surkis, J. 1996. 'No Fun and Games Until Someone Loses an Eye: Transgression and Masculinity in Bataille and Foucault', *Diacritics* 26 (2): 18–30.
Tremayne, S. 2001. 'Introduction', in S. Tremayne (ed.) *Managing Reproductive Life: Cross-cultural Themes in Sexuality and Fertility.* Oxford: Berghahn Books, pp. 17–29.

CHAPTER 2

SEXUALLY ACTIVE VIRGINS: NEGOTIATING ADOLESCENT FEMININITY, COLOUR AND SAFETY IN CAPE TOWN

*Marie Rosenkrantz Lindegaard and
Ann-Karina Henriksen*

In South Africa, adolescent girls are subject to stringent social and moral controls over the management of their sexuality and sexual practices (Mørck 1998; Gammeltoft 2002; Salo 2004). In the poor, coloured townships of Cape Town, discourses of respectability and virginity render adolescent femininity safe. As adolescent girls become sexually mature, they enter a morally contested space in which they must deny their emerging sexuality by demonstrating sexual restraint. Such restraint secures their 'social safety' by ensuring that they are accepted into the wider networks of kin and neighbours that underwrite daily life in the townships. Although respectability is a signifier for women of all ages, this chapter will focus primarily on how respectability informs the everyday dispositions of adolescent girls.

In the moral landscape in which these girls live, every adolescent sexual act is transgressive, because it subverts the notion of respectability that underpins local networks of economic and social support. We examine this contested space by looking at the moral discourses about young girls' behaviour in public, and about their involvement in sexual activity. We argue

that the maintenance of 'respectability' and 'virginity' are crucial
to the social safety of adolescent girls, whose sexual welfare may
be compromised if they do not behave according to these moral
precepts. Yet, at the same time, the need to be seen as
'respectable' and sexually innocent can lead to ignorance, the
outcome of which is a failure to practise safe sex, and this
eventually puts girls at risk of HIV/AIDS and teenage pregnancy.

Respectability is analysed as a discourse of asexual femininity,
which can be traced back to the historical and political
construction of the local coloured population. Respectability
informs the lived experiences of South African women partly as
something they are, i.e. as embodied knowledge (see Bourdieu
1990), and partly as something created through bodily discourse
(see Butler 1993). We show how girls negotiate others'
perceptions of the tension between their asexual and sexual
subjectivities and how they express their sexual awareness in
sexual practices. Finally, we discuss how wider cultural notions of
respectability in South Africa become a form of symbolic violence,
that jeopardises adolescent girls' ability to negotiate safe sex.

Being or becoming respectable

Like gender and race, respectability is not a fixed category or
something you are, but is something you do. However, this
approach to respectability cannot always account for how young
coloured women in Cape Town themselves see respectability, for
they do sometimes experience it as a 'fixed' condition that they can
do nothing about. Some young Cape Town women, for example,
complain that they are regarded as disreputable whatever they do,
so that an absence of respectability is experienced by them as part
of their very being. Drawing on Butler (1993) and Bourdieu
(2001), we try to incorporate into our analysis both these aspects of
respectability, combining a consideration of respectability as
something enacted with local South African perceptions of it as
something you are. Butler and Bourdieu represent two different
approaches to gender and thus different views on how to approach
respectability. Their varying perceptions of gender are
distinguishable in their writings on the body.

Butler (1993) argues that the body is a blank surface that is
only ascribed meaning through discourse. Outside discourse, the
body is seen as an object but it gains subjectivity within discourse,
i.e. a girl is not a girl, but gendered discourses invite her to
become a girl. The body is thus understood as regulated and

subjectivised through discourse, and the meaning attached to the body changes according to discursive constructions. Analysing respectability as articulated through discourse opens up a dynamic perspective on gender as contextual and negotiable and as a process of becoming rather than being. Bourdieu (2000) provides a different perspective by drawing attention to the inertness of subject positions. His approach to gender is preoccupied with power and reproduction. Many contemporary feminist scholars have characterised his approach as simplistic and objectivist due to its lack of any interpretative element (Järvinen 1999: 31; McNay 2004: 183). Bourdieu (2000), on the other hand, has criticised the constructivist feminists, such as Butler, for their 'linguistic universalism', where gender is perceived as a discursive construction with no social or historical specificity: 'It is naïve, even dangerous to suppose and suggest that one only has to "deconstruct" these social artefacts in a purely performative celebration of "resistance" in order to destroy them' (Bourdieu 2000: 108).

Bourdieu (2001) approaches gender as a material relationship between dominant (men) and dominated (women) and not as a symbolic construction, where the relationship is one of recognition and misrecognition. This approach is related to his understanding of the body as a path of access, loaded with meaning, which is deeply inherent in the body. Bourdieu (2001) refers to the embodied version of accumulated experiences (habitus) as 'hexis': 'Bodily hexis ... is assumed to express the "deep being", the true "nature" of the "person", in accordance with the postulate of the correspondence between the "physical" and the "moral" which gives rise to the practical or rationalized knowledge whereby "psychological" or "moral" properties are associated with bodily or physiognomic indices' (Bourdieu 2001: 64). Bodily hexis is the way people 'carry' their body, the way they walk, talk, eat or run, and it is through hexis, Bourdieu argues, that social categories such as class, sexuality, gender, race and age are expressed. Respectability and the maintenance of racialised bodies is an example of such embodied knowledge and practice. Bodily hexis is not written on the surface of the body, but is deeply grounded in its very being, expressed in every move and part of the corporeal disposition. Class, gender and race are embedded in the body and provide analytical possibilities for understanding social categories ascribed through discourse, including the potential to misrecognise the power and impact these categories have in people's lived existence (see Bourdieu and Wacquant 1992). However, in Bourdieu's approach to gender there is limited space for interpretation and negotiation, that is, for people to carry their bodies in different ways depending on shifting contexts. In most of Bourdieu's other writing this would be accounted for through his concept of field; the body engages in different fields and is thereby articulated in different ways. In regard to gender the dynamic of the field is left out of his writing (Lovell 2000: 18).

Søndergaard's (1996: 89) concept of 'bodily signs', which is inspired by semiotics, emphasises the importance of recognising the shifting meanings of the material body and thus acknowledges both Butler's and Bourdieu's approaches to gender. When colour is ascribed to a body, it has material consequences for how this body can interact in particular situations. Søndergaard (1996) perceives the body as marked by signs, although these signs are not visible in all contexts. Studying 'bodily signs' instead of 'bodies' emphasises that having a biologically female body marked by female signs is not necessarily the same as always being perceived as feminine. Adolescent girls are marked by signs of sexual maturity, which can be manipulated, altered, made highly visible or invisible depending on the context of their engagement. Bodily signs, such as breasts, hips, buttocks, lips, long hair, maturity, colour of skin, ways of walking and sitting and ways of looking at other people provide different possibilities for expressing sexualised or asexualised femininity.

Cape Flats: the dark side of Cape Town

This chapter is based on five months' fieldwork carried out in the first half of 2003 in Heideveld, a predominantly coloured residential area on the outskirts of Cape Town. During apartheid, coloured and black people were forced to live outside the city centre, and the sandy, barren land surrounding Cape Town was designated as a non-white residential area. During the 1950s, the area known as Cape Flats was populated through forced removals and rural–urban migration, and developed into racially segregated black and coloured residential zones. Today a lack of economic resources, rather than a discriminating political system, prevents residents from moving elsewhere. In the public imagination, Cape Flats is known mostly for its gang wars and high rates of domestic and sexual violence (Jensen 2000; Salo 2000; Gibson 2003). However, Cape Flats is highly heterogeneous in terms of income level, population density, forms of housing and levels of violence. Some residents have escaped apartheid-inflicted poverty and, by improving their level of education and income, have moved from shacks or communal housing to owner-occupied single-family dwellings in the same residential area.

The girls described in this chapter live in an area on the Cape Flats characterised by poverty and high rates of violence. During fieldwork, gang warfare claimed the life of at least one gang member a week. The area houses about 20,000 people, most of whom live in two-room flats shared with ten to fifteen other family members. The research was carried out at a high school using semi-structured interviews, workshops, focus groups, questionnaires and photography. The most intensive study was undertaken among girls in the fifteen to nineteen age group. We also visited students in their homes and accompanied girls and their friends to the local shopping malls and clubs.

Constructions of Cape coloureds

The racial constructions of the apartheid regime are still significant in Cape Town. The political construction of the category 'coloured' is central to understanding the dispositions of the young girls. During apartheid, coloureds were constructed as being in between whites and blacks, as both a metaphorical and a spatial buffer zone. This was evident in the workplace and in residential areas, where coloured neighbourhoods separated blacks from whites. Being coloured implied striving to 'become' white through a range of practices that created proximity to whiteness rather than blackness (Wicomb 2000: 4). Coloured bodies could signal being more or less civilised by a light tone of skin, straight rather than curly hair and choosing clothes, food and drinks preferred by whites. Coloured women were perceived as responsible and as having the capacity to save the group as a whole from becoming like the local black population (Jensen 2001; Salo 2003). In contrast, the stereotype of coloured men, in black, white and coloured imagination, was characterised by lazy, drunken and criminal behaviour (Jensen 2001: 63). As a result, it was coloured women rather than coloured men who were entrusted with the health and well-being of their home and family and who received the welfare support from the state (Salo 2003: 349; Steinberg 2004: 113). Responsibility became a core attribute of acceptable femininity among coloured women.

The process of 'becoming' white through the ways in which the body is presented in public is still evident amongst the coloured residents today. However, it is a highly embodied practice of adhering to 'good' taste (see Bourdieu 1984), rather than a conscious attempt to deny one's racial background. For example, many coloured people now regard it simply as fashionable to straighten one's hair, rather than as an effort to be seen as white (Erasmus 2001: 17). Many coloured boys still struggle to overcome the stereotypical image of the lazy and criminal coloured man, and girls struggle to uphold ideals of respectability (Henriksen and Lindegaard 2004).

Staging coloured femininity through photography

Halfway through the fieldwork we supplied a group of girls with disposable cameras. We asked them to take photographs of people and places in their everyday lives that made them feel both comfortable and uncomfortable. The photographs focused on the negative aspects of their daily lives. They took photographs of gangs selling drugs in playgrounds, young boys flashing money and guns, women drinking and gambling accompanied by their children, girls hanging out on street corners and pregnant teenagers. Their comments on the pictures provided valuable insights into how negative representations of coloureds (Steinberg 2004: 113) continue to be reproduced and used to create social distinctions in their lives.

Many of the photographs are staged to represent the reality in which the girls live. Figure 2.1 shows a woman standing in her living room drinking beer. The photographer made her neighbour

Figure 2.1. *The* sleg *woman*

Figure 2.2. *Drinking and gambling in a* shebeen

pose with the beer, because as she explained: 'This is what she always does. Also there are always fights in her house. She is a *sleg* woman.' The participants distinguished between *ordentlike*, which is Afrikaans for 'respectable', and *sleg* women, which means 'bad' women. The distinction is used to describe an array of female behaviours seen as either morally acceptable or reprehensible. *Ordentlike* women are essentially responsible housewives who take care of domestic chores, keep a clean and tidy house, take good care of the children, attend church and display bodily, emotional and social self-control. *Ordentlike* women are never drunk or loud in public; they are only present outside their homes during the day and are always accompanied by friends.

Gambling is another recurring theme in the photographs. Gambling has been connected to negative representations of coloureds as far back as the early twentieth century, along with dancing and singing in the street, drunkenness, violence and sexual promiscuity (Ross 1999: 55). Figure 2.2 shows a group of men and a woman sitting in a tin shack playing dominoes, with a child idly watching them. The photographer comments on the photo: 'Gambling is a big problem here. It usually happens at the *shebeen* [local bar]. The women are particularly drunk and that is what children get to see.' The presence of the child makes the photograph significant, because it underlines the irresponsibility of the woman and exposes her as a *sleg*. The photographs thus reproduce the discourse of the *sleg* coloured women, while they

Figure 2.3. *Diana the 'taxi queen'*

also reflect the photographers' attempts to distance themselves and communicate their adherence to a different femininity, as *ordentlike* women.

Among peers the undeniable marker of respectability is the management of sexuality and sexual bodies. Figure 2.3 shows two girls smoking on a balcony and one of the girls is allegedly a taxi queen. Taxi queens are girls who date taxi drivers and spend many hours driving with them in the taxi dressed up in fashionable clothes, SMS-ing on their new cellphones. The girls are provided for and bought expensive clothes in return for sexual favours. Among peers they are both admired for their clothes, money and mobility and looked down upon for their overt sexual activities. The photographer spoke at length and in great detail about the sexual history of the alleged taxi queen, exposing the level of gossip pertaining to the sexual lives of young girls. The significance of gossip was expressed in many other contexts too, and gossip mainly revolved around sexual partners and activities, along with real or imagined pregnancies. Figure 2.4 is a staged picture of two pregnant girls. As the photographer said: 'This represents one of the big problems in Heideveld. These two girls are only fifteen and sixteen years old and already pregnant. They are not even married and now their future is spoiled. They cannot continue with school.' Placed in front of a plastic couch, the girls are made to testify to their *sleg* behaviour. Looking slightly guilty they become representations of teenage promiscuity as examples not to be followed. Their clothes are also

Figure 2.4. *Teenage pregnancy*

at odds with respectable dress codes. Girls must wear dresses or skirts below the knees, loose-fitting trousers and headscarves over straightened hair. Exposing bare skin, such as the girl with the short top, is shameful, and in conjunction with her pregnancy reveals her lack of respectability.

Respectability is a category of social control that serves partly to define the ideal and partly to define its opposite, which is the *sleg* woman, who does not take care of the household, spends money on herself instead of her children, and hangs out in the street and local bars. Skeggs (1997: 115) argues that in Britain respectability distinguishes middle-class women from working-class women, who are seen as 'sexual, vulgar, tarty, pathological, tasteless and without value'. In South Africa, respectability can be traced back to British colonialism, where respectable women were Christian whites (Ross 1999: 34). During the apartheid regime, respectability was also associated with white women, while coloured women were constructed as lacking whiteness and, by implication, also lacking respectability, although they could become respectable through the proper management of their racially defined bodies (Salo 2004: 254). Whereas in Britain respectability defines socio-economic class, in contemporary South Africa it has strong racial connotations, as coloured and black women lack respectability by default, and need to make themselves respectable by modifying their behaviour. In contrast, white women in South Africa can more readily behave like a *sleg* and still be considered *ordentlike* due to their status as whites.

White women have historically accumulated more experiences of being respectable than coloured women, which offers them more space to negotiate varying ways of being feminine. The fact that South African women have different access to respectability depending on, among other things, class and race shows that approaching gender as a singular relationship of suppression, as Bourdieu suggests, is not analytically constructive. Women do gender in various ways, as Butler suggests, but their doing depends on their accumulated experiences; on their access to power and thus on their historically developed position (see Bourdieu 2001).

Staying safe by staying respectable

Among less affluent adolescent girls in Cape Flats, virginity is significant. Virginity is a signifier of a woman's respectability and that of her family. Salo (2004: 175) writes about respectability as follows: 'A woman's ability to control her own as well as her daughter's sexuality is the constitutive sign of respectability... A respectable mother would not allow her daughter to be sexually active, use birth control methods, or become pregnant out of wedlock.' If a girl sleeps around, her actions reflect on the family name and suggest that her parents have no control over her. Good girls stay at home. They are quiet, polite and sexually inexperienced. Shireen, a sixteen-year-old girl living in a poor part of Heideveld, commented: 'My mum brags about me not having a boyfriend, always staying home, never having friends over and she buys stuff to keep me happy, like clothes and jewellery, like they are rewarding me for not having a boyfriend, but dressing me up for one [laughs].' Shireen used to spend a lot of time on the street, 'which made me bad in Heideveld', as she puts it. Now she tries to communicate respectability and sexual unavailability by staying inside, and her mother has taken responsibility for her respectability in the eyes of their community.

   If girls 'misbehave', i.e. if they cast doubt upon their respectability, by dancing with men they meet at a nightclub, being drunk or 'performing', flirting and eating too much, kissing their boyfriends in public, or walking in dangerous places at dangerous times, they will be strictly censured by their parents or boyfriends. Adolescent girls must demonstrate sexual abstinence in order to validate their social position in relation to their mothers and other powerful women in the community (Salo 2004: 177). Fulfilling ideals of respectability is a means of accessing support networks, which assist with food, money, services in times of hardship and, most importantly, jobs, which are provided through these networks. The social safety of girls and their families is strongly influenced by how they choose to manage their sexual bodies and sexual practices. Shireen referred to an incident that illustrates this. Her mother had taken her shopping, and later Shireen decided to parade through the neighbourhood to show off her new clothes. When her mother discovered this, she rushed to bring Shireen home. Her mother yelled at her in public, telling her to come inside and stop 'modelling and showing off'. Shireen was very upset at her mother for making a public scene. However, her mother seemed to have chosen to reprimand her daughter publicly in order to communicate to other women that she did not condone Shireen's behaviour. She demonstrated her own respectability through her attempts to manage the sexuality of her daughter.

Sexual closure through domestication

Shireen was forced to stay inside to communicate her sexual unavailability. Her power to negotiate personal space was severely inhibited, not only by her past actions in hanging out on street corners, but also by a range of other factors, including the fact that her parents were divorced and her father was an alcoholic who lived in another equally poor neighbourhood. Shireen's mother is not widely perceived as respectable, but she tries to improve her reputation by managing the reputation of her daughter. Sixteen-year-old Shireen must struggle to demonstrate her respectability, but she feels unable to control her appearance:

> They can see if you are a virgin – like if your bum is loose, then you are not a virgin. Tight bums and small breasts are virgins ... they [the guys] will say you are not a virgin, even the girls say that. The girls will just watch you from behind, and say you are not a virgin any more, but I don't know how they know that.

A loose bum and big breasts, essentially a matured body, communicates that a girl is sexually active. Shireen has a feeling that her body is not respectable, and that it exposes her as immoral. Virginity is not only about behaviour but also about bodily expression. It does not matter how girls like Shireen behave, since their bodies tell their story. She feels that she lacks virginity and thus respectability but she can do nothing to change what other people see in her. Shireen's body communicates openness, and she therefore has to stay at home to be respectable; she exposes her own vulnerability every time she leaves the house. Shireen is very aware of how her clothes and her body communicate respectability or the lack of it:

> Sometimes I regret wearing tight jeans, but it's all I have. I don't like wearing long clothes and why should I wear certain clothes because of other people? Sometimes I wish I were living in Vanguard, that posh place, where people don't have to look at you. So I walk with my hands on my back to hide my bum, or I will sneak out when there are not so many people there, like men hanging out at the shop yelling at you, 'that bum is just right for me' and touch you and stuff. And people walk past and just laugh, or they think I like it.

Shireen is struggling against being categorised as lacking respectability, but she refuses to wear 'longer clothes' such as dresses and loose shirts. She talks about Vanguard as a place where people 'don't have to look' and she can walk undisturbed. Vanguard, a neighbouring residential area about 500 metres down the road, consists almost exclusively of owner-occupied housing. The more prosperous residents of Vanguard enjoy a higher standard of living than the inhabitants of Heideveld, and they do not have to legitimise their respectability to quite the same extent as their poorer neighbours (see also Bourdieu 1990; Skeggs 1997).

Generating personal space through respectability

Shireen's friend Shamielah is sixteen and also lives in Heideveld. In contrast to Shireen, she has been able to negotiate a lot of personal space, mobility and parental trust. As she put it, 'My mother thinks I'm an angel.' Shamielah is often allowed to go out during weekends to her cousin's house and to stay over. Her cousin has older friends and they have been clubbing in town a few times. Shamielah related this with excitement and fear, because the men who had taken them out were related to gangsters and the taxi driver who had carried them free of charge was a well-known gang member in her neighbourhood. Shamielah was concerned that people had seen her in his taxi, and was anxious about what people might think and what they might say to her mother. As a result, she decided to refuse any more lifts to preclude any gossip:

> It's like you have to care about what your parents and people say. People will say, 'I saw you with that girl and that boy,' but it was just this once, so it's not a big thing, people know I am not in that category. The next few weekends, I will spend time with my family and then we will see what happens, maybe they will ask me again and I will say yes.

She knew that people perceived her as respectable, and that it would take more than a single instance of misconduct to jeopardise this status. Shamielah is perceived as being essentially more respectable than Shireen; and as a result has more licence in what she does; she has more space to be feminine in different ways and not solely in the strictly respectable manner which Shireen struggles to uphold. By staying at home with her family, she could 'bank' her good behaviour and use it sometime in the future to create space for going out again, having a boyfriend or hanging out with those considered less respectable.

It is not only the disdain of close kin that can influence youth perceptions of virtue and shame; gossip networks between families and across communities also serve to exercise social control and maintain social hierarchies. Strategies of social control resulting from gossip have been well documented in the anthropological literature (see Gluckman 1963; Hannerz 1967; Stadler 2003) and, in the Cape Flats context, the girls' fears of being ridiculed, criticised and subjected to public shame meant that they took account of the rumours circulating about them. Gossip circulated around ideas of promiscuity relating to potential boyfriends, sexual practices, suspected pregnancies or being caught at inappropriate times in certain locations. Despite the fear of gossip and ridicule that their actions could bring, the girls still held other girls who behaved properly in contempt. Gossip thus maintains the ideology of respectability and acts as a vehicle for defining the girls' sexual transgressions.

Rape: sex or violence?

Lacking respectability can threaten survival (Salo 2004: 295), as it can invite physical and sexual violence, which is widespread in Cape Town's townships. Cape Town is notorious for some of the

highest crime rates in the world and, without economic resources
to invest in security measures such as private guards and alarm
systems, social networks are central to safety (Henriksen and
Lindegaard 2004). Most people living on the Cape Flats relay
information about crimes via neighbours and friends. As already
mentioned, respectability is the key to these networks and,
therefore, the key to personal safety, since the support of family
and neighbours is contingent on the reputation of the victim of
violence. In rape cases, many girls struggle to convince their
families that they were violated. If the girls have had boyfriends or
have often been seen outside the house, then they are likely to be
seen as sexually promiscuous rather than the victims of violence.

At the Rape Crisis Centre in Heideveld, we spoke to Janine, a
woman in her late thirties who had been raped at the age of
seventeen.[1] She had been dating a man for several months, which
was widely known and accepted by her parents: 'They knew I had
very high morals and would never do anything,' she told us.
When she ended their relationship, however, he raped her. She
never told anyone, because she was terrified of what people
would think:

> Because he was my boyfriend, people were going to say I
> allowed it, you know I can never tell people I was raped,
> they will never believe me, that's how I was thinking. It's
> not supposed to happen, like my father said, the first
> person you have sex with must be your husband, so he's
> not my husband, and then I made up my mind – he's going
> to be my husband, 'cause he is the only man who knows I
> was a virgin when he met me, this is how I was
> indoctrinated – otherwise people can point a finger and say
> you've been with many men – he is the only one who
> knows. (Janine, age 38, Heideveld)

Janine married her rapist because he was the only one who knew
that she had been a virgin. She was acutely aware that there was
no in-between. She was in no position to convince everyone that
it had been a violent act; rather, having had a boyfriend exposed
her as potentially disreputable. Rape could only be turned into a
legitimate sexual act through marriage to avoid contamination
and the loss of respectability. In Janine's case, then, the violence
associated with marrying the rapist was experienced as less
painful than the violence associated with being socially
stigmatised. Many girls would never report a rape case because
the social stigma of being sexually active could be more

detrimental to the girl's social safety than the rape itself (see also Gibson 2005).

Many girls were similarly unable to make a case for having been raped. At the Rape Crisis Centre they struggled with perceptions of rape as sex, expressed most acutely in situations where sexually active girls had been raped by a family member. One Rape Crisis counsellor commented, 'See now the family doesn't understand why she presses charges against her uncle, when she doesn't press charges against her boyfriend who she also has sex with.' Girls who lack the symbolic capital to legitimise their sexual status because they have a boyfriend risk being defined as disreputable if they are raped. Respectability is not only a strategy of safety protected by networks of mothers, but also a strategy that resists the social stigma of being defined as promiscuous if a woman is sexually harassed or raped.

Having sex without being there

Many of the girls tried to mediate between being both respectable and sexually active. According to our survey of 500 high school pupils in the sixteen to nineteen age group, 18 per cent of the girls and 28 per cent of the boys had had sexual intercourse. One must be careful when evaluating whether these numbers reflect actual behaviour. The survey was completed during class, and the answers may reflect how respondents wished to represent themselves. It is likely that girls hid their sexual experiences due to ideals of respectability, while local constructions of masculinity might encourage the boys to exaggerate their sexual exploits (Jewkes et al. 2001; Swart et al. 2002). A study conducted by LoveLife among adolescents throughout South Africa suggests that 48 per cent of a sample of 4,731 adolescents aged fifteen to nineteen have had sexual intercourse (LoveLife 2004: 13). In Cape Town, the average age of sexual initiation (without gender specification) is 16.4 (Jewkes et al. 2001: 734).

Women in their late twenties use the expression 'sexually active virgins' to refer to adolescent girls who pretend to be virgins even though they are sexually active. They claimed that within small groups of friends, girls would admit to being sexually active, but outside these circles they pretended to be virgins. Jewkes et al. (2001: 733) note that one-third of all pregnancies in South Africa are teenage pregnancies, which not only suggests that premarital sex is common but also that sexual practices among adolescents are connected to unsafe sexual habits.

Irrespective of whether girls claimed to be sexually active or not, some expressed the view that sexual intercourse was mostly the result of being manipulated by boys, rather than choosing to have sex:

> It's like when you are in the mood – you flirt now, and now you are in the mood and your hormones are going, so he asks you at that moment [when they are about to have sex], but he didn't ask you before you were going into the mood – some girls say when you are in the mood, you can't say no. Just go with the flow ... But I don't go with that. (Shamielah, age 17, Heideveld)

> Girls are softer than guys ... it's different; I don't actually know how a boy is... Here in Heideveld we say that girls have a weak spot, like the boys know where that weak spot is, and the guys just make the girls more ... and then the girls cannot control it and go with the flow. And regret it afterwards. (Shireen, age 16, Heideveld)

The girls speak about the sexual act as a black hole, an act that happens without their complete knowledge and participation. The boys just touched their 'weak spot', which resulted in a temporary loss of control. Abdicating responsibility and knowledge of the act becomes a strategy to regain respectability. The girls did not take part actively; they were tricked, which makes it less a choice and therefore more respectable. In other words, the girls try to fulfil ideals about respectability, which means sexual abstinence, at the same time as they engage in sexual relations. They regain a sense of respectability by participating as little as possible, by letting the man decide how and when sex takes place. However, by abdicating responsibility for the act, they also abdicate the power to negotiate safe sex.

Pretending not to be present in the sexual act and believing that it did not actually happen might be seen as psychological denial. When girls say they are not sexually active, this is not necessarily due to an unwillingness to reveal their deepest secrets to a researcher, but rather reflects their experience of not really being present in the act itself (Kirmayer 1994; Cohen 2001). This could stem from a fear of being regarded as disreputable, but it could also relate to different perceptions of sex. In the workshops we held among the school pupils, the boys accused the girls of having overly romantic expectations of relationships: as one boy put it, 'They think it's like those soaps they watch after school.'

The girls explained sexual abstinence as a moral issue. Abstinence was related to the threat of HIV/AIDS and pregnancy, both of which appeared to be out of their control. As expressed by a seventeen-year-old girl from Heideveld, 'My opinion is not to have sex because of the AIDS virus... it's loose here in South Africa, I don't know with who did he sleep before.' Both boys and girls seemed to be well informed about various methods of birth control, but expressed a lack of confidence in these preventive measures. Several girls said that condoms were unsafe: 'They always break, so rather not have sex.' The myth of 'condoms always breaking' seemed to express a general fear about their lack of control over the sexual act. This is supported by other studies in South Africa which suggest that the power to negotiate sexual relations is held by men rather than women (Wood and Jewkes 1997; Gibson 2003). The consequence is that while respectability and a reluctance to talk about sex may operate as a survival strategy at one level, at another level they become a 'death strategy' as Farmer (1999: 79) suggests, since young women's lack of sexual knowledge increases the likelihood of them being exposed to HIV/AIDS. For girls like Shireen in particular, practising respectability means being unable to negotiate safe sex. The respectability that offers social safety to young women in one context might thereby jeopardise their health in another.

Symbolic violence with real consequences

Engaging in unsafe sexual relationships has become life-threatening in South Africa, where it is estimated that, at the current rate of infection, 50 per cent of South Africans under the age of fifteen will die of AIDS-related causes (LoveLife 2001). The message communicated by governmental as well as non-governmental campaigns is that AIDS is a sexually transmitted disease that kills.[2] The million-dollar LoveLife campaign was launched in 1999, using large billboards, national radio and TV broadcasting, monthly magazines and the establishment of youth centres. The aim was to reach South African youth with a clear message concerning the urgency of accepting sexual responsibility, preferably by abstinence or by using condoms. The LoveLife campaign also tapped into the notion of female respectability by presenting girls as responsible for saying no to sex and rejecting boyfriends who have had multiple sexual partners. The campaign reproduced the cultural discourse of uncontrollable male sexuality and controllable female sexuality (Stadler and Hlongwa 2002:

374). However, the message seemed to ignore the extensive research that stresses the limited negotiating power of women in sexual relations (Wood and Jewkes 1997; Gibson 2003, 2005; Henriksen and Lindegaard 2004). It fails to address the fact that a majority of adolescent relationships are characterised by male dominance and that the use of physical and sexual violence is common. About 2 per cent of South African women aged between seventeen and forty-eight are raped every year (Jewkes and Abrahams 2002: 1235); five women are killed every week by an intimate partner (Mathews et al. 2004: 1); about 30 per cent of girls between fifteen and nineteen years old have been forcibly introduced to sex (Jewkes and Abrahams 2002: 1237); and about 50 per cent of teenagers' dating relationships include physically violent interaction (Swart et al. 2002: 389).

The construction of masculinity in the campaign not only jeopardises the safety of girls, it also puts boys at risk. In an anthropological study conducted by Lindegaard in 2005, boys described their sexuality as far from uncontrollable; they expressed feeling under pressure in terms of taking the initiative and being in charge in relation to girls (Gibson and Lindegaard 2007). Unlike girls, boys nevertheless said they were aware of their power to negotiate safe sex. They are in control in the sexual act, as the girls suggested, and control gives them the potential to insist on safe sex. Whether they are able to make use of this potential depends on their social position. If boys think about condoms 'when things are getting hot', they are regarded as weak men, not sexually expressive when they are supposed to be. For boys, sexual abstinence runs counter to dominant perceptions of masculinity. Boys who practise sexual abstinence are regarded as churchgoers and 'mummy's boys'; they are not real men. Suggesting safe sex in the 'heat of the moment' entails negotiating dominant perceptions of masculinity and it is only some boys who are able to do so without being regarded as weak men.

It is difficult to criticise a politics of abstinence considering the magnitude of the HIV/AIDS pandemic. However, our research suggests that girls have various reasons for not taking responsibility in sexual matters. They attempt to negotiate the tensions between being respectable and sexually active by abstaining from any responsibility. Further, the social stigma attached to adolescent sexuality makes it stigmatising to seek information on safe sex, and adolescent girls are consequently ill-informed about the possibility of assuming responsibility. As Gammeltoft (2002: 493) concludes on sexual risk-taking among adolescents in Vietnam:

The societal negation of young people's sexual activity thus produces a violence, which is both symbolic and real. It is symbolic in its power to define youth as sexually innocent, and real in its negative implications for the reproductive health and well being of young people who are brought to expose themselves to sexual risks that could have been averted.

The outcome of the discourse of respectability outlined here is a symbolic violence that has real consequences in the everyday lives of adolescent girls. Teenage pregnancy is common and sexual violence on the Cape Flats is more frequent than virtually anywhere else in the world. Bourdieu (2001) argues that just like physical violence, symbolic violence is the effect of a relationship of domination. The two differ only in that with symbolic violence there is rarely a clear violator and victim. Symbolic violence is embodied, and becomes powerful through misrecognition precisely because it is not recognised as violence (Bourdieu 2001). Girls are not equipped with the necessary knowledge or social power to negotiate safe sex, as any interest in sexual matters is perceived as a sign of sexual activity and, by implication, promiscuity (Gibson 2005). Respectability guarantees safety in one sense because it gives access to social networks, yet in another sense this very notion of respectable, asexual femininity clashes with everyday experiences, and places girls at risk of HIV/AIDS and teenage pregnancy.

Notes
1. During fieldwork we spent two weeks at the Rape Crisis Centre in Heideveld interviewing counsellors and activists.
2. An example of a government-sponsored campaign is LoveLife (www.lovelife.org.za). An example of a non-governmental campaign is the Treatment Action Campaign (www.tac.org.za).

References
Bourdieu, P. 1984. *Distinction: a Social Critique of the Judgement of Taste.* London: Routledge.
―――. 1990. *The Logic of Practice.* Cambridge: Polity Press.
―――. 2000. *Pascalian Mediations.* Cambridge: Polity Press.
―――. 2001. *Masculine Domination.* Cambridge: Polity Press.
Bourdieu, P. and L. Wacquant. 1992. *An Invitation to Reflexive Sociology.* Chicago: University of Chicago Press.
Butler, J. 1993. *Bodies that Matter.* London: Routledge.
Cohen, S. 2001. *States of Denial. Knowing about Atrocities and Suffering.* Cambridge: Polity Press.

Erasmus, Z.E. 2001. 'Re-imagining Coloured Identities in Post-Apartheid South Africa', in Z.E. Erasmus (ed.) *Coloured by History, Shaped by Place: New Perspectives on Coloured Identities in Cape Town*. Cape Town: Kwela Books, pp. 13–28.

Farmer, P. 1999. 'Invisible Women: Class, Gender and HIV', in P. Farmer (ed.) *Infections and Inequalities*. Berkeley: University of California Press, pp. 59–93.

Gammeltoft, T. 2002. 'Seeking Trust and Transcendence: Sexual Risk-taking among Vietnamese Youth', *Social Science and Medicine* 55: 483–96.

Gibson, D. 2003. 'Rape, Vulnerability and Doubt', *Medische Antropologie* 15 (1): 43–64.

———. 2005. 'Of Victims and Survivors. Health Care, Legal Intervention and Women's Responses to Rape', *Medische Antropologie* 17 (1): 23–40.

Gibson, D. and M.R. Lindegaard. 2007. 'South African Boys with Plans for the Future, and Why a Focus on Dominant Discourses Only Tells Us a Part of the Story', in T. Shefer, K. Ratele, A. Strebel, N. Shabalala and R. Buikema (eds) *From Boys to Men: Social Constructions of Maturity in Contemporary Society*. Lansdown: UCT Press, pp. 128–44.

Gluckman, M. 1963. 'Gossip and Scandal', *Current Anthropology* 4: 307–16.

Hannerz, U. 1967. 'Gossip, Networks and Culture in a Black American Ghetto', *Ethnos* 32: 35–60.

Henriksen, A. and M.R. Lindegaard. 2004. *Vulnerable Women and Men at Risk: Safety and Gendered Experiences of Violence among Adolescents in Cape Town*. M.A. thesis. Copenhagen: University of Copenhagen Press.

Järvinen, M. 1999. 'Pierre Bourdieu on Gender and Power'. *Sociologisk Rapportserie* 7. Copenhagen.

Jensen, S. 2000. 'Of Drug Dealers and Street Gangs: Power, Mobility, and Violence on the Cape Flats', *Focaal* 36: 105–16.

———. 2001. *Claiming Community – Negotiating Crime: State Formation, Neighbourhood and Gangs in a Capetonian Township*. PhD Dissertation. Roskilde: University of Roskilde Press.

Jewkes, R. and N. Abrahams. 2002. 'The Epidemiology of Rape and Sexual Coercion in South Africa: An Overview', *Social Science and Medicine* 55: 1231–44.

Jewkes, R., C. Vundule, F. Maforah and E. Jordaan. 2001. 'Relationship Dynamics and Teenage Pregnancy in South Africa', *Social Science and Medicine* 52: 733–44.

Kirmayer, L.J. 1994. 'Pacing the Void: Social and Cultural Dimensions of Dissociation', in D. Spiegel (ed.) *Dissociation, Culture, Mind and Body*. Washington: American Psychiatry Press, pp. 91–122.

LoveLife. 2001. *Hot Prospects – Cold Facts: Portrait of Young South Africa*, Program for Health and Development in South Africa.

———. 2004. *Report on Activities and Progress 2004*, http://www.lovelife. org.za/corporate/research/AnnualReport_2004.pdf.

Lovell, T. 2000. 'Thinking Feminism With and Against Bourdieu', *Feminist Theory* 1 (1): 11–32.

Mathews, S., N. Abrahams, L. Martin, L. Vetten, L. van der Merwe and R. Jewkes. 2004. *Every Six Hours a Woman is Killed by Her Intimate Partner*. Cape Town: MRC Policy Brief, Centre for the Study of Violence and Reconciliation.

McNay, L. 2004. 'Agency and Experience: Gender as Lived Relation', in L. Adkins and B. Skeggs (eds) *Feminism after Bourdieu*. Oxford: Blackwell.

Mørck, Y. 1998. *Bindestregsdanskere: Fortællinger om Køn, Generationer og Etnicitet*. Frederiksberg: Sociologi.

Ross, R. 1999. *Status and Respectability in the Cape Colony*. Cambridge: Cambridge University Press.

Salo, E. 2000. 'Gangs and Sexuality on the Cape Flats', *African Gender Institute Newsletter* 7: 8–9.

———. 2003. 'Negotiating Gender and Personhood in the New South Africa: Adolescent Women and Gangsters in Manenberg Township on the Cape Flats', *European Journal of Cultural Studies* 6 (3): 345–65.

———. 2004. *Respectable Mothers, Tough Men and Good Daughters: Producing Persons in Manenberg Township, South Africa*. PhD dissertation, Department of Social Anthropology, Emory University.

Skeggs, B. 1997. *Formations of Class and Gender: Becoming Respectable*. London: Sage.

Søndergaard, D.M. 1996. *Tegnet på Kroppen: Køn, Koder og Konstruktioner blandt Unge voksne i Academia*. Copenhagen: Museum Tusculanum.

Stadler, J. 2003. 'Rumor, Gossip, and Blame: Implications for HIV/AIDS Prevention in the South African Lowveld', *AIDS Education and Prevention* 15 (4): 357–68.

Stadler, J. and L. Hlongwa. 2002. 'Monitoring and Evaluation of LoveLife's AIDS Prevention and Advocacy Activities in South Africa 1999–2001', *Evaluation and Programme Planning* 25: 365–76.

Steinberg, J. 2004. *The Number. One Man's Search for Identity in the Cape Underworld and Prison Gangs*. Johannesburg: Jonathan Ball Publishers.

Swart, L., M. Stevens and I. Ricardo. 2002. 'Violence in Adolescents' Romantic Relationships: Findings from a Survey amongst School-going Youth in a South African Community', *Journal of Adolescents* 25: 385–95.

Wicomb, Z. 2000. *You Can't Get Lost in Cape Town*. New York: The Feminist Press at the City University of New York.

Wood, C. and R. Jewkes 1997. 'Violence, Rape and Sexual Coercion: Everyday Love in a South African Township', *Gender and Development* 5 (2): 41–46.

CHAPTER 3

SUMMER SEX: YOUTH, DESIRE AND THE CARNIVALESQUE AT THE ENGLISH SEASIDE

Suzanne Clisby

In the UK, there have been recurrent moral panics about the promiscuity of young people, teenage pregnancy and the rise of sexually transmitted diseases (see also Roche, this volume). Any increase in the number of teenage parents is presented as an indicator of moral decline. Because young people's sexuality and erotic desire can be constructed as transgressive and deviant, they become subject to state intervention in a highly politicised arena. This chapter is concerned with situations in which young people confront, negotiate and utilise this putatively transgressive sexuality in specific geographical and embodied spaces. Drawing on research conducted amongst young people in an English seaside resort between 2000–1 and 2002–4 (Clisby and Craig 2001; Bell et al. 2004), I explore the ways in which casual sex is created and sustained as a defining feature of the carnival atmosphere and experience of the seaside as well as part of its economic base.[1] However, while transgressive desire is experienced by holidaymakers and seasonal workers as a temporary thrill, for the local young people who live and work by the seaside throughout the year it is part of the permanent context of their daily lives. The effect of this situation is to empower and disempower them, simultaneously, in gender-specific ways.

I am particularly concerned with the constructions of young, white working-class women's sexuality and the ways in which these are reinforced and extended in the context of the liminal space of the seaside. Referring to both historical and contemporary debates, I argue that white, working-class teenage girls are positioned in popular discourse as the symbolic 'primitive' other to the middle class ideal (Russo 1995; Skeggs 1997, 2004; Stoler 1997; Lyons and Lyons 2004; Lawler 2005). Their perceived transgressive sexuality arises not simply from the fact that historically they have been associated with openly promiscuous behaviour that seemingly flouts public middle-class morality, but also because as the triply abject 'other' – in terms of age, class and gender – they are not reproductively authorised either by the state or in mainstream popular culture.

The chapter focuses on the collision and potential exacerbation of two interrelated social and cultural sites of transgression. The first is of young people generally, and of white, working-class girls in particular as potentially transgressive anomalous bodies, whose reproductive capacity is regarded as both symbolically polluting and socially disruptive (see, for example, Bullen et al. 2000; Tincknell et al. 2003). The second is that of the liminal sphere of the seaside: the hedonistic, transgressive sexual mores of the holiday resort as a place where sexual desire can be pursued outside the normal constraints of everyday life.

Gender, class and whiteness in constructions of transgressive sexuality

The issue of teenage sexuality in Britain is shrouded in controversy, being generally perceived by formal state institutions and the national media as transgressive, deviant and problematic behaviour. The idea that young people should not be sexually active seems to be the crux of the issue, despite the fact that teenagers are quite clearly sexual beings. There are important gender and class differences in these attitudes. For example, whilst the activities of sexually active young men who engage in serial holiday sex are not condoned, they are not the central focus of state sanction or media vitriol. Rather, they tend to be accepted as an aspect of cultural constructions of hegemonic British masculinity. When young women engage in casual sex, by contrast, a double standard is discernible in cultural attitudes. It is girls, not boys, who carry visible markers of such liaisons. Whilst sexually transmitted infections (STIs) are a genuine concern, they can be concealed by individuals. It is obviously more difficult, however, for a woman to hide her pregnancy in the longer term. Thus, the fear is that young women – and, in the context of this study, white, working-class young women – will become teenage parents whose children will have to be supported by taxpayers and the state.

Teenage pregnancy and young parenthood are political and policy issues that receive much anguished attention in the UK, particularly in the media (Bullen et al. 2000; Bell et al. 2004: 1). At the heart of this moral panic, the 'folk devils' (Cohen 1972) are working class girls and the 'problem' of control over their young female bodies.[2] As Tincknell et al. (2003: 47) argue:

> Moral panics over teenage sex in Britain have been a recurrent feature of the nation's media culture for much of the post-war period. Tending to be marked in turns by 'permissive populism' and prurient speculation, public accounts of shifts in sexual behaviour and attitudes have frequently combined nostalgia of the 'traditional' family with an anxious focus on female adolescent sexuality as the source of national moral degeneration.

In the UK there is widespread debate about the rights and wrongs of sexual health education in schools, the availability of contraception and abortion services for young people, and the 'deviance' of teenage parenthood. A report in the national *Daily Mail* newspaper epitomises much of the tone of this debate. Entitled 'Relentless Rise in Teenage Pregnancies', the article criticises the government's teenage pregnancy strategy for spending £138 million since 1998, and for:

> making the morning after pill, condoms and sex education more easily available ... Contraceptives are being offered to boys as young as 11 and teenagers are told they have the 'right to a fulfilling sex life' ... The Government [welfare] benefit policies have also been blamed for encouraging pregnancies among young women. One recent study showed that a single mother of two children relying entirely on benefits is now just £1 a week worse off than a working couple with two children living on an average income. (Doughty 2005)

Similarly, Ferrari (2005), writing in the *Sun* newspaper, adds his contribution to the 'scandal' under the banner 'Yeah but No but

...We've BECOME Little Britain'. The report begins with a critique of a middle school in Dorset in the south of England in which girls have been told that they must wear trousers rather than skirts to class and links this to a scheme funded through the Department for Education and Skills, costing '£3.4 million of OUR money' (Ferrari 2005: 11). He explains that, '[a]s part of the Sure Start Plus scheme, pregnant schoolgirls and teenage mothers will get free beauty consultations, makeovers and shopping vouchers ... this means the career path for these girls is to get pregnant as soon as they hit their teens, get a council flat, live off state handouts – and have their personal shopper thrown in!' (Ferrari 2005: 11). Then, in reference to the girls at the school in the (presumably) middle-class area of Dorset, he continues, 'But, how is it right that decent girls who do the unthinkable and use schools for education as opposed to copulation are denied these luxuries?' (Ferrari 2005: 11). He concludes, 'We pay millions in benefits each year and the hordes of scroungers continue to take us for an increasingly expensive ride' (Ferrari 2005: 11).

Both of these reports illustrate how the issue of young people's sexuality inextricably intersects with notions of class and gender, where 'transgressive' sexuality is defined in relation to the control, or perceived lack of control, over young women's reproductive capacity and to the authorisation of certain kinds of reproductive bodies and not others. As Skeggs (1997) and Lawler (2005) indicate, tangible 'disgust' exists amongst the middle classes towards the working classes. Within the class context, there is an issue of whiteness. The focus of this chapter is on white working-class young people, because they constituted the majority of the young people in the seaside resort where the research was carried out. However, the focus on whiteness is not merely a practical strategy arising from the data. Rather, as Lawler (2005: 430) argues, 'there is, increasingly, an implicit coding of "the working class" *as* white. Of course, working class people are not exclusively white, but their emblematic whiteness might be necessary to their continuing disparagement' (Lawler 2005: 430; see also Haylett 2001; McRobbie 2001). Lawler identifies a creeping, almost insidious, tolerance of expressions of disgust at white working-class existence within the British media and other public forums, which simultaneously 'work to *produce* working-class people as abhorrent and as foundationally "other" to a middle-class existence that is silently marked as normal and desirable. But ... they also work to produce *middle-classed* identities that rely on *not* being the repellent and disgusting "other"' (Lawler 2005: 431, emphases in original).

The construction and categorisation of white working-class women as socially disgusting or morally degenerate are by no means recent phenomena. At the height of Europe's colonial expansion in the nineteenth century there was an explicit attempt to prevent European middle-class colonists from being biologically 'contaminated' by both the non-white colonial subjects and white working-class Europeans (Arnold 1979, cited in Stoler 1997). Moreover, the potential for both racial 'pollution' and moral degeneracy was ultimately a female embodiment. As Stoler (1997: 24) argues:

> Whites had to guard their ranks – in quantity and in kind – to increase their numbers and to ensure that their members blurred neither biological nor political boundaries. In the metropole the socially and physically 'unfit', the poor, the indigent, and the insane, were either to be sterilized or prevented from marriage. In the colonies it was these very groups among Europeans who were either excluded from entry or institutionalized while they were there and eventually sent home...Measures were taken to avoid poor white migration.

Similarly, Levy explored the cross-cultural analysis of sexual customs in Henry Mayhew's *London Labour and the London Poor* (1861–62), which, Levy argues, 'transferred a notion of female sexual deviance to the urban working classes as a whole' (Levy 1991: 48, cited in Lyons and Lyons 2004: 44). According to Lyons and Lyons (2004: 44), Mayhew's account 'equates virtually every variation from mid-Victorian middle-class norms with prostitution ... the familiar "social evil"'. They conclude that the significance of links between 'primitive' and working-class women's sexuality lay in the fact that:

> [i]ssues of class, gender, disease, and the sexual secrets of 'respectable' men touched several raw nerves for the Victorians, giving urgency to discourses, from the scholarly book to the music hall lyric, that threatened to expose them. It was in this context that the sexuality of primitives became a foil for debates that had their origins much closer to home. (Lyons and Lyons 2004: 50)

The extent to which contemporary constructions of white working-class women depend upon, or are constructed in relationship to, other non-white bodies is the subject of another debate. The point here is to show that the perceived transgression of young women's sexuality is not simply about issues of control over their bodies and reproductive capacities but about which kinds of bodies are reproductively authorised. Moreover, a critical arena for these debates continues to be the British press. Mayhew first published his account of sexual deviance and moral deficiency amongst the 'other' in the *Morning Chronicle* in 1849. Marrin (2006), writing for the *Sunday Times* over 150 years later, evokes similar constructions of 'deserving' and 'undeserving' women. In her article 'Only the Middle Class Can't Afford Babies', she articulates these uncomfortable middle-class concerns that the wrong women are reproducing the nation:

> First we are told that not enough women are having babies ... Next we learn that some women are having too many babies and the government's best efforts to discourage them have proved an expensive and scandalous failure: '£150m plan has failed to cut teenage pregnancies' screamed a [recent] news splash ... It's not that there is a shortage of babies. It's that there is a shortage of babies in respectable middle-class, middle-income families ... Among the poor it is perfectly possible to have babies with or without a man or a job; the state will pay ... The women who are not having children are what would have been called in the 19th century the deserving mothers; they are hard working, competent and responsible. (Marrin 2006: 5)

Marrin encapsulates here the recurrent anxiety or moral panic that is both contemporaneous and historical. As she argues, the kinds of women who should be encouraged to reproduce (the 'deserving', white, adult middle classes) are failing to do so and these are juxtaposed to the white, working-class young women who 'have lots of babies' and who – in a categorisation that evokes the Victorian typologies of Mayhew – 'are what you might call the undeserving mothers' (Marrin 2006: 5).

White, working-class teenage girls and their reproductive capacity have thus come to epitomise the abject other in the moral panic surrounding teenage pregnancy. Furthermore, as I argue below, when the putative transgressive sexuality of white working-class young girls is played out in the carnivalesque arena of the seaside resort, the collision between the potential 'sexual promiscuity' of young girls and the hedonistic, carnivalesque context can serve to exacerbate the sense of moral panic.

The lure of the sea

The seaside has a long tradition as a site of hedonism, pleasure and illicit and even transgressive desire. The edge of the land is a liminal zone, not merely geographically, but also in providing a sociocultural liminality, a sense of otherness, of detachment and of suspension in which 'people have been able to eschew the constraints of social *mores*' (Morgan and Pritchard 1999: 60, original emphasis). This quality has been noted by various authors. Shields (1991: 74–75) shows how over the course of the nineteenth and twentieth centuries Brighton on the English south coast 'came to be associated with pleasure, with the liminal and with the carnivalesque' and how the British seaside 'came to be a topos of a set of connected discourses on pleasure and pleasurable activities'. Similarly, Walton (2000: 97) describes the seaside as:

> a liminal environment ... a 'place on the margin' where the usual constraints on respectability and decorum in public behaviour might be pushed aside in the interests of holiday hedonism, and of carnivalesque escape from petty restrictions of everyday life in displays of excess, challenging authority and flouting the everyday norms which restrained bodily exposure and recommended civilised moderation in consumption and demeanour.

The seaside resort has also been a locus in which white, working-class women have been constructed and utilised as objects of illicit erotic desire since at least the eighteenth century (Corbin 1994). In this historical context, Corbin comments on the role of 'local' (i.e. white, working-class) young women as being integral to this eroticism. He explains that it was common for young men to bathe naked in groups whilst local young women held their clothes, gave them a rub down as they came out of the water and helped them to dress. Corbin (1994) also documents accounts of male tourists enjoying watching groups of 'local' young women bathing naked in the sea as part of their holiday fun.[3]

There is then a long association of the seaside with eroticism, transgression and the carnivalesque. The notion of carnival itself is often associated with the work of Mikhail Bakhtin. In *Rabelais and His World* (1984), Bakhtin describes the carnival experience as one of utopian radicalism in which 'there is a suspension of all hierarchic distinctions and barriers'; the 'norms and prohibitions of usual life' are suspended so that an 'atmosphere of freedom, frankness and familiarity' reigns; and there is a 'temporary liberation from the prevailing truth and from the established order' (Bakhtin 1984: 10, 15, cited in Webb 2005: 122). Whilst Bakhtin's construction of the carnival as a form of utopian radicalism is understandable, if not unproblematic, in the context in which he writes, I do not believe this continues to be the case, if it ever were, in contemporary seaside contexts. I would argue for a more critical reading of the carnival, one in which there may exist sanctioned liberation from social norms but in which social hierarchies are simultaneously reinscribed. Nevertheless, as Webb (2005: 121) states, 'the utility of the concept of carnival lies in its capacity to illuminate potentially transgressive elements within popular social and cultural practices'.

There has been a tendency to argue 'that pre-industrial popular recreations in England were typified by many of the transgressive features characteristic of the Bakhtinian carnival' (Webb 2005: 123, citing Malcolmson 1973; Reid 1982; Rule 1986; Rojek 1995). How then has the seaside come to be one of the few remaining socio-geographical spaces associated with carnival in contemporary British society? A range of authors point to the rise of the industrial revolution, during the first decades of which, they argue, the carnivalesque features of popular recreations were suppressed as a result of a combination of factors. These included the increasing regulation of both labour and leisure within the industrial system and the rise of new Protestant movements such as Methodism (Thompson 1967; Malcolmson 1973; Storch 1977; Cunningham 1980; Webb 2005: 123, citing Billinge 1996).

According to Rojek (1995), the carnival did not wholly disappear but was pushed to the margins over the course of the latter half of the nineteenth century, when there began a 'rise of new centres of "carnival" on the coastal periphery in the development of seaside resorts' (1995: 86, cited in Webb 2005: 123). This analysis is supported by a number of writers, including Shields (1991), Billinge (1996) and Walton (2001), and by detailed studies of particular resorts such as Brighton (Shields 1990, 1991) and Blackpool (Bennett 1983, 1986, 1995). According to Bennett, both the traditional wakes and newer urban forms of popular recreation such as fairs which came under considerable attack in the inland towns at the time, 'had been displaced to Blackpool beach where they were able to thrive in an excess of unbridled vulgarity' (1986: 138, cited in Webb 2005: 124). With the development of the mass entertainment industry, however, there has been 'a programme of ideological and cultural re-formation' (Bennett 1986: 140–41, cited in Webb 2005: 124) 'which sought to re-order the carnivalesque aspects of popular recreation, render them complicit with the dominant ideology of progress and modernity and thereby destroy their transgressive and utopian dimensions' (Webb 2005: 124).

In contrast to Webb's suggestion that the modern entertainment industry has led to a destruction of notions of transgression, I would take a more nuanced approach, one that allows for the integration of transgression into the norm within the liminal context, but one in which notions of transgression never entirely dissipate. As such, in the context of my research, I argue that the liminality and carnival of the seaside do not represent radical and utopian possibilities, as represented by Bakhtin. Whilst it is important to recognise the power and agency of the young women who are the focus of this chapter, and the possibilities for fun and enjoyment in their lives at the seaside, they have not and will never experience a utopian 'suspension of all hierarchic distinctions and barriers' (Bakhtin 1984: 15, cited in Webb 2005: 122). What closes down their utopian possibilities in the longer term is their construction as the marginal, abjected feminine other, and, as we have seen, this is by no means a recent construction.

As Russo (1995: 56) argues in her exploration of the female grotesque, 'an examination of the materials on carnival can also recall limitations, defeats, and indifferences generated by carnival's complicitous place in dominant culture'. In particular, she warns of 'especial dangers for women and other excluded or marginalized groups within carnival [that] may suggest a redeployment of taboos around the female body as grotesque (the pregnant body, the aging body, the irregular body) and as unruly when set loose in the public sphere' (Russo 1995: 56). Russo (1995: 60) goes on to argue that the marginal position of women and others in the everyday, mundane world makes their presence in the 'topsy-turvy carnival' particularly dangerous, citing historical evidence of women raped during carnival festivities. She concludes, 'in the everyday indicative world, women and their bodies, certain bodies, in certain public framings, in certain public places, are always already transgressive – dangerous, and in danger' (Russo 1995: 60). Russo's arguments have particular resonance for the young, white, working-class women who are the subjects of this chapter, and for the ways in which they may be empowered by the hedonistic extension of social mores in the context of the seaside and simultaneously disempowered and even endangered by their positionality as the 'already transgressive' and 'grotesque' other against the middle-class norm.

Experiences of carnival in an English resort

The seaside town in which I did research has all the elements of the British coastal resort—funfairs, big dippers, bars, arcades, pleasure domes and donkeys on the beach. It is a relatively small resort in the east Midlands, with a permanent population of between 18,000 and 22,000 (Office of National Statistics 2001; Regional Government Office 2005). This population quadruples in the peak holiday season and the area has up to three million visitors annually (Regional Government Office 2005).[4] The town has a predominantly white, working-class population and high levels of deprivation and unemployment (Craig et al. 1998). For example, according to the 2001 Government Census 98.7 per cent of the population is white and 46 per cent of sixteen- to seventy-four-year-olds have no qualifications (Office of National Statistics 2001). The area is geographically isolated from large cities and industrial conurbations, being surrounded by an extended rural hinterland with limited transport links. It is perceived by some people from outside the area in a very disparaging way:

> What's here in [seaside town]? I think there's a lower class of people of England, not all of them. You can definitely see a big difference between the people in London, yeah.
>
> Q: What kinds of difference?
>
> Erm. Well [pause] here is so much people with syndromes and stuff? Syndromes, syndromes, do you know what I mean? More people that like are something wrong with. [pause] And they are all fat, here. [pause] They're really not very clean up here. And they don't really give a damn about the way they live, because they're the really fat girls wearing the little tops. [pause] I just think that they don't know any better. It's just that. Yeah. (Migrant seasonal worker, female, 19)

These perceptions of place are important for the ways in which they inform local young people's identities and young women's identities in particular. The relatively negative light in which the resort is sometimes cast by both local and incoming young people can and does play a part in how young people behave in their environment. In other words, to identify oneself and to be identified with a place that is poorly regarded, a place that is seen as slightly seedy behind the entertainment dazzle and, ultimately, a place of little import plays a role in some young people's limited aspirations and negative evaluations of themselves and their bodies.

Among the young people with whom I worked, there was a range of significant social actors, all with differing but interrelated relationships to the area and with other social groups.[5] I have categorised these key social actors into five groupings. The first group comprises the 'locals', the young people who live permanently in the area and are frequently employed as seasonal workers in the tourist and entertainment industry, sometimes on the boundaries of legality. The second group consists of seasonal migrant workers who come into the area to work in the tourist industry in the peak season. These young people come from both within and outside the UK. The third group are 'transient' young people, whose lives are characterised by repeated relocation and changes in their living arrangements and family circumstances, as well as by their lack of connection to mainstream school or work. These young people may also be engaged in seasonal employment in the entertainment industry. The fourth group of significant actors are the holidaymakers, whose relationships to the area are characterised by the temporary but often repeated nature of their visits. Finally, the fifth group comprises the entertainment industry which is threaded through these groups, connecting them and playing a significant role in both their working and social lives across a range of contexts, as considered below.

Seasonality and employment

> The fair, the pier, the arcades, even now I get excited when summer comes. (Local young mother, 23)

The issue of seasonality is of particular importance in this area, where there is a distinct 'summer' season, which has recently been extended from Easter to November. The peak season is geared towards holidaymakers, and the population of the area increases significantly during this period. In winter, the population declines again and jobs become relatively scarce as the entertainment and tourist industry scale down their activities for several months. This ebb and flow of the seasons inevitably impacts upon young people's behaviour, as one local young man explained:

> It's a seasonal thing, you know, they're half the time, you know, for what four or five months of the year the place is effectively dead. You know, all the clubs are closed and everything. I think that doesn't help. I mean, there are a

few bars and, you know, clubs that open, but when the
season really does kick off, people's attitudes change. They
let go more. They feel they can. (Local seasonal worker,
male, 22)

The characteristics of seasonally available work create conditions
whereby young, single people are the preferred employees. The
work tends to be unskilled, relatively poorly paid (usually not
more than the minimum wage) and relatively insecure, with few
promotional prospects. It is often within the informal economy
and so may not benefit from employment rights legislation.
Another aspect of the availability of seasonal work is that local
young people frequently begin working in the entertainment
sector from the age of twelve or thirteen. This kind of work, in
arcades, at the funfairs and in cafes, introduces them to the
culture of earning, and, although they must work long hours for
low pay, it gives young people a disposable income to spend in
clubs and pubs at the weekends: 'You do get into a cycle, you can
earn a lot of money in a summer season, long hours and low pay
but you do lots of hours, and have two or three jobs, you get used
to earning money from a young age' (local young mother, 23).
      Access to a regular income appears to be a factor in
constraining young people's future aspirations, in so far as some
of them envisage continuing this pattern of unskilled, seasonal
work beyond their teenage years rather than broadening their
horizons. Thus, their habitual service to the carnival influences
their longer-term employment patterns. Moreover, it brings them
into contact with older people who come to the area in search of
casual sexual encounters.

The entertainment industry

The resort's holiday atmosphere, with its culture of clubbing,
drinking, having a good time and meeting new people for brief
friendships, has implications for young people's sexual behaviour,
be they locals or holidaymakers. The role of the entertainment
industry could be said to institutionalise this culture (Bell et al.
2004; Stanley 2005). Furthermore, the fact that there are influxes
of strangers into these seaside areas can contribute to the idea of
'no consequence sex', sex that may also be more likely to be
unprotected. 'Seasonal sex' and 'sex on the beach' were often
raised as factors in young people's lives in the resort:

> I broke into a chalet at sixteen to have sex with a summer
> holidaymaker, he was seventeen. (Local young mother, 23)

> Cos all the holidaymakers come down. It's the season to be
> jolly! Because they'll all be gone in a week. And at our age
> we've all got summer jobs so we've got money so we can
> all get drunk. And they'll be off in a week so...
> (Secondary school pupils, year 12 males, sixteen to seventeen)

> Cos you can like screw them and then just... You don't see
> them again. You just hope they don't get pregnant.
> (Secondary school pupils, year 10 males, fourteen to fifteen)

Local young people felt that they were pressured into becoming
part of a cultural stereotype of engagement in 'holiday
relationships' by participating in the 'good time' atmosphere.
Young people from many cultural and regional contexts feel that
they are pushed into having sex, or into being seen to have lost
their virginity, but in the seaside context this pressure becomes
more acute as a result of the particular nature of the holiday,
carnival atmosphere. This has particular ramifications for young
women, who must negotiate the double-edged sword of the
virgin–whore dichotomy in cultural constructions of femininity.
Young women should not be sexually promiscuous, but it has
become an aspect of the abjected working-class white girl to
expect her to be and simultaneously condemn her for being so.
Similarly, alcohol consumption amongst young people (and,
again, especially amongst young women) is at once culturally
deviant and encouraged by the entertainment industry as an
integral aspect of the holiday atmosphere, and can affect young
people's attitudes to casual and, reportedly, unprotected sex,
reducing their inhibitions:

> Oh, yeah. It's [underage drinking] real bad, around here it
> is anyway ...my sister was in there [nightclub] at eleven
> drinking alcohol. Loads of kids, holidaymakers ...Yeah, it's
> all just pubs.

> Q: What about people's attitudes to contraception and
> casual sex?

> Well, a lot of them think it's a load of fun, don't they? I
> mean, they don't take it seriously ... they aren't bothered
> around here. They do it and they're not bothered about the
> consequences. (Local seasonal worker, female, 25)

Transience is also significant, the nature of which can be specific to the seaside context. There is a sense of people attempting to run and hide at the edge of the land. Some young people come to the resorts to escape lives that in some way had gone wrong, running from family problems and relationship breakdowns. They may have spent family holidays in the area in the past and have memories of happier times from their childhood that they are attempting to recapture:

> The resort is a bit like the village of the damned, once you enter you can't leave! You get a lot of people coming on the run from the police, from family, from their former lives. They come [here] like it's the end of the world, to escape. They may have been here once on holiday and liked it for a week so they made their way back to escape whatever horrible lives they have, but they don't realise it's horrible here too, full of rough people and it all closes down in winter. I like the isolation of the place myself but that's not why they come really, they wanted to relive their fun times. (Local seasonal worker, female, 25)

Behind the big dipper: perpetuating liminality and reinscribing transgression

Seasonality, temporality and transience thus characterise the lives of many young people in the seaside context. The holiday atmosphere removes the young people from their mundane, everyday lives, at least temporarily, creating a fantasy world in which the normal order is suspended. These issues of fantasy, carnival and impermanence are directly significant for the social relations manifested by and between these young social actors. In turn, these contexts and behaviours have important implications for their attitudes towards casual and unprotected sex – sex that is seen by the state and the media as 'transgressive'. Relationships are often brief, casual and with strangers. This adds to the excitement of the moment, the excitement of risk and danger for which a ride on the roller coaster might be an appropriate metaphor.

For the young people who live permanently in the resort this sense of carnivalesque temporality becomes a condition of their lives and can affect their perceptions of the longer-term consequences of having casual, unprotected sex, placing them at greater risk of potential negative consequences of such behaviour. Young holidaymakers are at 'risk' too, inasmuch as they also suspend reality for the duration of their time in the holiday resorts, potentially encouraging less responsible attitudes towards sexual relationships. In all cases, these social groups reinforce the expectations of the other to 'let go' in a perpetuation of the carnival:

> Because when you're young all you can wait for is the season starting and all the lads coming to the holiday camps. Or the fair lads will be starting ...and you start to go out to work and get a bit of dosh so that you can dress up and it does feed that atmosphere and you get excited like oh there's going to be fresh lads in town ...That's how I would think a lot of pregnancies come about when you're young. And it is that attention, because the local lads treat you in one way because you're there all the time and the summer lads would spend money on you.... It's that old notches on the bedpost business ... let's see how many lads we can get off with this summer. And along the line somewhere there might be one that's unlucky enough to fall pregnant. It's not deliberate, it just happens, but you don't think of it because you're just acting recklessly really cos the lads are down for the season. We're bored with the local lads – let's see what we can find out there. When you're younger that is what you feed off .... It's that buzz. There is a buzz about the place when the season starts. (Local professional, Traveller Education Service, female)

These young people engage in unprotected sex with relative strangers not because they are unaware of sexual health messages or the risk of unplanned pregnancy, but because sexual experimentation becomes an aspect of the suspension of reality and consequence in the carnival context. An analogy might be drawn here with the annual Brazilian *carnaval* in Rio, perhaps the most widely known association of carnival with sexual promiscuity, hedonism, transgression and inversion. Whilst the carnival in an English seaside resort may seem a poor relation to the colourful parades, celebrations and excesses of the Rio *carnaval*, there are nevertheless some similarities. As Parker (1997: 367) explains, in Rio, '[i]mpersonal sex between strangers who may never see one another again, sex in groups, sex in the streets or on the beach, sex in public ... all become part and parcel of the play of *carnaval*'. In reference to Bakhtin, Parker (1997: 375) acknowledges that the vision of the Rio carnival is utopian, an experience of the world as it might be rather than as it is, but, importantly, '[i]t is also, of course, an illusion, and no matter how fully they throw themselves into its peculiar reality, its participants never completely lose sight of its fleeting quality'.

That the Rio carnival is a time-bound event is significant. I am arguing that, when one lives 'the carnival' on a more permanent basis, as do young people who live in seaside resorts, it can become more difficult to separate the 'fleeting quality' of the carnival from the lived realities of their everyday existence. Whilst the fantasy is more clearly defined for those young people who move in and out of the resort, as tourists, as migrant seasonal workers or as part of transient families, for the youth for whom the seaside is a permanent 'home', it becomes simultaneously fantastic and the norm, the mundane and the extraordinary. As such, despite the fact that this sense of impermanence may well be relatively permanent, they may continue to perceive their lives as moving within this temporal carnival:

> It could be that with some of these transient populations that come in ... they come for a few weeks in the summer, they stay and they do have a feeling that they're constantly on holiday and therefore throw all caution to the wind. I know when I first moved here, for a year I thought I was on holiday. You just get that holiday feeling and I think you do, you act differently when you're on holiday to what you do when you are actually living ... You do tend in the summer – locals tend to spend more time on the beach and doing holidaymaker things because it's there. Whereas if you lived in a city you would continue with your daily life and you wouldn't have them holidaymakers there. (Local professional, Youth Service, female)

Young people's lives are located in a world that is part of a ritual calendrical event for the holidaymakers, a place holidaymakers come to 'let go' and in which there is little desire to allow their 'normal lives' to encroach. Within this world young men and women are active agents drawn almost inevitably into the carnival culture. The holidaymakers come to have fun and they expect the local young people to participate, whether by providing services, entertainment or even casual sexual relations in the nightclubs or pubs or on the seafront. However, neither the holidaymakers nor the seasonal migrant workers have an enduring attachment to the place. For them, it is a temporary arena in which to holiday or earn money, have a good time – including a good sexual time – and leave. Even when they revisit, they have little sense of responsibility towards, or ownership of, the area and its residents. For them, there is no sense of 'home', and, like the transient young people, they do not see their future being located there in the longer term.

In contrast, for 'local' young people the resort is seen as 'home', even if this sense of permanence is tempered by the seasonality of their carnival employment. Local young people also have conflicting aspirations for the future, inasmuch as they do not expect this life to be permanent; they expect change, possibly relocation, but definitely a transition to a new permanence in later adulthood. At the same time, their aspirations are limited and they frequently expect to remain in the area, and to continue working in the tourist and entertainment industry. This seeming contradiction may be linked to an acknowledgement that their ability to transcend their situation is structurally constrained. These structural constraints combine a range of factors, including limited cultural and educational capital and social and geographical exclusion.

Whilst white, working-class young men and women experience both social and geographical liminality arising from their spatial and class position, young women are further constrained by an embodied liminality as the abject feminine other. As Skeggs (1997, 2004) demonstrates, working-class women are symbolically constrained to the extent that:

> [t]heir ability to move through metaphoric and physical social space is limited, because their cultural dispositions are inscribed and read on their body as symptoms of pathology. This marking and value attribution restricts their ability to convert their cultural resources, which of course have been acquired through classification (by such dimensions as sexuality, race, class and gender) and have been read and valued as worthless by those who institutionalise the dominant systems of exchange. (Skeggs 2004: 293)

Because of the social and economic perpetuation of a marginal existence in the liminal space of the seaside, and because they are confronted with a discourse that continually reinscribes their perceived gender and class deviance as a fundamental condition of their bodies, such young women do not experience 'carnival' as the liberating radical utopianism suggested by Bakhtin (1984). This is not to suggest that these young women are passive victims of a rigid set of social values. Within the carnival context, young women are able simultaneously to undermine and reinforce the existing social structure through appropriating the caricatures of femininity that they are ascribed. As Davies states in the context of carnival in early modern Europe: 'The image of the disorderly woman did not always function to keep women in their place. On the contrary, it was a multivalent image that could operate, first, to widen behavioural options for women ... and, second, to sanction riot and political disobedience' (Davies 1965: 131, cited in Russo 1995: 59).

What clearly emerged from the research with young women was their conscious complicity with these stereotypes of disorderly women, not only because they knew that this was expected but because they were fun to enact, and in doing so they gained a sense of power, at least in the short term. Nevertheless, whilst negotiating, subverting and utilising the social categories and cultural perceptions within which they are yoked, they are ultimately compromised by them.

Conclusion

This chapter has grown out of a larger multi-sited research project funded by the UK government's Teenage Pregnancy Unit (see Bell et al. 2004). Press coverage of the research findings was interesting, if predictable. The focus of the headlines was on the sexual transgression of the teenage girls and on the high rate of teenage pregnancy. Under the headline 'By the Sleaze-Side', the *Sun* reported, 'Teen pregnancies boom at "partying resorts". Seaside resorts have the highest teenage pregnancy rates because of their partying atmosphere ... Blackpool has 74.8 teenage conceptions per 1000 girls aged 15 to 17 compared with a national average of 42.6' (Whittingham 2004: 12). The point here is not that the press misrepresented the research, but rather that they were highly selective in what they did report. The locus of attention becomes the problem of (white, working-class) young women's sexuality and not, for example, the role of younger or older men or the entertainment industry itself. And so yet again, the same old stereotype of the young, working-class female 'slapper' was reinforced by partial reporting of the findings of our study.

The research also raised a dilemma over how to deal with the idea that the entertainment industry itself benefits from casual teenage sex. Neither the media nor the government seems to want to critique openly an industry that is a fundamental economic base of a seaside resort with an already high rate of deprivation.[6] The seaside entertainment sector not only employs young people to work in the clubs, arcades, restaurants and funfairs, but it also benefits from their sexuality. For many men and women a holiday at the seaside would be incomplete without casual sex. For adults, this is a permitted, if somewhat illicit, desire, precisely because it does not fundamentally destabilise the everyday order of regulated adult sexuality, although there are concerns about the rise of STIs. For teenagers, and teenage girls in particular, it is transgressive and a cause for moral panic, especially when pregnancy results and they become a 'burden on the state'. These are young female bodies that are 'out of control'. This returns us to the point made at the outset, that the crux of the debate, and that which most defines sexual transgression, is about the control, or perceived lack of control, over the reproductive bodies of white working-class young women, and about who is reproductively authorised.

The connection between transgressive sexuality and the control over young people's bodies is heightened in the seaside context described above. As Rubin (1993), Skeggs (1997) and Tincknell et al. (2003) have suggested, transgressive sexuality is that which is seen to violate the norms of monogamous, long-term, reproductive (and middle-class) heterosexuality: all other forms of sexuality and sexual relations can be constructed as occupying an excluded and transgressive 'other' category. Here I suggest that transgressive sexuality is permitted, and even encouraged, among certain people in certain contexts, so long as it remains outside the geographical and temporal boundaries of the reproductive norm (i.e. the brief holiday fling in the liminal sphere of the seaside resort).

Where that sexual activity becomes culturally unacceptable is when it seeps from the liminal space – the temporal sphere of the holiday – into the mundanity of the permanent, everyday lived realities of local people. This crossing occurs not in any geographical space, but in the bodies of young women. Young women are constructed as standing at this boundary, and in this context, specifically white, working-class young women. At that point, the line between sanctioned transient pleasure and perceived social deviance has been transgressed.

Notes

1. The research for this chapter was carried out as part of a larger study commissioned by the UK government's Teenage Pregnancy Unit (see Bell et al. 2004).
2. It is significant to note that the folk devils at the centre of Cohen's (1972) analysis are the (white, male working-class) Mods and

Rockers in the 1960s, and that the moral panic focused on their violent and hedonistic behaviour, which was often played out in seaside resorts, such as Brighton. See also Presdee (2000) for an exploration of the links between carnival, crime and constructions of working-class masculinities.

3. Although Corbin does not make their class and ethnicity wholly explicit, it seems that these 'male tourists' were mainly white and middle- or upper-class (Walton 1983).

4. I have referred here to the Regional Government Office (2005). This information was sourced from local government documentation but in order to maintain anonymity the full reference cannot be cited. This is similarly the case for Craig et al. 1998.

5. The following discussion draws on qualitative research conducted in the region for the *Living on the Edge* study and developed initially in Bell et al. (2004: 9–14).

6. The report was presented to the government in July 2004, at the same time as the government announced the relaxation of gambling laws to encourage 'Las Vegas style' entertainment complexes in British resorts, which it was hoped would generate employment.

References

Arnold, D. 1979. 'European orphans and vagrants in India in the nineteenth century', *Journal of Imperial and Commonwealth History* 7 (2): 133–58.

Bakhtin, M. 1984. *Rabelais and His World*, Bloomington, IN: Indiana University Press.

Bell, J., S. Clisby, G. Craig, L. Measor, S. Petrie and N. Stanley. 2004. *Living on the Edge: Sexual Behaviour and Young Parenthood in Seaside and Rural Areas*. Hull: University of Hull.

Bennett, T. 1983. 'A Thousand and One Troubles: Blackpool Pleasure Beach', in T. Bennett, L. Bland, T. Davies, J. Donald and S. Frith (eds) *Formations of Pleasure*. London: Routledge, pp. 138–55.

———. 1986. 'Hegemony, Ideology, Pleasure: Blackpool', in T. Bennett, C. Mercer and J. Wollacott (eds) *Popular Culture and Social Relations*. Buckingham: Open University Press.

———. 1995. *The Birth of the Museum*. London: Routledge.

Billinge, M. 1996. 'A Time and Place for Everything: an Essay on Recreation, Re-creation and the Victorians', *Journal of Historical Geography* 22 (4): 443–59.

Bullen, E., J. Kenway and V. Hay. 2000. 'New Labour, Social Exclusion and Educational Risk Management: the Case of "Gymslip Mums"', *British Educational Research Journal* 26 (4): 441–56.

Clisby, S. and G. Craig. 2001. *Performing Parenthood: Choices and Constraints, Young Parenting in Lincolnshire*. Lincoln and Hull: Lincolnshire County Council and University of Hull.

Cohen, S. 1972. *Folk Devils and Moral Panics: the Creation of the Mods and Rockers*. London: MacGibbon and Kee.

Corbin, A. 1994. *The Lure of the Sea: the Discovery of the Seaside in the Western World 1750–1840*. Cambridge: Polity Press

Craig, G., M. Elliott-White, and N. Perkins. 1998. *Mapping Disaffected Youth*. Regional Training and Enterprise Council (full reference withheld to maintain anonymity).

Cunningham, H. 1980. *Leisure in the Industrial Revolution*. London: Croom Helm.

Davies, N. 1965. *Society and Culture in Early Modern France*. Stanford, CA: Stanford University Press.

Doughty, S. 2005. 'Relentless Rise in Teenage Pregnancies', *Daily Mail*, 25 February, p. 7.

Ferrari, N. 2005. 'Yeah but No but...We've BECOME Little Britain', *Sun*, 24 June, p. 11.

Haylett, C. 2001. 'Illegitimate Subjects? Abject Whites, Neoliberal Modernisation and Middle-class Multiculturalism', *Society and Space* 19: 351–70.

Lawler, S. 2005. 'Disgusted Subjects: the Making of Middle-class Identities', *Sociological Review* 53 (3): 429–44.

Levy, A. 1991. *Other Women: the Writing of Class, Race and Gender, 1832–1898*. Princeton: Princeton University Press.

Lyons, R. and H. Lyons. 2004. *Irregular Connections: a History of Anthropology and Sexuality*. Lincoln and London: University of Nebraska Press.

Malcolmson, R. 1973. *Popular Recreations in English Society, 1700–1850*. Cambridge: Cambridge University Press.

Marrin, M. 2006. 'Only the Middle Class can't Afford Babies', *Sunday Times*, 26 February, p. 5.

Mayhew, H. 1861–62. *London Labour and the London Poor: a Cyclopaedia of the Condition and Earnings of Those That Will Work, Those That Cannot Work, and Those That Will Not Work*, 4 vols. London: Griffin, Bohn.

McRobbie, A. 2001. 'Good Girls, Bad Girls? Female Success and the New Meritocracy', in D. Morley and K. Robins (eds) *British Cultural Studies*. Oxford: Oxford University Press, pp. 361–72.

Morgan, N. and A. Pritchard. 1999. *Power and Politics at the Seaside: the Development of Devon's Resorts in the Twentieth Century*. Exeter: University of Exeter Press.

Office of National Statistics 2001. *Census 2001*, www.statistics.gov.uk/census2001/ons, accessed 23 February 2006.

Parker, R. 1997. 'The Carnivalization of the World', in R. Lancaster and M. di Leonardo (eds) *The Gender/Sexuality Reader: Culture, History, Political Economy*. London: Routledge, pp. 361–77.

Presdee, M. 2000. *Cultural Criminology and the Carnival of Crime*. London: Routledge.

Regional Government Office. 2005. *Structure, Plan, Policies: Issues and Strategic Themes*. Area County Council (full reference withheld to maintain anonymity).

Reid, D. 1982. 'Interpreting the Festival Calendar: Wakes and Fairs as Carnivals', in R.D. Storch (ed.) *Popular Culture and Custom in Nineteenth-century England*. London: Croom Helm, pp. 125–53.

Rojek, C. 1995. *Decentring Leisure: Rethinking Leisure Theory*. London: Sage.

Rubin, G.S. 1993. 'Thinking Sex: Notes for a Radical Theory of the Politics of Sexuality', in H. Abelove, M.A. Barale and D.M. Halperin (eds) *The Gay and Lesbian Studies Reader*. London: Routledge, pp. 3–44.

Rule, J. 1986. *The Labouring Classes in Early Industrial England*. London: Longman.

Russo, M. 1995. *The Female Grotesque: Risk, Excess and Modernity*. New York: Routledge.

Shields, R. 1990. 'The "System of Pleasure": Liminality and the Carnivalesque at Brighton', *Theory, Culture and Society* 7 (1): 39–72.

———. 1991. *Places on the Margin: Alternative Geographies of Modernity*. London: Routledge.

Skeggs, B. 1997. *Formations of Class and Gender*. London: Sage Publications.

———. 2004. 'Uneasy Alignments, Resourcing Respectable Subjectivity', *Gay Lesbian Quarterly* 10 (4): 291–98.

Stanley, N. 2005. 'Thrills and Spills: Young People's Sexual Attitudes and Behaviour in Seaside and Rural Areas', *Health, Risk and Society* 7 (4): 337–48.

Stoler, A. 1997 'Carnal Knowledge and Imperial Power: Gender, Race, and Morality in Colonial Asia', in R. Lancaster and M. di Leonardo (eds) *The Gender/Sexuality Reader: Culture, History, Political Economy*. London: Routledge, pp. 13–36.

Storch, R.D. 1977. 'The Problem of Working-class Leisure: Some Roots of Middle-class Moral Reform in the Industrial North', in A.P. Donajgrodski (ed.) *Social Control in Nineteenth-century Britain*. London: Croom Helm, pp. 138–62.

Thompson, E.P. 1967. 'Time, Work-discipline, and Industrial Capitalism', *Past and Present* 38: 56–97.

Tincknell, E., D. Chambers, J. Van Loon and N. Hudson. 2003. 'Begging For It: "New Femininities," Social Agency, and Moral Discourse in Contemporary Teenage and Men's Magazines', *Feminist Media Studies* 3 (1): 47–63.

Walton, J.K. 1983. *The English Seaside Resort: a Social History 1750–1914*. Leicester: Leicester University Press.

———. 2000. *The British Seaside: Holidays and Resorts in the Twentieth Century*. Manchester: Manchester University Press.

———. 2001. 'Respectability Takes a Holiday: Disreputable Behaviour at the Victorian Seaside', in M. Hewitt (ed.) *Unrespectable Recreation*. Leeds: Leeds Centre for Victorian Studies, pp. 176–93.

Webb, D. 2005. 'Bakhtin at the Seaside: Utopia, Modernity and the Carnivalesque', *Theory, Culture and Society* 22 (3): 121–38.

Whittingham, S. 2004. 'By the Sleaze-side', *Sun*, 2 August, p. 12.

CHAPTER 4

A CURIOUS THREESOME: TRANSGRESSION, CONSERVATISM AND TEENAGE SEX IN THE 'FREE HOUSE' IN NORTHERN IRELAND

Rosellen Roche

It was just a few days before Saint Patrick's Day, 17 March 2000, when the conversation started about 'free houses' and where they were going to be that year. 'What time?' and 'Where is it?' were the most commonly asked questions among the teenagers drifting in and out of the National Vocational Qualification (NVQ) tuition room, a facility for young people who had left school at age sixteen, training them in skilled and semi-skilled trades. After all, everyone was going to have the day off and that meant a party, and, potentially, a free house. For the young people I came to know while working and living in deprived working-class areas of Northern Ireland's second largest city, Derry/Londonderry,[1] a day off from training and a free house meant more than just the ability to have a party; it meant an opportunity to meet, mingle and have sexual contact with members of the opposite sex in a house with no authority figures.

During this conversation with the young people about their impending day off, an example of the shenanigans that occur in a free house was provided by Columba,[2] who recalled for us how his parents returned to find their home transformed by a party in full swing. Emphasising how multiple familial and societal rules

were broken in youthful cunning and frivolity, such as illegal
drinking and drug-taking, Columba also described how he had
helped a young couple to a room by picking the lock to his
parents' bedroom. In the quotation below, Columba tells how
young people aged eleven to eighteen from both Catholic and
Protestant backgrounds were involved in the revelry of the free
house, and the punishment that can follow when caught:

> I remember the whole thing, like [when the parents came
> home] … There were these two wee girls opening these
> bottles of beer, sort of here [demonstrating] and then he
> [Columba's father] just busts right through the door.
> And everyone in the front room, they're smokin'
> [marijuana] and all. And my ma and da, they don't allow
> no one to smoke. And they have their feet up on the table
> and all, like that [demonstrating]. This one, he doesn't
> know who came to the door and he thinks it is Mark
> [Columba's older brother] and he says: 'Go on and go to
> the fridge and get me a beer, will ye?' And it's my ma. And
> my ma is like: 'You fucking cunt, get out of my house, you
> bastard!' [Laughing.]
> The really bad part was we gave my wee brother money
> to go out and they don't allow him, like. He's only eleven.
> He's gone out and shows up home full [drunk] and walks
> in the door and says: 'Beers all round!' And my father goes
> up to him and bang, bang, bang, gives him good ones
> across the face. And he's [younger brother] 'Oh I'm in it
> now, I'm in it now!' and he runs upstairs.
> Then Ma goes upstairs, and says, after everyone's gone:
> 'At least they didn't get up here.' They lock their door [to
> their bedroom], ye see. But I had picked the lock for these
> two upstairs … And they had gone in and then locked it
> from the inside. So my ma, she's poundin' on the door and
> gets inside and then there's this wee girl … I'm sorry I'm
> not goin' to tell ye what she was doin', but she's pullin'
> something up, and there she is like: 'Ahhhhhhhh!'
> And my ma, yells: 'Ahhhhh!' And there's all this
> screamin' and she's like: 'What are you doin' in here?!'
> And the wee girl is [demonstrating nodding sideways]
> 'cause he's in the toilet. And my ma goes in and is like:
> 'What are you doing in here, you bastard?' And the wee
> girl, she's up and out into the hall already.

If transgressing can be conceived of as going beyond a set limit, or violating a prescribed rule or law, Columba's story recalling his experience of the free house describes the situation well. For Columba, and particularly for his parents, the gathering held in what Columba and his brothers thought was going to be a free house (their free house) was a violation of the rules both of Columba's family and their wider community. Discovery resulted in Columba's younger brother being struck by their father, and in the oldest sibling, who was ultimately responsible for the house in his parents' absence, being forbidden to engage in any social activity for several weeks. The fact that the young people had transgressed the rules was clear to both the young people involved in the party and to the parents who inflicted the punishment.[3]

In further conversations, Lori, a nineteen-year-old Protestant, described a free house to me as 'a house that's empty [of authority figures]. C'mon, Rose, *ye know*, a house where people have a wee party and some people go to cop off [have sexual contact] and *go* together [get together romantically].' Lori's brief explanation captures very well how both Catholic and Protestant young people describe the free house. Early in my fieldwork I understood only that a free house entailed a party. It was only much later that I realised that what distinguished 'free' houses from ordinary party houses was the freedom young people felt they had over their own sexual choices, away from the authoritative gaze of home, church and school. For the young people I came to know, the free house meant much more than just a party – it meant a 'free' space for 'free' choices and a space where sexual contact was possible. Of course, anyone coming to a free house engaged in the usual teenage party activities, such as drinking and/or taking illegal substances, but a free house also entailed the potential for sexual contact and sexual intercourse. Sometimes this sexual contact was between established young lovers escaping to the 'privacy' of a room, yet often this sexual contact included two new partners going 'upstairs to one of the rooms', an act that 'publicly' signalled their union. In both cases, other partygoers are aware that sexual contact is taking place. In a highly conservative Christian-based society, where sexual contact outside marital or consensual 'grown-up' conditions is discouraged, having this type of contact is perceived as fun by the young people, not least because it is forbidden. By including the potential for sexual contact, a free house for the young people is something that can be shared and communally relished among them, whether assisting a young couple in a relationship, or when the rooms are used for a one-off liaison.[4]

What young people see as a space for transgression and choice, however, may be viewed differently by the anthropologist. While young people can negotiate access to such space, and transgress familial and societal rules in the process (such as lying to get there), free houses are not always the wholly transgressive spaces that young people perceive them to be. Indeed, while young people may take advantage of the free house's availability for sexual contact in the midst of a party atmosphere, in the end the choices they make are shaped by the conservative ideologies of the wider society.

This chapter explores the free house in light of the recent 'moral panics' (Goode and Ben-Yehuda 1994; Cohen 2002) about the decreasing age for sexual activity among young people in Northern Ireland. I begin by outlining the relative paucity of research regarding the sexual habits of Northern Ireland's young people against the growing disquiet at the trend for sexual activity at an ever younger age, situating this within the region's continuing conservatism and comparing Northern Ireland's teenage sexual habits (Shubotz et al. 2002) with those elsewhere in the United Kingdom and in the Irish Republic.

The chapter then focuses on the free house as understood by working-class young people living in deprived urban areas.[5] Using case examples, I consider how some young people perceive the free house as too 'public' for sexual experimentation, while others use its 'privacy' to escape parental control. Notions of the boundaries (Harding 1998) between public and private spaces where sex feels comfortable are shown to be subjective and shifting depending upon who is involved in the process of decision making, such as parents and siblings, and what options young people have available to them. While sexual boasting is common, even in the free house sex is bound by notions of 'permitted' sexual partners and peer approval. I argue that, although the free house is conceptualised by young people as a space for transgression, they often bring with them their own socially and personally approved moral histories (Foucault 1979; Weeks 1995). Thus, while this 'free' space can be seen as a bounded heterotopian moment when teenage energy and choice can be explored in full (Foucault 1984), the free house is also a space where wider social mores continue to constrain sexual partnerships.

As young as twelve:
Northern Ireland's teenage 'sex crisis'

'1,321 Teens Are Treated in Ulster Sex Clinics' (2 November 2005), 'Teen Sex Crisis Must Be Tackled' (3 November 2005), 'Broader Approach Needed to Tackle Teen Sex Crisis' (9 November 2005) cried the headlines of a series of articles and editorials in the *Belfast Telegraph*, one of Northern Ireland's leading daily newspapers. All of a sudden, Northern Ireland's teens were having sex (and catching sexually transmitted infections) and the rest of Northern Ireland knew about it. This 'moral panic' in autumn 2005, one of a spate of news clusters about the teenage sex topic, followed some of the first empirical studies of young people's sexual health in Northern Ireland. Why was Northern Ireland so slow to conduct research on the sexual attitudes and habits of its citizens? Two factors would seem to explain this: the first relates to Northern Ireland's continuing political and moral conservatism, and the second to the fact that for over thirty years everyday issues such as the sexual health of Northern Ireland's young people were overshadowed by a focus on ethnic conflict.

Although Northern Ireland constitutionally remains part of the United Kingdom, its physical location is on the island of Ireland, and it continues to be divided along ethno-nationalist and ethno-religious grounds. Despite efforts to address residential segregation and divisions in school and workplace (Office of the First Minister and Deputy First Minister 2003, 2006), repeated interruptions in devolved power-sharing government since October 2002 indicate the ongoing political difficulties in creating a shared society, and sectarian segregation remains a reality for much of Northern Ireland.

Church attendance has historically been high for both Catholics and Protestants in Northern Ireland, with middle-aged and older women from both traditions being the leaders in service attendance (Boal et al. 1996). Although trends show a decrease in attendance, with Catholics demonstrating a more dramatic decline (McAllister 2005: 1), as recently as the early 2000s half the population continued to attend services weekly or more regularly, and the majority of the population continue to self-identify as either Catholic or Protestant (McAllister 2005).

This combination of political and religious conservatism affects much of the legal, policy and social regulation of sexual practice. Like the Republic of Ireland, where the moral and political domination of the Roman Catholic Church affected attitudes towards sex and sex education until the 1990s (Inglis 1998),

Northern Ireland trailed behind England, Scotland and Wales both in academic research on sex and in policy formation. Much of Northern Ireland's policy in relation to sexual health now remains more in line with the Republic than with the rest of the United Kingdom, such as the legal age of consent for heterosexual contact and the prohibition on abortion. Although the age of consent in England, Scotland and Wales is sixteen, in Northern Ireland, as in the Republic, it is seventeen,[6] while abortion is similarly prohibited in both places despite its legalisation in England, Scotland and Wales since 1967.

It is within this context of sexual conservatism that the sexual practices of Northern Ireland's young people have recently been creating a wave of uneasy concern. News reports, such as 'Prevent Teen Sex Schools Are Told' (*Belfast Telegraph*, 17 May 2006), state that young people 'as young as twelve' are having sexual intercourse, and that sexually transmitted infections (STIs) increased by 30 per cent between 2000 and 2004 across Britain and Northern Ireland (Family Planning Association 2005). Initiatives have been advocated or introduced to combat everything from Northern Ireland having one of the highest European teenage pregnancy rates (Department of Health, Social Services and Public Safety (DHSSPS) 2002) to demands from prominent organisations such as the National Society for the Prevention of Cruelty to Children (NSPCC) for a comprehensive curriculum review of Northern Ireland's Personal, Social and Health Education (PSHE) (NSPCC 2006).

However, young people in Northern Ireland are having sex in their teens at or before the age of consent, just as they are in the Republic of Ireland, England, Scotland and Wales. A cross-sectional national survey in the Republic of Ireland of 3,000 adults aged eighteen to forty-five revealed that age at first sex had decreased for men from nineteen to seventeen and for women from twenty to eighteen (Rundle et al. 2004: 7). In England, Scotland and Wales, however, the results of the National Survey of Sexual Attitudes and Lifestyles show that the age has decreased for both sexes to the age of consent (Wellings et al. 1994; Wellings 2005).[7] Indeed, age of first experience has decreased for men aged twenty to sixteen and for women aged twenty-one to sixteen over a forty-year period. Discussing these shifts, Wellings (2005) indicates that the proportion of young people who have had sexual intercourse before the age of sexual consent is also shifting. Over the same forty-year period, the percentage of young women who have experienced sexual intercourse before the age of consent rose from fewer than 1 per cent to 25 per cent (Wellings 2005: 16).

In Northern Ireland, the absence of comprehensive data regarding sexual behaviour makes it difficult to comment definitively on whether young people have increased or decreased their age of first sexual experience. However, recent evidence suggests that Northern Irish young people are very similar to those in Britain and the Republic. In a 1997–98 survey (Health Promotion Agency for Northern Ireland 2000), approximately 15 per cent of the 4,465 young people between twelve and sixteen years who were contacted indicated that they were sexually active, while a Family Planning Association (FPA)-sponsored survey showed that 53 per cent of 1,013 respondents between fourteen and twenty-five had experienced sexual intercourse and, of these, almost 37 per cent had sex before seventeen (Schubotz et al. 2002; Family Planning Association 2005; see also Northern Ireland Statistics and Research Agency 2002). In the FPA survey almost 27 per cent reported that they had had sex before age sixteen. Young males reported having sex on average one year earlier than their female counterparts (at approximately fifteen years compared with sixteen years), while the average age of the first steady sexual partner varied even more between the sexes, with young men reporting an average age of sixteen years and young women an average age of eighteen years (Schubotz et al. 2002: 35–46).

Revealingly, the FPA survey shows that most young people's first sexual encounter occurred in what they perceived to be a steady relationship, with approximately 77 per cent stating that they were in a steady relationship or had known their partner for a while. Young women were significantly more likely than young men to have sex in a steady relationship. Only 9 per cent noted that they had had sexual relations when they had met their partner for the first time (Schubotz et al. 2002: 35–46), illustrating that, although young people are engaging in sex in their early teenage years, and are having sex perhaps earlier than the previous generation, they still consider themselves to be having sex in what they see as committed relationships.

Too many people about: family homes, free houses and sex in 'public' spaces

Although we now know more about the age at which young Northern Irish people become sexually active, we still know very little about where they engage in sexual contact. While some young people from working-class areas with whom I have conducted research related incidents of sexual contact, experimentation and intercourse in open fields, sheds, dance clubs and cars, most reported that sexual contact occurred when parents or authority figures were absent either in their own homes or in the homes of others (Roche 2003). That many young people from working-class areas live at home well into their twenties is confirmed by recent research on young, working-class school leavers in the Derry City Council District areas (Roche 2003, 2005a, b). From a sample of 486 males and females aged fifteen to twenty-five, 71 per cent stated that they lived in parental or natal home environments: 82 per cent of young people eighteen and under, 65 per cent of those nineteen to twenty-one-years-old, and 52 per cent of young people between twenty-two and twenty-five reported being in the natal home (Roche 2005a: 71). Young people, therefore, are living within housing environments that have many people living within them, often including extended family members, such as grandparents, as well as siblings, parents, step-parents and others.

With so many family members around, especially parental figures, having sex is a problem for these young people. For example, when I asked Richard, a seventeen- year-old Protestant who works in a local abattoir, where he and his girlfriends engage in sexual activities, he mentioned 'waiting for' and 'getting' a free house. He explained that 'ye wait', because 'ye just don't do that with people [family] about'.[8] Young people abstain from sex at home not just because the presence of authoritative parental figures may interfere with feeling comfortable and 'private' about sex, but also because some of them are concerned that other family 'people', such as younger siblings, may be influenced by their sexual behaviour. Richard, for example, had a deep feeling of responsibility towards his younger sister, Amanda, which functioned not just within the family home but also inside the free house. In the process of 'getting' his own house as a free house, Richard often made promises to his parents to mind his younger siblings:

> You wait for a free house [to have sexual contact]. I would say, like, 'I'll mind them [brothers and sisters]. Ye can have the night away, a weekend, like.' It works, like. And then, there's a party, a party and all and people come round. It happens then. They stay or whatever. Go into the [bed]rooms ...When Amanda [sister] was younger, I wouldn't do it like, but now, everyone knows. She knows like. It happens around her, her friends like. Well, between

us, like, we all know about it. It's that you go to other people's houses too. It works itself out.

Here the free house is something occasionally engineered by Richard and something understood among peers to be a place where sexual contact occurs. Even though the house may be filled with people, it is, as Richard suggests, not filled with 'people' – family people. When Richard's sister was younger, he felt responsible for keeping the potential for sexual contact out of the family home and he stepped into the role of being one of the 'people'. Now, however, as Amanda enters her middle teens, Richard and his brothers accept Amanda into their peer network as part of the 'we' who 'know' and 'hear' about 'it', even though his parents still perceive Amanda as young enough to be 'minded' by her older siblings. For both Richard and Amanda, the free house is a private space that now 'between us' is a place where sex can happen and is understood to happen, and this fact is accepted between them. No longer belonging to the strict category of 'people', Amanda joins Richard, and they become partygoers alike at the free house.

On some occasions, young people in especially committed relationships, such as those who are engaged, can 'stay' in the same room in the family home with the blessing of their parents. In these circumstances, there is negotiation between parents and the young people involved about whether their lover can 'stay' in their bedroom overnight. Such decisions not only reflect the parents' own morality, but again involve the sense of stewardship over others in the house. A typical case involved Assumpta, a twenty-two-year-old Catholic whom I have known since the start of my fieldwork in 1999. Assumpta has had countless beaux in the time I have known her, but, now a receptionist at a local charitable organisation, she has been going steady with Niall, a twenty-one-year-old night clerk at a nearby hotel. Assumpta explained to me that, since they have been in a long-term relationship for 'almost two years', both sets of parents agreed to let the lovers 'stay' in the same room together in their respective homes. Although the couple are not engaged, this decision was made after approximately two months of negotiation, and after she and her parents felt her youngest sister was 'old enough to understand that Niall and she were together, forever'. Assumpta continued:

> We are together now, Rose. Well, I hope forever, like. My parents, they think he's wile [very] good and all. It was just about my wee sister and all. But she's old enough now,

like, to understand. It's just better we're together and no one talks about it, like. He gets up and just eats wi' [with] us and all. It's grand. We never had nowhere to go and it was a problem, so it was. We would wait for a [free] house like, but I just was wile uncomfortable with that. So was Niall. It was wile [very], I don't know, open. There were too many people about, so there were.

Assumpta and Niall's sexual experiences are now tolerated and accepted inside their own family homes. By saying that 'no one talks about it', Assumpta emphasises that her activity in the bedroom with Niall is a private act between the two of them, whereas both Assumpta and Niall found sex in the free house an uncomfortable experience, more 'open' and public.

Other young people also echo sentiments of feeling too 'public' while having sex in the free house, and stress the importance of setting a good example to younger siblings. Dympna, an eighteen-year-old Catholic, is open about sex and has moved out of the natal home to be able to have sex with her boyfriend on a more regular basis. Dympna and her boyfriend now live in a young persons' Foyer, a housing system devoted to giving rooms to young teenagers who have left home. Dympna left her family home because of 'too many arguments' about her behaviour (sexual and otherwise) with her parents. Echoing both Richard and Assumpta, Dympna's move was not just based on her personal preferences, but reflected concern for other family members as well. 'It was too much with the other wains [children] … I guess I understand that now.'

Regarding sex and the free house, Dympna explains that different people use the space of the free house in different ways, and that having sex in the free house is a matter of personal preference. Like Assumpta, Dympna sees the free house as too public a space, particularly if one is 'really with somebody' and in a committed relationship:

It's just I think it's, if you're goin' steady it's a lot different. If you're really wi' [with] somebody. If you're just wi' them a couple of nights here and a couple of nights there, and sleeping wi' them here and sleeping wi' them there, or some people only do it if they're at parties and if they're here or they're there, if there's a free house. If there's something going on and they'd just, say it was somebody that they would go wi' [kiss or further] every week, if he was there then they would go in and have sex or whatever.

I seen it happening many a night, most parties it always happens. But naw, I wouldn't be, I don't think sex is for something te do at a party. I think it's more intimate, it's more personal than that.

And it's, anybody could walk in on ye and then everybody'd be talking about ye and then, I don't know. Maybe it's just me, some people just don't give a shite ... Like, [a girl] came down [from upstairs]. And everybody didn't know what they were gonny do or whatever [when they went upstairs]. But then she came down wi' her trousers on the wrong way. And everybody said te her: 'Aw, naw inside out.' ...And somebody said: 'Ye'd need te fix your trousers.' And then everybody knew. You know, that kind of way. If she really didn't want anybody te know, she would make sure. Know it's, it's just funny the way some people are.

Harding (1998: 37) has argued that the boundary between public and private domains of sexuality is interdependent and shifting:

Transgressions of this border help to constitute categories of sexual experience and perform a normative function, since representations of private sex made public are accompanied by an indication of whether or not they should be tolerated. Sexuality, in turn, gives meaning to and links the domains of the private and public and, through this, links the individual to broader cultural and political structures in a way that makes social (dis)order possible.

Harding's sentiments resonate when thinking about the free house. When young people seek out sexual contact, the interpretation of what is a 'public' or a 'private' space can vary, and, as Weeks (1995: 38) also suggests, is dependent upon much personal and situational evaluation. Young people's perceptions of where is a good place to have sex are dependent on many factors such as the moralities of the families, how many 'people' are around, responsibilities to younger siblings and the length of the relationship. Sexual acts and the spaces in which they happen are subject to shifting situational interpretations regarding 'public' or 'private'. Although sex at home and in the free house may both at times be defined as 'public', the particular personal and situational circumstances of those involved may ensure at other times that both are seen as 'private'.

Such changing definitions of social space can be illustrated by the preferences and practices of young people as they decide where to have sex. For instance, while Richard sees the free house as a space where he and his girlfriends can have sexual contact, he is also comfortable with having his own house available for a free house (if he can get it), as his sister now 'knows about it'. For Richard, the free house is shared and 'public' in that many people can be present, but it is also a place that he, his girlfriends, his peers and his sister share 'privately' together, rather than 'publicly' with their parents. Conversely, although Assumpta and Niall tried having sex in a free house, they found the experience 'wile uncomfortable' and too 'open'. Their family homes offer a more private solution for the young lovers, and they have attained an acceptable status as a 'couple'. For Assumpta and Niall, the 'privacy' of the free house was just too 'public' and having 'people' around now is no problem because they are one of them. Finally, Dympna and her boyfriend fit into neither category, and have sought privacy away from 'anybody' or curious peers and from family 'people' by creating their own space.

Under the covers: transgression and conservatism in the heterotopia

I turn now to consider those who use the free houses. Many working-class young people do use free houses for sex, and feel comfortable doing so. Even if a young person does not enjoy using the free house, it creates an opportunity 'when there is nowhere to go'. Transgressions, such as lying to one's guardians, are integral to accessing a free house. Sixteen-year-old Teresa, a Catholic, and trainee hairdresser, disgruntled with the fact that she is forbidden to have sexual contact in her own house, explained how easy it is to get a free house:

> But the way it is, there's gonny be a way around it. No matter what, there's always a way around everything. Like say if I wanted to stay over with a boy somewhere? I'd look about and see who has a free house that night, and: 'Aw mammy, I'm stayin' in such and suches.' And then he'd stay over too. There's a way around everything. Know, if you're gonny do something you're gonny do it. If someone says to ye: 'He's not stayin' in the same room as you,' you're not gonny let … you're just gonny do it.

For these young people, lying about what they intend to do is merely a necessary risk they must take when getting to the 'free' space and they see deceitfulness as part of the risky transgression they feel about the free house. As Judith, a twenty-one-year-old Protestant secretary noted when discussing parental control over her behaviour: 'Ye have to lie to them. Especially if ye are young, like. It's not as if ye are gonny get anywheres if ye just say to them like: "Oh, aye. I'm going to go take Es, get absolutely fucking hammered, or cop off," or something like that.' For the young people, this is the first step in entering a situation that will separate them from what they see as the wider world where rules forbidding sexual conduct apply.

Once in the free house, however, young people use the space as they see fit. The stuff of teenage television drama plays itself out: heartache, revenge, love and raw sexual gratification are all on the agenda. In this 'free' space, young people are granted access to sexual contact and sexual intercourse. However, despite what is seen as liberation from authority figures, judgement is still prevalent. Who has sex with whom is subject to peer approval or disapproval according to personal codes of moral conduct. In a conversation with seventeen-year-old Emer and me, sixteen-year-old Christine talks about getting the attention of a desired lover (Mick) by having sex with another young man (Aidan). Having had access to a free house attended by both Catholic and Protestant young people over the weekend, both young women had engaged in sexual intercourse. Emer had slept with her new boyfriend, Ronan, while Christine had had intercourse with someone with a 'steady' girlfriend. Describing this as 'nothing to be fucking proud of', Emer condemns Christine for her actions because Christine's desire for a particular young man is played out by using another person for sex. Here, Christine uses sex and the space of the free house to her advantage:

Emer	She can't remember how she got a lump in the head, or was it plump in the bed [laugh]. Last night at the party she went with a fella that she shouldn't went with 'cause he is going steady for five and a half years. And his girlfriend's a motherfucker of a bitch, so she is.
Christine	Aye, but I went with him before, sure.
Emer	Aye, you went with him before but this time you *went* with him.
Christine	I talked to him …
Emer	[To Rosellen] That just goes to show that you've shagged [had sexual intercourse with] him. [Laugh.]
Rosellen	What happened?

Christine   I was going with him, right ...
Emer   [Interrupting] And she shagged him and he
           dumped her. [Laugh.]
Christine   That's basically the story ... I don't know, hi, one
           minute we were sitting talking ...
Emer   Aye, and the next minute he fell forward with his
           trousers down and you fell back wi' [with] yours
           down too.
Rosellen   Did this all go on at the party?
Emer   Aye, and she called *me* a slapper [promiscuous
           woman] ...
Rosellen   Was this upstairs?
Emer   It's a bungalow, like a one-bedroom bungalow. I
           was in that bedroom last night along with Ronan
           and about twenty people must've walked in before
           we actually put something up against the door. We
           put the chair up against the door thinking, right if
           they push it, the fucking handle will get caught on
           the top of it. They pushed it and the chair went
           flying to the other end of the room, and I thought,
           'Bastards' [jokingly].
           [Back to Christine] I don't know, give over about him.
           [To Rosellen] She slept with one person last night
           and she wouldn't fuck up about Mick and it wasn't
           Mick she slept with, it was Aidan ...
Rosellen   And Aidan is the one with the girlfriend?
Emer   Yeah, five years ...
Christine   'Cause he [Mick] looked at me and he was all like
           'What the fuck were you and Aidan at last night?'
           And I was all: 'Happy days! He got something that
           you're not getting!'
Emer   But Christine, that there is nothing to be fucking
           proud of, know what I mean. Like you came out of
           the bedroom and all you heard was: 'Has anybody
           got a fag [cigarette]?'

While this example illustrates the humour that accompanies sex in the free house, it also shows that certain kinds of sexual relations can be censured. Sexual conduct in the free house is subject to 'public' viewing by one's peers and while it may be something to boast about, depending upon what occurred and with whom it occurred, it can also be considered morally reprehensible. While Emer's behaviour is acceptable and taken as an opportunity by others to ogle and make mischief, Christine's antics are found morally unacceptable by some in the house. Accusations that she has 'nothing to be fucking proud of' suggest that a code of practice has been broken, even inside the free house. Here, 'public' and 'private' aspects of sexual conduct are again mingled and individualised. Free house sex is subject to rules that young people often do not recognise as reflecting those of the wider society. When conduct is considered improper by those in the free house, such as when Christine has sex with another's long-term boyfriend, young people are illustrating that they still rely upon and are following many of the same standards that would apply outside the free house, whether they realise this or not. Rather than an uninhibited, anything-goes environment, the space of the free house thus sometimes makes visible the hidden societal rules that the young people themselves are not always aware of following. Consequently, it would be misleading to equate the free house and wider society with private and public, or good and bad (see Harding 1998: 26).

While the free house may be a space that young people perceive as wholly discrete, it is in fact an arena in which erotic desire and societal norms meet, conflict and overlap. In this sense, the free house bears much resemblance to Foucault's (1984) idea of the 'crisis heterotopia'. For Foucault (1984: 23), the heterotopia is in contrast to the utopia, and is a separated site nestled in reality, where 'all the other real sites that can be found within a culture are simultaneously represented, contested and inverted'. However, it is a place 'outside all places'. Thus, the heterotopia has elements that are both 'mythic' and 'real' (Foucault 1984: 25). Foucault (1984: 23–27) outlines the following six principles of heterotopias: all societies have them; they can change according to the synchrony of the culture and over time; they juxtapose many sites in one space; they are intimately linked with slices of time; they have a system of opening and closing that both isolates them and makes them penetrable; and, finally, they have a function in relation to all space that remains. In the first principle, Foucault (1984: 24) describes what he terms a 'crisis heterotopia', a sacred or forbidden place 'reserved for individuals who are, in relation to society and to the environment in which they live, in a state of crisis'. Amongst these individuals, Foucault includes adolescents, menstruating women and the elderly.

The free house has all the elements of a heterotopia, and fills a need for those who find themselves in 'crisis'; those young people who have 'nowhere to go' to have sex. What is most compelling considering this theoretical model, however, is that linked to this slice of time, which, by its very nature, is porous only to those who seek and are permitted entry, is the fact that the free house is influenced by history, including the personal histories of the young people who interact within it (Foucault 1979, 1985; Weeks 1986, 1995). While young people see this space as a space of savvy, wilfulness, transgression, creativity and choice, the wider society influences their actions within it (see also Giddens 1991).

Indeed, the free house is not wholly independent of the social expectations that surround the young people, but rather, like the crisis heterotopia, is a place 'reserved' for young people, intimately linked with a slice of adolescent time and located very much within the reality of the young people's worlds.[9] Incorporating much societal and moral dialogue and teaching, young people talk about what happens in the free house and use the free house in a way that shows they consider it to be a forbidden place apart for them, as well as a place that is inevitably subject to many of the norms that come from 'outside' and which penetrate the 'free' space. And it is the free house's very ability to be simultaneously both 'mythic' and 'real' (Foucault 1984: 25) that allows young people to work out their personal agendas in relation to and within this space. For example, while Emer and Dympna see their sexual involvement as quite different from each other, both expressed concern over issues connected to free house sex in terms of commitment to a relationship. Both their perspectives are embedded in societal norms of monogamous commitment and reflect the trend for young people in Northern Ireland to see themselves in terms of a steady relationship. Although both examples entail sexual activity before marriage, the idea of a 'committed' relationship applies even within the free house. Similarly, although Emer's and Ronan's only concern inside the free house appeared to be whether the chair was strong enough to barricade the door from curious onlookers, Dympna did not think that sex was something to do at a party. Subscribing to a notion that sexual intercourse is 'intimate' and therefore 'private', Dympna tried to adhere to 'rules' created and expected of her by the wider society, the Catholic Church and her family.

The reality and myth of transgression in the free house

Transgression and the free house make a unique couple. Moreover, transgression and the free house relate to each other on many different levels. Not only do young people transgress many rules to get to the free house, as well as transgressing many rules when they are there, but the 'free' space is also seen by them as in itself forbidden. This perception that the free house is risky and taboo makes the space transgressive in the eyes of the young people. For them, getting there and what they do there feel very transgressive indeed.

At the same time, however, the free space is also nothing but a reserved 'crisis' space where societal expectations are worked out in a different setting. When in the free house, young people make a variety of decisions that reflect both their own first tentative sexual and moral choices, and wider social realities. Thus, while having sex in a bedroom of someone else's house can be exciting and transgressive, certain rules still apply. For example, it is important not to cheat on partners and not to show oneself up sexually in public or be talked about in a morally negative way.

In this sense, the transgression that is connected to the free house is simultaneously actual and mythic, fulfilling a heterotopology. In actuality, when a free house is available, many young people will lie to their parents to get to it. It is anticipated that rules about underage drinking and substance abuse will be broken when inside the free space. Sexual experimentation is also anticipated. Some may seek to participate in sexual contact on the night, while others may merely 'see' young people moving to bedrooms. In sum, the young people perceive the free house as transgressive.

On the other hand, beyond this actuality of the transgression of social rules and perceptions of a forbidden place is another reality – the fact that rules of the wider society are often carried into this space by the young people. An uninvited partner, moral conservatism, also often sneaks under the covers amongst those who choose to use the free house. The free house is not just a space of imagined taboo behaviour, encouraging and providing space for sexual liaisons among teenagers. It is also an actual space that combines both perceptions of and realities of a place set apart, where young people can work out both their own relationships to sex and their relationship to the wider society's beliefs about sex.

While Northern Ireland swings into the occasional moral panic regarding underage sex and teenage pregnancy, values regarding commitment between sexual partners that can be seen as rooted in the 'traditional' teachings of both Christian communities in Northern Ireland are apparent even in the free house. Equally, young people's sexual behaviour in Northern Ireland parallels that of their contemporaries in the rest of the United Kingdom and the

Republic of Ireland, and their sexual liaisons are no further out of bounds. Regarding these concerns, it can be said that young people will make their own choices when it comes to having sex in the free house. Often, these choices are influenced by outside events or people. However, in many instances, these choices, like many other youthful choices, are made at the time. What is understood, encouraged and even engineered is the expectation that the free house will provide the space for this choice, and that young people see the space as somewhere over which they can preside; it is a space 'reserved' for them (Foucault 1984: 25). The free house may thus be seen as a place where societal and personally adapted rules and regulations can be tried out, transgressed or tabooed, and where the sexual energy of young people can be subject to an array of choices for just that night.

Notes

1. Northern Ireland's second largest city was first known by its Irish Gaelic name, 'Dóire' (meaning 'oak grove'), or 'Derry'. In the seventeenth century the city was officially renamed 'Londonderry' due to the London Livery Companies' financial interests there. Catholic Nationalist and Protestant Unionist factions still argue over the official naming of the city, and the most common expression used in research and local documentation is Derry/Londonderry, as used here.
2. All names are pseudonyms. The age of the respondents given in the text is that at the time of interview. Transcription follows the dialect and individual nuances of the young people's speech patterns.
3. Not every free house hosts such large parties. On some occasions, young people have a few friends over and use the rooms for sexual intercourse at the end of the evening. This chapter discusses those free houses that have more of a party atmosphere and have many young people attending them.
4. This chapter covers consensual heterosexual contact only and does not include sexual contact that is forced or unwanted. In my experience, young people discussed the free house in relation to desired sexual contact and not in terms of force or rape, although this too could happen in the free house. Homosexual contact was also never mentioned.
5. Fieldwork was carried out in Derry/Londonderry in 1999–2002, 2003–5 and 2006, and, while this chapter primarily draws on data collected then, recent dialogue with young people in Belfast supports my interpretations of the free house. Fieldwork was supported as follows: in 1999–2002 by Peterhouse College, Cambridge, and H.F. Guggenheim Foundation and in 2003–5 by EU Peace II Funding/Community Foundation for Northern Ireland, the Derry Youth and Community Workshop, the Northern Ireland Policing Board, Derry City Council, the Ireland Funds and the Honourable

The Irish Society. The chapter was written while the author was an ESRC Postdoctoral Fellow (PTA-026-27-0865) in the School of History and Anthropology, Queen's University, Belfast, in 2005–6.

6. Statutes regarding homosexual contact also follow the same pattern, although Northern Ireland contains no specific legal act for lesbian sex (Family Planning Association 2006).

7. Throughout England, Scotland and Wales, the main source on trends of sexual behaviour is the National Survey of Sexual Attitudes and Lifestyles. The Survey, conducted once in 1990 and again in 2000, examined trends in sexual lifestyles across almost five decades, focusing on respondents aged fifteen to sixty (Wellings et al. 1994, 2001; Johnson et al. 2001). Northern Ireland was never included in these surveys.

8. This expression is a variation of the common expression 'my people'. Young people often described parents and siblings in a possessive and family-oriented form of speech, such as 'my Bronagh' or 'our Michael' when discussing siblings, or when with siblings describing family, 'our people'.

9. Foucault (1984: 25) continues with his description of the 'crisis heterotopia' as:

> privileged or forbidden places, reserved for individuals who are, in relation to society and to the human environment in which they live, in a state of crisis … For example, the boarding school, in its nineteenth-century form, or military service for young men, have certainly played such a role, as the first manifestations of sexual virility were in fact supposed to take place 'elsewhere' than at home.

Foucault considers these crisis heterotopias to be places where young people go 'elsewhere' and yet he does not see them as abnormal. Foucault (1984: 26) states that these types of heterotopias are 'disappearing today' and being replaced by what he terms 'heterotopias of deviation' characterised by 'individuals whose behaviour is deviant in relation to the required mean or norm', and he notes cases of deviant heterotopias as rest homes, psychiatric hospitals and prisons. The free house fits the crisis heterotopian agenda well in that, although young people may perceive the space to be transgressive and risky, they are acting within the norms of society, creating and using a space 'reserved' for them.

References

Boal, F., M. Keane and D. Livingstone. 1996. *Them and Us? A Survey of Catholic and Protestant Churchgoers in Belfast*. Belfast: Central Community Relations Unit of the Northern Ireland Office.

Cohen, S. 2002 [1972]. *Folk Devils and Moral Panics: the Creation of the Mods and the Rockers*. London: Routledge.

Department of Health, Social Services and Public Safety (DHSSPS) 2002. *Teenage Pregnancy and Parenthood: Strategy and Action Plan 2002–2007*. Belfast, Castle Buildings: DHSSPS.

Family Planning Association. 2005. *Sexual Behaviour and Young People (December Factsheet)*. Accessed at http://www.fpa.org.uk/about/info/NIsexbehavyoung.htm.

———. 2006. *Teenagers: Sexual Health and Behaviour (September Factsheet)*. Accessed at http://www.fpa.org.uk/about/info/teensexhealth behaviour.htm.

Foucault, M. 1979. *The History of Sexuality: Volume I, An Introduction*. London: Allen Lane.

———. 1984. 'Des espaces autres', *Architecture/Mouvement/Continuité* October, 22–27.

———. 1985. *The Use of Pleasure: the History of Sexuality*. Vol. II. New York: Random House.

Giddens, A. 1991. *Modernity and Self-Identity: Self and Society in the Late Modern Age*. Cambridge: Polity Press.

Goode, E. and N. Ben-Yehuda. 1994. *Moral Panics: the Social Construction of Deviance*, Oxford: Blackwell.

Harding, J. 1998. *Sex Acts: Practices of Femininity and Masculinity*. London: Sage.

Health Promotion Agency for Northern Ireland. 2000. *The Health Behaviour of School Children in Northern Ireland: a Report on the 1997/1998 Survey*. Belfast: Health Promotion Agency.

Inglis, T. 1998. *Lessons in Irish Sexuality*. Dublin: University College Dublin.

Johnson, A., C. Mercer, A. Copas, S. McManus, K. Wellings, K. Fenton, C. Korovessis, W. Macdowall, K. Nanchahal, S. Purdon and J. Field. 2001. 'Sexual Behaviour in Britain: Partnerships, Practices and HIV Risk Behaviours', *The Lancet* 358:1835–42.

McAllister, I. 2005. *Driven to Disaffection: Religious Independents in Northern Ireland*, Research Update No. 41. Belfast: The Social and Political Archive.

National Society for the Prevention of Cruelty to Children (NSPCC). 2006. 'Pressure to Have Sex Highlights the Need for Better Sex Relationships Education', *Childline*, May. Accessed at http://www/chidline.org.uk/extra/alcoholteensex_casenote.asp.

Northern Ireland Statistics and Research Agency. 2002. *Northern Ireland Health and Social Wellbeing Survey 2001 – Bulletin Number 5*. Belfast: Central Survey Unit, Department of Finance and Personnel.

Office of the First Minister and Deputy First Minister. 2003. *A Shared Future: a Consultation Paper on Improving Relations in Northern Ireland – January 2003*. Belfast: Community Relations Unit, Office of the First Minister and Deputy First Minister.

———. 2006. *A Shared Future First Triennial Action Plan 2006–2009: Policy and Strategic Framework for Good Relations in Northern Ireland*. Belfast: Community Relations Unit, Office of the First Minister and Deputy First Minister.

Roche, R. 2003. 'The Inheritors: an Ethnographic Exploration of Stress, Threat, Violence, Guts, Fear and Fun Among Young People in Contemporary Londonderry, Northern Ireland', PhD dissertation, University of Cambridge, England.

————. 2005a. *Something to Say: the Complete TRIPROJECT Report on the Views of Young School Leavers in the Derry City Council District Areas.* Belfast: Blackstaff.

————. 2005b. *Something to Say Condensed: a Condensed TRIPROJECT Report on the Views of Young School Leavers in the Derry City Council District Areas.* Belfast: Blackstaff.

Rundle, K., C. Leigh, H. McGee and R. Layte. 2004. *Irish Contraception and Crisis Pregnancy Study: a Survey of the General Population.* Dublin: Irish Contraception and Crisis Pregnancy Study.

Schubotz, D., A. Simpson and B. Rolston. 2002. *Towards Better Sexual Health: a Survey of Sexual Attitudes and Lifestyles of Young People in Northern Ireland.* Belfast: Family Planning Association.

Weeks, J. 1986. *Sexuality.* London: Ellis Horwood and Tavistock.

————. 1995. *Invented Moralities: Sexuality in an Age of Uncertainty.* Cambridge: Polity Press.

Wellings, K. 2005. 'Lust: Changing Sexual Behaviour in the UK', in I. Stewart and R. Vaitilingham (eds) *Seven Deadly Sins: a New Look at Society Through an Old Lens.* London: Economic and Social Research Council, pp. 16–19.

Wellings, K., J. Field, A. Johnson and J. Wadsworth. 1994. *Sexual Behaviour in Britain: The National Survey of Sexual Attitudes and Lifestyles.* London: Penguin.

Wellings, K., K. Nanchahal, K. Macdowall, W. McManus, S. Erens, B. Mercer, C. Johnson, A. Copas, A. Korovessis, K. Fenton and J. Field. 2001. 'Sexual Behaviour in Britain: Early Heterosexual Experience', *The Lancet* 358:1843–50.

CHAPTER 5

ZOOSEX AND OTHER RELATIONSHIPS
WITH ANIMALS

Rebecca Cassidy

> In our culture, the decisive political conflict, which governs
> every other conflict, is that between the animality and the
> humanity of man. That is to say, in its origin, Western
> politics is also biopolitics. (Agamben 2004: 80)

Zoosexuality, a sexual orientation towards animals, is one of a
number of identities that emerged on the Internet during the
1980s and 1990s, alongside distinct but related groups of furries,
plushies and therians (weres).[1] The anonymity of the Web created
a space in which people who enjoyed sexual relationships with
animals could discuss their activities unencumbered by the anxiety
of discovery. By the mid-1990s, one could marry one's animal
partner at the First Church of Zoophilia, receive practical
instructions on how to have sex with a wide variety of species of
animals, and conduct a discussion as to the pros and cons of 'coming
out' as a zoo. Human–animal sex was no longer confined to the
psychological literature where it had been treated as a paraphilia,
practised by voiceless social inadequates. Zoos introduced
themselves, tentatively at first, on blogs, including alt.sex.bestiality
(which has since been replaced by alt.sex.zoophile – this change in
domain is highly significant), and began to create a distinctive
sexual identity and to form an international community.[2]

As zoos became an increasingly confident presence on the Internet, they attracted the attention of the mainstream media. In 1999, *Hidden Love: Animal Passions* (Spencer 1999), a film about a Missouri zoo known as Mark Matthews (and also 'The Horseman' or 'Hossie'), was shown on British terrestrial television (Channel 4). It provoked a wide range of responses from viewers in the UK, including seventy-five complaints to the television regulator (Ofcom 2004: 14), who defended the programme as 'a serious documentary exploring a rare minority sexual orientation'. Matthews was one of the first zoos to 'come out', in his autobiography published in 1994, and had also featured in an episode of Jerry Springer alongside Pixel, a strawberry roan pony that he referred to as his wife. The episode was shown in the UK in 1998. In the US, the trailer caused such a furore that the show was pulled. In 2000, an article in the *Independent on Sunday* described the loving relationship between Brian, 42, and Trey, his golden retriever: '"I would lay down my life for him without thinking", says Brian. "He is always there for me. We sleep in the same bed ... and he wakes me in the morning with a kiss. The sex", he adds, "is great"' (Bird 2000). The article argues that, 'for most people, bestiality is far from being the horrifying taboo that it once was'. Soon afterwards, in 2001, Peter Singer, controversial Princeton Professor of Bioethics and author of the 'Bible' of the animal rights movement, *Animal Liberation* (1975), wrote a review of a book about bestiality, suggesting that because we are animals (great apes, to be precise) 'sex across the species barrier' should no longer be seen as 'an offence to our status and dignity as human beings' (Singer 2001). Like *Hidden Love: Animal Passions*, the review prompted huge volumes of contributions to newspapers and Internet forums, some of it supportive, much of it outraged (Beirne 2001).

During this flurry of activity on the Internet and elsewhere, zoos anticipated their eventual acceptance by society, using the language of the gay rights movement in their Web-based discussion groups. Zoo gatherings (zoocons) were openly advertised.[3] Individuals planned coming out parties and informed families of their sexual orientation. By 2005, this had changed. Although pornography involving animals was widely available on the Internet, zoo sites were less numerous and individuals more guarded about their activities.[4] At the same time, a great deal of energy was invested in the creation of laws prohibiting bestiality. During the 2000s, anti-bestiality laws were introduced in Missouri, Oregon, Maine, Iowa, Illinois and Indiana. Zoosex has been recast as 'interspecies sexual assault' (Beirne 1997: 317), a lobbying issue for animal welfare organisations including People for the Ethical Treatment of Animals (PETA) and the Humane Society of the United States (HSUS). The celebratory attitude of zoos writing on the Net has been replaced by a bitter sense of disappointment at an opportunity that they feel has been missed. In some ways, the debate currently taking place mirrors others surrounding sexual practices that are presented as transgressive. Zoos hide behind anonymous tags on the Internet, afraid of being 'outed' and prosecuted under the laws created by those who consider their activities to be a moral outrage or a form of abuse. At the same time, many references to sex between humans and animals are couched in a ribald tone that would be out of place in relation to other kinds of sexual transgression. In the 2001 film *The Animal*, for example, a man looking lustily at a goat when convinced he is an animal himself is expected to provoke laughter, not condemnation. Edward Albees's play *The Goat, or Who is Sylvia?* described an affair between a married man and a goat and received the Tony Award and rave reviews in London and New York in 2002. The range of responses provoked by references to sex between humans and animals creates a peculiarly productive space in which to consider the nature of human–animal relationships, and, more broadly, the relationship between individual sexuality and public morality. The aim of this chapter is not, of course, to advocate or to condemn the act of having sex with animals. Nor is it to understand the reason why people might choose to do so. It is to consider a variety of responses to zoosexuality and to place these in the wider context of other relationships between humans and animals in order to assess what is at stake when people choose animals as sexual partners.

Understanding human–animal sex

There are several possible explanations as to why the UK television watchdog and broadsheet press might be comfortable representing zoosexuality as a minority sexual preference, rather than an aberration. Giddens (1991) has argued that a 'transformation of intimacy' has taken place in Euro–America. He relates 'confluent love', which is 'active, contingent love, and therefore jars with the "forever", "one-and-only" qualities of the romantic love complex', to the 'pure relationship', 'a situation where a social relation is entered into for its own sake, for what can be derived by each person from a sustained association with another; and which is continued only in so far as it is thought by both parties to deliver enough satisfactions for each individual to stay within' (1991: 58, 61). Alongside these new kinds of relationship that are contingent, open and negotiated, he identifies the emergence of plastic sexuality. The transformation of intimacy implies that people will actively pursue relationships that reject the connection of sex with reproduction and marriage. This argument and similar arguments by Fukuyama (1992) and Castells (1996) have been criticised by anthropologists for their exaggeration of change, technological determinism, lack of historical depth and conflation of several distinct elements. Despite this, the idea that the family, sex and intimacy have entered a radically new phase has become commonplace (Cherlin 1992; Crompton 1999; Peterson and Steinmetz 1999; Teachman et al. 2000). According to this argument, zoosex can be understood as one amongst many newly emerging identities that are no longer restrained by a patriarchal, reproduction (both biological and social)-focused system.[5] As with all arguments that claim to identify broad historical trends, it is possible to identify countervailing tendencies. Perhaps most obvious are the rise of the conservative 'family values' associated with the Christian Right in the United States (something that was tried by the Conservative party in the UK under John Major with mixed results) and the sexual traditionalism of many institutions within the West, including the armed forces and the Church. The gentrification of spaces that were once havens for sexually transgressive behaviour, including Times Square in New York and Soho in London, epitomise the recent desexualisation that is currently taking place in the centres of many Euro-American cities (Delany 1999).

The reality, causes and implications of demographic changes are contested. The idea that sexual values are socially constructed is less controversial, and descriptions of sexual practices including zoosex as perversions, deviations and paraphilia in the work of sexologists in the 1950s are commonly deconstructed. The historical study of sexuality eschews universal and essentialist explanations of behaviour based upon a singular and fixed 'nature', in favour of accounts that invoke 'the specifics of any sexual phenomenon: the histories and narratives that organise it, the power structures which shape it, the struggles which attempt to define it' (Weeks 1995: 6). Bestiality, and in particular the emergence of zoosexuality, as well as the recent drive for legislation against these activities should be understood in this way.

Few anthropologists have considered bestiality (exceptions include Devereux 1948 and Beidelman 1961). Incest and its prohibition attract far more attention (Meigs and Barlow 2002).

There is no agreement as to the universality or otherwise of an incest taboo, or on the biological or cultural basis of particular prohibitions. Lévi-Strauss described the incest prohibition as 'culture itself' (1969: 12), on the basis that it forces out-marriage and in doing so creates links between procreating units. More recently, sociobiologists have argued that it is a response to the loss of adaptive potential that results from inbreeding (see, for example, van den Berghe 1979: 29). Both of these arguments may also be applied to proscriptions against sex with animals, which does not create links between human individuals or groups, perpetuate genetic survival or improve evolutionary fitness. In a sense, both incest and zoosex are, literally, antisocial. However, I would argue that a universal argument accounting for the prohibition of sex between humans and animals is unlikely to suffice. Both prohibitions and the practice of human–animal sex appear to relate to historical and cultural moments, each of which requires specific, contextualised understandings.

Peter Singer (2001) suggests that human–animal sex should no longer provoke disgust, since we now recognise that there is no biological or philosophical basis for the barrier between humans and animals (we share genetic material and the ability to experience pain) and this barrier is therefore morally irrelevant. He regards the treatment of animals and humans with unequal regard as 'speciesism' (Singer 1975). I will argue that, although there are a number of activities taking place on the boundary between humans and animals that challenge any simplistic dichotomy between the two, it is not the case that this is part of an unproblematic unidirectional process of undifferentiation. Humanity's animality has always been contested and competing visions of its significance have always coexisted. Conflicting and contradictory relationships with animals in Euro–America are the backdrop to both the emergence of zoosexuality and the determination to legislate against bestiality. Such energetic reactions suggest that there is more at stake than mere animal welfare: the management of the sexual lives and indeed the mortality of animals is explicitly exempt from the moral disapprobation of mainstream campaigners for animal welfare (but not all zoosexuals).

The abominable and detestable crime against nature

In 1601 sixteen-year-old Claudine de Culam was tried for bestiality in Rognon, France. Apparently uncertain as to whether such an act was anatomically possible, the judge appointed a number of female assistants in order to put the dog and the girl to the test. As the women undressed Claudine, the dog leaped upon her. On the basis of this evidence both the dog and the young woman were strangled, their bodies burned and scattered to the four winds, 'that as little trace as possible might remain to remind mankind of their monstrous deeds' (Masters 1973). Bestiality has often attracted savage penalties for human and animal participants. These penalties both reflect and seek to impose particular conceptions of humanity and animality. Where this separation is most marked, or emerging, enforcement becomes a matter of public concern. Salisbury (1994) has described how in Europe in the sixth and seventh centuries animals were perceived as objects and bestiality no worse than masturbation. By the late eighth century, she detects a change in attitudes towards animals that led to bestiality being treated as a crime involving two equally guilty partners. At this time, she argues, having sex with animals threatened our status as humans (Salisbury 1994: 90). Where a more flexible conception of the human–animal boundary is in place there may be a lack of censure, as amongst the Mohave in the 1940s, where bestiality was apparently seen as a childish failing, rather than a crime (Devereux 1948).

Prehistoric depictions of bestiality have been found in Siberia (Taylor 1996), Italy (Taylor 1996), France (Rosenberger 1968), Fezzan (Néret 1995) and Sweden (Dekkers 1994) and are used by zoosexuals as evidence of the naturalness of their activities, based on its wide distribution through time and space. As one zoosexual told me:

> People have always fooled around with animals...In paintings and the books that have been written about zoo you get an idea that loneliness has played a part in this, so shepherds were particularly likely to boff their animals, but now anyone can be a zoo. It is natural to have sex with animals. God made us all, didn't he?

Those who oppose bestiality use its existence in prehistoric times as evidence that it is a practice associated with primitive society and has no place in modern civilisation:

> All the rock paintings show you is that this was something that cavemen did and that we should have grown out of. No one goes around dragging women by the hair or carrying a big club anymore do they? We should have left bestiality behind with all of the other childish things that went on before we knew any better. (contribution by anti-zoo campaigner to zoo blog, 2004)

Despite the Flintstones version of prehistory, the sentiment is clear. Bestiality is an ancient affliction that should have been eradicated by the civilising process. Opponents of bestiality often refer to its prohibition in Leviticus:

> And you shall not lie with any beast and defile yourself with it, neither shall any woman give herself to a beast to lie with it: it is a perversion (Leviticus 18: 23) ... If a man lies with a beast, he shall be put to death; and you shall kill the beast. If a woman approaches any beast and lies with it, you shall kill the woman and the beast; they shall be put to death, their blood is upon them (Leviticus 20, verses 15–16)

Laws against animal sex established and reinforced boundaries between neighbouring, competing identities, in this case Hebrew and pagan, and in doing so established a category of sinful behaviour that is still widely recognised in Euro–America.

Other examples from classical antiquity make mythic work out of blurring boundaries between humans and animals. Metamorphosis and interspecies reproduction is a recurring motif of ancient Greek mythology. Complicated genealogies combine and recombine the animal and human, according to a variety of reproductive formats. Zeus, as a bull, rapes Demeter, who produces Persephone. In a combination of at least two taboos, Persephone is then raped by Zeus as a serpent. Perhaps the most frequently depicted example of this genre is Zeus, as a swan, having sex with Leda, who produces a batch of eggs, one of which contained Helen (see works by da Vinci and Michelangelo, for example). Although they involve sheep, goats, pigeons, horses and women laying eggs, these queer stories are not really about bestiality but about the possibilities of divinity. Ancient Greek bestiality is, however, reported with slavering enthusiasm by a number of authors (Davis 1954; Bagley 1968; Masters 1973). The Greeks are described as 'notorious' in this regard, particularly the Sybarites, 'all of whom are known to have had sex with dogs' (Bagley 1968: 21). Similar examples are reiterated throughout the literature, one author referring to another, with few making use of any primary sources. The Greeks are sexualised in a manner that fits comfortably alongside their traditional association with other kinds of transgressive (homosexual, commercial, slave and master) sex.

Ancient Egyptians are also portrayed as combining a fantastic array of human–animal hybrid gods with a liberal attitude towards sex with animals. The most frequently cited case of bestiality in ancient Egypt involves the Goat of Mendes, described by Herodotus as worshipped by sexually submissive humans. Much is made of Plutarch's reports that Egyptian women locked in pens with goats subsequently refused the advances of men. In this grand tour of ancient empires, Rome is credited with having created the bestial spectacle: public orgies and ritualised ordeals apparently including the rape of slaves by dogs, baboons and horses. Consensual bestiality is also reported amongst shepherds and shepherdesses, and the nobility (Rosenberger 1968; Masters 1973). A satisfactory history of bestiality has not been written. Contemporary authors (Miletski 2002, 2005a, b) cite out-of-date sources without offering any guidance to the reader as to how they should be interpreted. Psychologists, sexologists, historians, classical scholars and sensationalists are lumped together without comment, their books plundered for examples of bestiality that are presented as 'facts' when they are really data, to be analysed and understood in relation to the contexts that produced them. The written history of bestiality reproduces and reinforces existing stereotypes. In short, evidence is not subjected to the same critical attention as it would require in the present, especially where this evidence supports an existing idea of a particular society as sexually alternative. This flaw is also apparent when comparisons are made through space.

Euro–American discussions of bestiality project the activity onto those who are culturally and geographically distant. Predictably, it is a practice associated with the exotic, or 'primitive', in a way that maps onto other kinds of Orientalist discourses about sexuality. In 2002, for example, Miletski used the work of Rosenfeld (1967) and Rosenberger (1968), to make the statement that 'the Arabs are the most dedicated bestialists in the world' (Miletski 2002: 25), without offering any kind of analysis as to how this statement might relate to the present, or to the maintenance of ethnically or religiously significant boundaries in the past. A homogeneous, timeless 'Arab' identity is constructed on the basis of observations that are out of date and of questionable derivation. Within the US, bestiality continues to be associated with the rural underclass, the 'hayseeds' of Kansas and Kentucky, following the problematic work of Kinsey and others (Kinsey et al. 1948; Ford and Beach 1951; Masters 1973). The difficulty of relying upon these kinds of sources for information about any sexual practice is neatly summed up by Havelock-Ellis's opinion that 'Bestiality…is … the sexual perversion of dull, insensitive, and unfastidious persons. It flourishes among primitive peoples and among peasants' (1925: 103).

Recent discussions of bestiality and zoophilia have emerged primarily from psychology (Peretti and Rowan 1983; Beetz 2002; Miletski 2002, 2005a, b; Williams and Weinberg 2003). These six authors gathered material from groups contacted via the Internet (with the exception of Peretti and Rowan's informants, who were referred by their doctors, and interviewed face to face) and their findings are summarised by Beetz (2005). Psychological investigations into zoosex tend to produce an ever finer categorisation of zoosexuals and their preferences. As Williams and Weinberg (2003) make clear, these kinds of descriptions are incapable of supporting generalisations, as they are based on small numbers of self-selected individuals, though they may suggest research questions for the future.

More recently, authors have sought to go beyond describing the nature of zoosex among small groups by relating it to sexual violence and animal abuse. Like attempts to write the history of bestiality, this work is limited by an absence of verifiable data. Bolliger and Goetschel (2005: 24, 25), for example, combine general statements about zoosex, including 'As not all animals comply with the humans' wishes and do not let sexual intercourse occur, it is frequently effected by using physical force', with an acknowledgement that the data necessary to make these kinds of observations are strikingly absent: 'many, if not most, cases [of zoophilic contact] remain undiscovered'. Discussions of bestiality, and particularly attributions of bestiality, reflect conflict, reify boundaries and establish a moral hierarchy, almost always to the disadvantage of the zoosexual. A different approach, one that analyses responses to and perceptions of zoosex, rather than the invisible practice itself, is warranted. This approach re-examines zoosexuality as one of a number of possible relationships between humans and animals.

What is a human?

Arguments about human distinctiveness formed the basis for the prohibition against bestiality that was enshrined in religious and legal documents. Recently, this distinctiveness has been challenged. Darwin's (1859) theory of evolution made humans and animals subject to the same impersonal forces. The idea that humans were made in God's image, but animals were not, which had been pervasive without ever having been completely dominant, was replaced by an image of a single 'kingdom' that included all animals. The evolutionary paradigm that currently dominates biological thinking (though not without competitors; see, for example, Dembski and Kushiner 2001) deplores the kind of essentialism that a human–animal boundary requires.

There is currently no convincing definition of species identity, nor is there any agreement as to how to distinguish formally the class of living creatures that is commonly identified as human from other creatures that share many of its apparently definitive qualities (Robert and Baylis 2003). While all humans appear to recognise categories of human, animal and object (Atran 1999), it is much more difficult to establish a formal definition of the species 'human' without producing some counter-intuitive exclusions and inclusions. Robert and Baylis (2003: 3) estimate that there are between nine and twenty-two definitions of species currently featured in the biological literature, and add that, 'of these, there is no one species concept that is universally compelling'. Attempts to define a particular species, homo sapiens, are equally problematic, even using recent technology. Apart from identical twins, each human genome is different from every other and there is 'no single, standard, "normal" DNA sequence that we all share' (Lewontin 1992: 36, quoted in Robert and Baylis 2003: 4). Moreover, the ability to distinguish between creatures we would intuitively recognise as of different species, say chimpanzees and humans, cannot be reproduced at the level of DNA. This leaves us with the surprisingly lame conclusion that, despite the progress of biotechnology during the past two decades, 'the unique identity of the human species cannot be established through genetic or genomic means' (Robert and Bayliss 2003: 4). Recent work in the natural sciences taking place at the genetic level has complicated, rather than clarified, the distinction between humans and animals that is invoked in many arguments about zoosex.

Ethology has recently adopted the term 'culture' (now out of fashion with social anthropologists) to describe behaviour specific to particular groups of animals. Jane Goodall's observations of spontaneous displays of pleasure at the discovery of a waterfall were the basis for a systematic study of chimpanzee 'culture' (Whiten et al. 1999), which also includes 'social customs', particularly tool use and grooming, which are learned and restricted to certain populations. If a chimpanzee squashes the parasites it has removed from its mate's skin on a leaf before eating them, one may assume that it is from Gombe. Chimps from the Tai forest squash the insects on their forearms. Neither biology nor ethology has offered a resolution to the problem of defining humans, or distinguished them from other animals. Biology cannot replace intuitions regarding likeness or difference between humans and animals with an objective measure that confirms some and reveals others as mere superstition. In fact, ethology suggests that some of the traits once considered to be uniquely human are anything but. Those intent on understanding the nature of the boundary crossing that takes place in human-animal sex must look elsewhere.

Pets

During the seventeenth Annual Pet Week in the UK a survey by Direct Line Pet Insurance claimed that British people are more likely to take time off work to care for their pets than for their partners or relatives (Brown 2005). Amongst those interviewed, Amanda Pitkethly argued that, 'If you have pets, most people would agree that they are part of the family and therefore you should do for them what you would do for your children. Harry (a collie terrier cross) is like my second child' (Brown 2005). In the same week, Zollie, a twenty-two stone mastiff from Aberdeen, began a 'healthfood diet' (O'Hare 2005), and my local Health Authority in Lewisham initiated a scheme under which patients could apply for funding for a pet on medical grounds. Hadley Freeman, deputy fashion editor of the *Guardian*, was dispatched to report on the launch of the latest canine fashion, dog coats from Burberry and Gucci that included a (fake) fur-trimmed parka, a poncho and a mint-green velour tracksuit (Freeman 2005). Pet store Pets at Home announced a 45 per cent rise in earnings, and unveiled plans to open twelve new superstores (Press Association 2005).

Pets should not be seen solely as a late modern or Euro-American idiosyncrasy. Pet keeping was widespread in classical antiquity (Bodson 2000), and is practised by many indigenous societies in the Americas (Serpell 1996; Erikson 2000). It is the recent rapid explosion of pets in Euro-America since the 1960s that has been described as 'unprecedented' (Serpell 1996: 23) and related to a loss of 'ontological security', the result of the decline of traditional social institutions, including the family and the state (Franklin 1999). Numerous authors have recorded the tendency of owners to refer to their animals using kin terms, or to invoke properties usually associated with relationships between kin in order to describe their relationships with their pets (Cain 1985; Voith 1985; Bonas et al. 2000). These arguments downplay the importance of the species involved in intimate relationships in order to emphasise their significance; Bonas et al. (2000: 234), for example, observe that 'what goes on between people and their pets has a lot in common with social relationships between people'. Pets have long been named, buried, clothed, bejewelled and identified as beneficiaries in wills. However, the sheer scale of contemporary pet keeping is impressive, leading some to speculate about a change in demography, from the nuclear family to the single 'parent' of one cat or dog. These family units are an important sector of the commercial enterprise that surrounds pet keeping and the focus of much of the advertising that could equally apply to the family pet, the working dog or the show dog. The status of the kinship involved is contested. As within step- or gay families, the idea of 'fictive kinship' may be rejected, on the basis that this is a label for relationships that are somehow inauthentic compared with those based on biogenetic ties. People demand equal consideration for their pets, and the idea that 'pets are people too' is deeply ingrained and continually reiterated. Discussions amongst committed pet keepers on animal-focused weblogs revolve around the human qualities of pets, and are in this sense very similar to discussions that take place between zoosexuals.

As in biology and ethology, the definitive qualities that once marked a boundary between humans and animals are now attributed to both. Pets are described as rational, reflexive, humorous and deceptive in turns. They 'speak' to their owners, who 'understand' them. Pets dream, have memories and an identity over time; they are individuals. They are 'part of the family', often 'my baby', and as such they are cared for, their rites of passage are celebrated, they are named, dressed and treated by specialists. At the end of their lives they are cared for in nursing homes, buried and remembered as humans would be (though it is also no doubt significant that many will be 'put to sleep', presumably unlike their human 'kin'). Academic descriptions of pet keeping and arguments about the obsolescence of barriers between species do not lead to discussions of zoosex, and, though pets may be thought of as rational individuals in need of stimulation, their sexual needs are rarely considered (except by zoosexuals, who campaign against neutering). Arguments for the acceptance of animals as kin do not support their recasting as sexual partners, but rather the existence of sometimes contradictory, but usually simply context-dependent, definitions of animals. Pets may be 'just like' kin, but, as this expression implies, in important respects they are also 'not quite' kin. They are not eaten, thus relative to (most) farm animals they are person-like. However, their reproductive destinies are controlled in a way that would presumably be unacceptable in human–human relationships, as is their mortality. The equivalence that is stressed by many pet owners is tempered by the imposition of profoundly differentiating acts on the bodies of pets, including a denial of their status as potential sexual partners.

Perspectivism

At the same time as scientific discoveries and everyday practices in Euro–America question previously held assumptions about the human–animal boundary, research by anthropologists amongst hunting and gathering people has revealed the variety of ways in which humans and animals are conceptualised elsewhere. Robert Brightman's (1993) study of the Rock Cree of northern Manitoba describes ritual attitudes towards animals that cast them as subjects, rather than objects. Animals are viewed as intelligent and powerful, and capable of making decisions that can alter the outcome of their interactions with humans. As a result, prey is killed quickly, and bodies are either consumed or disposed of in what is considered to be a respectful fashion, while the Master of Animals is thanked for his generosity so that he might be inclined to make a further gift to the hunter. Relationships with animals are at times adversarial, at other times cooperative. These attitudes are held in various combinations and expressed in myths, dreams, songs and the stories that hunters tell about their encounters with animals.

Other anthropologists have described societies in which the distinction between humans and animals is apparently lacking (Arhem 1996; Howell 1996; de Castro 1998; Willerslev 2004). This is often contrasted with 'Western' (Descola and Pálsson 1996: 96; Howell 1996: 128), 'dualist' (Howell 1996: 128), 'Cartesian' (Descola and Pálsson 1996: 97) or 'naturalist' (Descola and Pálsson 1996: 96) thought. However, the fact that, according to Howell (1996: 131), the Chewong do not have a word for 'animal', but rather a 'class of beings which is constituted on the basis of presence or absence of consciousness', does not mean that their perception of humans and animals (or 'personages' in Howell's terms) is undifferentiated at all times. The Euro–American concept 'animal' includes humans, hence the necessity of the cumbersome 'non-human animal'. However, this does not mean that humans are always animals unless stated otherwise. In various contexts humans are: animals (various biological discourses), like animals (sociobiology, ethology), irreducibly different from animals (dualist, Judaeo-Christian thought), separated from animals by their possession of a soul (Cartesian), and morally inferior to animals (animal rights and heroic pet discourses). Animals are like infant humans or junior family members (when kept as pets) and sexual partners (in zoosexual relationships). Of course, this does not exhaust the possibilities, and perceptions are contextually variable and employed ad hoc. It is not possible to identify a unitary 'Western' (dualist, Cartesian or naturalist) human–animal distinction. The contrast, therefore, between societies in which a distinction is made between humans and animals and those in which it is not is dissolved. Attitudes towards, conceptual uses of and symbolic work done by animals are multitudinous both within and across societies. This variety is the necessary context in which sex between humans and animals may take place at the same time as prohibitions against it are strengthened.

Zoosex and animal welfare

The increasing closeness between humans and animals, in biological as well as social terms, combined with a loosening of the connection between sex and reproduction may provide support for the argument that zoosex is a potentially subversive and therefore liberating relationship between people and animals, which will gradually gain acceptance. The idea that animals are valid sexual partners may also be perceived as an implicit recognition of equality, which may be appealing to those campaigning for animal rights. However, zoosex is condemned by animal welfare organisations (Humane Society of the United States, People for the Ethical Treatment of Animals) as well as by the majority of mainstream pet owners on their numerous blogs (see, for example, pethub). The only organisation with a current Web presence that endorses zoosex is the North American Man/Boy Love Association (NAMBLA), presumably in order to advance its own controversial claims.

Animal welfare activists and zoosexuals do, however, use similar terms to describe their relationships with animals, emphasising autonomy and individuality:

> Animals are beautiful, perfect and equal to us. They should never be coerced into behaviour that is unnatural, and they will find ways of telling you exactly what they want. (Zoosexual)

> PETA believes that animals have rights and deserve to have their best interests taken into consideration, regardless of whether they are useful to humans. Like you, they are capable of suffering and have an interest in leading their own lives; therefore, they are not ours to use – for food, clothing, entertainment, experimentation, or any other reason. (http://www.peta.org/ 2005)

PETA president, Ingrid Newkirk, was the only high-profile animal welfare worker to consider Singer's (2001) argument, saying that: 'If a girl gets sexual pleasure from riding a horse, does the horse suffer? If not, who cares? If you French kiss your dog and he or she thinks it's great, is it wrong? We believe all exploitation and abuse is wrong. If it isn't exploitation and abuse, it may not be wrong' (quoted in Boxer 2001). Newkirk was roundly criticised for this opinion, and has recently restated her views in a response to a report about the death of a man following anal intercourse with a horse in Seattle: 'Let me be clear ... PETA and I are totally opposed to any exploitation and all bestiality ... Bestiality is cruelty to animals and PETA pushes for laws to outlaw it and prosecution when it occurs' (Canadafreepress.com 2005). A recent press release by PETA official Martin Mesereau (2005) went further, making an explicit connection between bestiality and violent sexual crimes against humans: 'offenders who commit bestiality often go on to commit sex crimes against humans. The community should follow this case closely because anyone capable of this kind of cruelty poses a definitive risk, not just to animals, but to fellow human beings.' This reasoning depends upon a flattening of the human–animal distinction (those likely to abuse animals are equally likely to abuse humans) at the same time as defending a strict distinction between the two (humans should not have sex with animals).

The degree of dissonance between these two groups, both of whom claim to have the animals' best interests at heart, is striking. About one-third of informants in Beetz's (2002) study of zoosex describe themselves as active in animal welfare, and the major zoo site that has endured throughout my research (http://www.zoophilia.net/) has a disclaimer condemning animal abuse and a link to the Animal Sexual Abuse Information Resource Site (ASAIRS) website for anyone who is unclear as to what constitutes animal cruelty. Some zoosexuals consider themselves to be primarily animal welfare activists. People United to Restore Eden (PURE), for example, have rejected the label 'zoo' in order to distance themselves from people who harm animals, and prefer to be referred to as 'zou' (Purehumanimal.com). Zous envisage a return to relationships between humans and animals as they were in the Garden of Eden.

The disagreement between zoosexuals and animal welfare campaigners crystallises in attempts to establish laws against bestiality. In Missouri, for example, reformed zoophile Mike Rollands, acting in his role as founder and administrator of ASAIRS, exposed two sociologists at the University of Indiana who had written to Members of the Missouri House of Representatives opposing the adoption of HB 1658, a law to prohibit bestiality. In his contribution to Green Vibrations, a Yahoo-hosted blog devoted to animal rights, Rollands provided the email addresses of the University of Indiana president, vice-president, admissions office and nine other council members, advising activists to 'Let them know you don't approve of their University hosting or being involved with providing services to these two doctors who are using this University's name and facilities to attempt to sway legislation in another state and to essentially promote bestiality':

> This is, as they say, 'war time' ... if you allow two zoophile friendly doctors who probably never met a zoophile in person nor saw their animals to stop legislation in a state they don't even live in, then you can expect they will try to remove the laws in ALL of the rest of the states using that as an example.

Rollands requested the help of fellow activists in suggesting 'animal rights/welfare activists who are psychiatrists, social workers, people who are heads of animal groups, anti porn, pro-family groups etc.' so that he might enlist their support for HB 1658, which eventually passed into law. Rollands was incredibly good at mobilising public opinion, and many zoos hold him largely responsible for the reduced zoo presence on the Net. Others are clear that he was the catalyst for a broader movement of religious and other conservatives:

> This is a holy war! The Christian right is terrified by anything like this. They get stoolpigeons like [Mike Rollands], therapy him up and produce a monster! He says that we are all perverts and animal abusers. I say, 'Of course, there are bestialists out there who do harm animals, and that is horrible to me.' He can't recognise that there are also many people who care very much about their animal partners and who would never harm any animal.

Conclusion

Despite the various activities taking place on the borderlands between humans and animals, zoosex continues to provoke outrage. Biologically, humans and animals are not distinguishable in any universal sense; socially animals are recognised, within certain contexts, as persons or kin-like. The 'pure' relationship does not seem species-specific. However, many of our most conventional relationships with animals demand that we continue to distance ourselves from them. Most obviously, we continue to eat animals and to exploit their labour. There are also conceptual barriers to the creation of interspecies relationships. If Agamben (2004) is right, and all politics is really biopolitics, concerned with distinguishing humanity from animality, then zoosexuality also constitutes a threat to the very basis of Euro-American culture. These contradictory inclinations have played themselves out on the Internet in the short history of zoosexuality.

The hopes of many zoosexuals, that they should be recognised and accepted by mainstream society, were dashed by the angry responses to Singer's (2001) review and by recent legislation against bestiality. Many have chosen to reduce their Net-based public activities. However, opposition to zoosex also appears to be on the wane. ASAIRS was disbanded in 2003, and Mike Rollands, for example, has removed himself from the scene, declaring that he now has 'zero interest' in the issue (ASAIRS.com). The flurry of activity that took place on the Web during the 1980s and 1990s provoked an equally lively response from people who opposed zoosex. Since the decline in zoo presence this energy has been redirected at the flourishing Internet-based animal pornography business. These depictions of human–animal sex often include cruelty as defined by HSUS and PETA; however, they do not make any accompanying claims to a particular sexual identity and are anathema to those zoos who are committed to animal welfare in general, and to monogamy in particular.

The treatment of animals as subjects or persons is not unique to zoosexuals. Many pets are treated in a similar way. Furthermore, people regularly intervene in animal sex without provoking moral outrage. Pets are neutered, some mating animals are doused in buckets of water while others are encouraged. In thoroughbred reproduction, the animal sex act with which I am most familiar (Cassidy 2002), the mare is restrained by human handlers using a selection of ropes and harness, including hobbles on its feet and a twitch on its nose. The stallion must cover the mare 'naturally' (according to the rules of horse racing), but human-assisted foreplay is tacitly permitted. Artificial insemination, banned for use in thoroughbred reproduction, permits a sexual manipulation of animals that differs only from zoosexual acts by virtue of its motivation (economic as opposed to sexual) and the context in which it takes place (down on the farm as opposed to in the bedroom). The transgression committed by the Internet generation of zoosexuals is not the treatment of animals as subjects, or their engagement with animal sexuality, but the elevation of this activity to the arena of identity formation, a definitively human zone. During the 1950s, when zoosex was considered as a paraphilia, zoos could be treated for their affliction, tolerated and even pitied. The new community of zoos that emerged on the Web in the 1980s and 1990s sought not treatment, but acceptance, and even recognition. This ambition reclassified zoosexuals as deviants, rather than victims or patients, and zoosex as an antisocial act that invited punishment, not therapy. The result has been extensive laws against bestiality. As zoosexuals retreat from the limelight once again, the message from the rest of society may be summed up in the advice one zoosexual told me he received from his father, who said, 'Have sex with animals, but keep it quiet, and don't you dare invite me to the wedding.'

Notes
1. The term 'zoosexual', or 'zoo', denotes a sexual identity and is distinguished from 'zoophilia', the term used by psychologists to refer to a sexual attraction towards animals. 'Bestiality' has been used to describe the act of having sex with animals, as has sodomy. Discussions of the definition of zoosex are often quite revealing. Bolliger and Goetschel (2005: 24), for example, exclude the 'petting and hugging of animals, riding and any conscious or unconscious fantasies of zoophilic acts...or the mere observation of intercourse between animals' from their definition. 'Furries' can be used to refer to fans of cartoons featuring anthropomorphic animals, or to people who dress up in fur suits. 'Plushies' love and/or are sexually attracted to stuffed animals. 'Therians' range from people who identify with a particular species of animal to those who consider themselves to be animals of a particular species trapped in a human body. Individuals who refer to themselves using these terms may or may not choose to engage in zoosex.
2. These blogs and subsequent one-on-one discussions via email and in person between 2002 and 2005 were the primary sources for this chapter. In keeping with the wishes of the majority of my informants, no zoosexuals will be identified in the chapter.

3. ZooCon '94, the first of these gatherings, took place at Mark Matthews's trailer and yard. ZooGathering '94 took place a few months later, at a Holiday Inn in New Mexico.
4. As well as individual zoos going underground, many zoo websites have disappeared and are only available as cached web pages.
5. In my experience, zoos often endorse a highly traditional template of sexual relationships based on ideals of romantic love, monogamy, etc. (albeit with animals). The only aspect of their sexuality that might be described as 'plastic' is their choice of a non-human partner.

References

Agamben, G. 2004. *The Open: Man and Animal.* Stanford, CA: Stanford University Press.

Arhem, K. 1996. 'The Cosmic Food Web', in P. Descola and G. Pálsson (eds) *Nature and Society: Anthropological Perspectives.* London: Routledge, pp. 185–204.

Atran, S. 1999. 'The Universal Primacy of Generic Species in Folkbiological Taxonomy: Implications for Human Biological, Cultural and Scientific Evolution', in R. Wilson (ed.) *Species: New Interdisciplinary Essays.* Cambridge MA: MIT Press.

Bagley, H. 1968. *The Beast Seekers.* Atlanta, GA: Pendulum Books.

Beetz, A. 2002. *Love, Violence and Sexuality in Relationships between Humans and Animals.* Doctoral dissertation. Aachen, Germany: Shaker Verlag.

———. 2005. 'New Insights into Bestiality and Zoophilia', in A. Beetz and A. Podberscek (eds) *Bestiality and Zoophilia: Sexual Relations with Animals.* West Lafayette, IN: Purdue University Press, pp. 98–119.

Beidelman, T. 1961. 'Kuguru Justice and the Concept of Legal Fiction', *Journal of African Law* 5 (1): 5–20.

Beirne, P. 1997. 'Rethinking bestiality: towards a concept of interspecies sexual assault', *Theoretical Criminology* 1 (3): 317–40.

———. 2001. 'Peter Singer's "Heavy Petting" and the Politics of Animal Sexual Assault', *Critical Criminology* 10: 43–55.

Bird, M. 2000. 'Beastly Passions', *Independent on Sunday*, 3 December.

Bodson, L. 2000. 'Motivations for Pet-keeping in Ancient Greece and Rome: a Preliminary Survey', in A. Podberscek, E. Paul and J. Serpell (eds) *Companion Animals and Us: Exploring the Relationships Between People and Pets.* Cambridge: Cambridge University Press, pp. 27–41.

Bolliger, G. and A. Goetschel. 2005. 'Sexual Relations with Animals (Zoophilia): an Unrecognised Problem in Animal Welfare Legislation', in A. Beetz and A. Podberscek (eds) *Bestiality and Zoophilia: Sexual Relations with Animals.* West Lafayette, IN: Purdue University Press, pp. 23–45.

Bonas, S., J. McNicholas and G. Collis. 2000. 'Pets in the Network of Family Relationships: an Empirical Study', in A. Podberscek, E. Paul, and J. Serpell (eds) *Companion Animals and Us.* Cambridge: Cambridge University Press, pp. 209–36.

Boxer, S. 2001. 'Yes, But Did Anyone Ask the Animal's Opinion?' *New York Times*, 9 June.

Brightman, R. 1993. *Grateful Prey: Rock Cree Human–Animal Relationships.* Berkeley: University of California Press.

Brown, A. 2005. 'Staff Take More Time Off for Ill Pets than Relatives', *Scotsman*, 28 April.

Cain, A. 1985. 'Pets as Family Members', in M. Sussman (ed.) *Pets and the Family*. New York: Haworth, pp. 5–10.

Cassidy, R. 2002. *The Sport of Kings: Kinship, Class and Thoroughbred Breeding in Newmarket.* Cambridge: Cambridge University Press.

Castells, M. 1996. *The Rise of the Network Society.* Cambridge, MA: Blackwell Publishers.

Cherlin, A. 1992. *Marriage, Divorce, Remarriage,* revised edn. Cambridge, MA: Harvard University Press.

Crompton, R. (ed.) 1999. *Restructuring Gender Relations and Employment.* Oxford: Oxford University Press.

Darwin, C. 1859. *On the Origin of Species.* London: Murray.

Davis, P. 1954. *Sex Perversion and the Law*, Vol. 1, 5th edn. New York: Mental Health Press.

de Castro, E. 1998. 'Cosmological Deixis and Amerindian Perspectivism', *Journal of the Royal Anthropological Institute* 4 (3): 469–88.

Dekkers, M. 1994. *Dearest Pet: On Bestiality,* trans. P. Vincent. London: Verso.

Delany, S. 1999. *Times Square Red, Times Square Blue.* New York: New York University Press.

Dembski, W. and J. Kushiner. (eds). 2001. *Signs of Intelligence: Understanding Intelligent Design.* Grand Rapids, MI: Brazos Press.

Descola, P. and G. Pálsson. 1996. 'Introduction', in P. Descola and G. Pálsson (eds) *Nature and Society: Anthropological Perspectives.* London: Routledge, pp. 1–22.

Devereux, G. 1948. 'Mohave Zoophilia', *Journal of the Indian Psychoanalytical Society* 2: 227–45.

Erikson, P. 2000. 'The Social Significance of Petkeeping among Amazonian Indians', in A. Podberscek, E. Paul and J. Serpell (eds) *Companion Animals and Us: Exploring the Relationships Between People and Pets.* Cambridge: Cambridge University Press, pp. 7–26.

Ford, C. and F. Beach. 1951. *Patterns of Sexual Behaviour.* New York: Harper and Brothers.

Franklin, A. 1999. *Animals and Modern Cultures: A Sociology of Human–Animal Relations in Modernity.* London and Thousand Oaks, CA: Sage.

Freeman, H. 2005. 'Latest Pet Trends Launched', *Guardian*, 29 April.

Fukuyama, F. 1992. *The End of History and the Last Man.* Harmondsworth: Penguin.

Giddens, A. 1991. *The Transformation of Intimacy: Sexuality, Love, and Eroticism in Modern Societies.* Cambridge: Polity Press.

Havelock-Ellis, H. 1925. *Studies in the Psychology of Sex*, Vol. 2. Philadelphia: F.A. Davies.

Howell, S. 1996. 'Nature in Culture or Culture in Nature? Chewong Ideas of "Humans" and Other Species', in P. Descola and G. Pálsson (eds) *Nature and Society: Anthropological Perspectives.* London: Routledge, pp. 127–44.

Kinsey, A. W. Pomeroy and C. Martin. 1948. *Sexual Behaviour in the Human Male*. Philadelphia, PA: W.B. Saunders.

Lévi-Strauss, C. 1969 [1949]. *The Elementary Structures of Kinship*. Boston, MA: Beacon Press.

Lewontin, R. 1992. 'The Dream of the Human Genome', *New York Review of Books*, 28 May, 31–40.

Masters, R. 1973 [1962]. *The Hidden World of Erotica: Forbidden Sexual Behaviour and Morality*. London: Lyrebird Press, originally published New York: Julian Press.

Matthews, M. 1994. *The Horseman*. Amherst, NY: Prometheus Books.

Meigs, A. and K. Barlow. 2002. 'Beyond the Taboo: Imagining Incest', *American Anthropologist* 104 (1): 38–49.

Mesereau, M. 2005. 'PETA Demands Jail Time, Psychiatric Intervention, If Alleged Neillsville Animal Rapist is Convicted', Press release accessed at: http://www.peta.org/Automation/NewsItem.asp?id=6048

Miletski, H. 2002. *Understanding Bestiality and Zoophilia*. Bethesda, MD: H. Miletski.

———. 2005a. 'A History of Bestiality', in A. Beetz and A. Podberscek (eds) *Bestiality and Zoophilia: Sexual Relations with Animals*. West Lafayette, IN: Purdue University Press, pp. 1–22.

———. 2005b. 'Is Zoophilia a Sexual Orientation? A Study', in A. Beetz and A. Podberscek (eds) *Bestiality and Zoophilia: Sexual Relations with Animals*. West Lafayette, IN: Purdue University Press, pp. 82–97.

Néret, G. 1995. *Erotica Universalis*. Munich: Taschen.

Office of Communications (Ofcom). 2004. *Programme Complaints Bulletin Standards and Fairness and Privacy*, Issue 14, 26 July.

O'Hare, P. 2005. '22-stone Dog Trades Meat for Herbs', *Irish Examiner*, 2 May.

Peretti, P. O. and M. Rowan. 1983. 'Zoophilia: Factors Related to Its Sustained Practice', *Panminerva Medica* 25: 127–31.

Peterson, G. and S. Steinmetz. 1999. 'Perspectives on Families as we Approach the Twenty-First Century-Challenges to Authors of Future Handbooks', in M. Sussman, S. Steinmetz and G. Peterson (eds) *Handbook of Marriage and the Family*. New York: Plenum, pp. 1–10.

Press Association. 2005. 'Pets Chain to Open More Stores', *Guardian*, 6 May.

Robert, J and F. Baylis. 2003. 'Crossing Species Boundaries', *American Journal of Bioethics* 3 (3): 1–13.

Rosenberger, J. 1968. *Bestiality*. Los Angeles, CA: Medco Books.

Rosenfeld, J. 1967. *The Animal Lovers*. Atlanta, GA: Pendulum Books.

Salisbury, J. 1994. *The Beast Within: Animals in the Middle Ages*. New York and London: Routledge.

Serpell, J. 1996. *In the Company of Animals: a Study of Human–Animal Relationships*. Cambridge, NY: Cambridge University Press.

Singer, P. 1975. *Animal Liberation*. New York: Avon.

———. 2001. 'Heavy Petting', *Nerve*, March/April, <www.nerve.com?Opinions?Singer?heavyPetting>.

Spencer, C. (dir.) 1999. *Hidden Love: Animal Passions*. Produced by Simon Andreae, Optomen TV/ Channel 4.

Taylor, T. 1996. *The Prehistory of Sex*. New York: Bantam Books.

Teachman, J., L. Tedrow and K. Crowder. 2000. 'The Changing Demography of America's Families', *Journal of Marriage and the Family* 62: 1234–46.

van den Berghe, P. 1979. *Human Family Systems. An Evolutionary View*. New York, NY: Elsevier.

Voith, V. 1985. 'Attachment of People to Companion Animals', *Veterinary Clinics of North America* 15: 289–95.

Weeks, J. 1995. *Invented Moralities: Sexual Values in an Age of Uncertainty*. Cambridge: Polity Press.

Whiten, A., J. Goodall, W. McGrew, T. Nishida, V. Renolds, Y. Sugiyama, C. Tutin, R. Wrangham and C. Boesch. 1999. 'Cultures in Chimpanzees', *Nature* 399: 682–85.

Willerslev, R. 2004. 'Not Animal Not Not–animal: Hunting, Imitation and Empathetic Knowledge among the Siberian Yukaghirs', *Journal of the Royal Anthropological Institute (NS)* 10: 629–52.

Williams, J. and M. Weinberg. 2003. 'Zoophilia in Men: a Study of Sexual Interest in Animals', *Archives of Sexual Behaviour* 32 (6): 523–35.

CHAPTER 6

DANCING SEXUALITY IN THE COOK ISLANDS

Kalissa Alexeyeff

One of the most startling events in my entire time conducting fieldwork in the Cook Islands occurred when I asked a male friend if he was gay.[1] This incident occurred directly after the annual Drag Queen Competition held at a nightclub on the main island of Rarotonga. After the competition, the resident string band played a final set which ended, as is commonplace, with a slow number to which men and women dance the 'last waltz' together. During this number, a man who fancies a woman will ask one of the following questions: 'Where do you stay?' or 'How did you come [get here]?' meaning, where do you live and can I get a lift home with you. As Rarotonga is a small island, the interlocutor generally knows exactly where the woman lives. The purpose of both questions is to elicit if the woman is interested in the male going home with her. On the night of the Drag Queen Competition, I was asked to dance the last waltz by Junior,[2] a man I knew relatively well as we lived in close proximity to one another. I was relieved to be dancing with him, as I knew he was having a relationship with another man, Rangi, who had been performing in the competition earlier, and I assumed I would not have to tackle the 'last waltz' questions. However, about halfway through our dance he asked the question 'How did you come?' I was surprised and without hesitation I replied, 'But I thought you were gay?' Instantly Junior raised his fist as if to punch me, but then decided to push me away and instead he screamed above the music, 'What the fuck are you talking about?!' Two of his male friends restrained him, as he continued to lunge and yell at me. I was grabbed by the women I was out with and quickly escorted from the nightclub.

Junior never spoke to me again. When I told my female friends what had made Junior so angry, they were horrified and annoyed with me. They could not understand why I had even suggested he was gay. 'But he is sleeping with Rangi,' I said. I could not understand why this was not obvious to them. Rangi had told me they had been in a relationship for three years and he obviously had deep feelings of attachment. But, instead of agreeing with the facts as I presented them, the only response that was made was *maniania koe* – you are making too much noise – a phrase used to silence those who raise deliberately provocative issues or inappropriate matters.

Until this incident, I had considered homosexuality (the cultural specificity of which I discuss shortly) as relatively unproblematic in mainstream Cook Islands life. Homosexuality appeared to be far less bracketed off than in Western societies as men who seemed to be openly gay were clearly integrated into a variety of workplaces and other social contexts. Some worked in a family business with their parents and siblings and they interacted with straight men and women across a range of contexts, including church and politics. These men were also highly visible in the lively performing arts scene as composers, singers and events managers. The regular occurrence of male-to-female cross-dressing and dancing performances also seemed to attest to widespread liberal attitudes towards homosexuality. These performances often occurred at the official Independence Day dance competitions, at fund-raising events for sports and church groups, and at more informal events such as nightclubs and parties. They draw on a long local history of cross-dressing and performing and often also reference Western-style drag performances.

In contrast to these images of tolerance was the violence provoked by my asking Junior about his sexuality. This chapter is an attempt to understand these seemingly incongruous attitudes towards homosexuality and Cook Islanders' notions of sexual transgression more broadly. As the above story begins to reveal, talking about homosexual sex can be a highly transgressive act, a prohibition that extends to the open display of homosexual desire and affection in the everyday public sphere. In sharp contrast, homosexuality is foregrounded in performance contexts such as drag queen competitions and other highly visible public events. In the analysis that follows, I draw on Sedgwick's (1990) insight into the interrelationship between homosexuality and heterosexuality and other binary categories, such as private/public, secret/ disclosure, knowledge/ignorance, in order to elucidate the culturally specific understandings of these terms in the Cook Islands. In the first section of the chapter, I posit that the norms surrounding the expression and identification of homosexuality are configured alongside understandings of public and private spheres of social life and public and private dimensions of personhood.

The second section of the chapter explores the related issue of the connection between sanctions on talking about homosexuality and the visibility of homosexual sexuality in performance contexts. Here I build on recent analyses that view performance spaces as arenas for the playing out of key social tensions to explain Cook Islanders' understanding of sexual transgression and social conformity (Murray 1998; Henry et al. 2000). In the Cook Islands, the ambivalence surrounding homosexuality and norms about public and private sexuality are elaborated in performance contexts. These performances, which primarily utilise dance and song, often flagrantly act out homosexual desire and sex acts, in ways that both articulate and eroticise the prohibition on homosexual sex in everyday Cook Islands social interaction. While I agree with analyses of cross-dressing which suggest that the mute facticity of these kinds of performance is potentially liberating (Butler 1990; Garber 1992), I will suggest in the concluding discussion that in the Cook Islands context these cross-dressing performances serve to reiterate hegemonic notions of masculinity and heterosexuality.

The Cook Islands are a group of fifteen islands in central Polynesia. Rarotonga, the administrative capital of the group, has a population of around 9,000. The other 3,500 inhabitants reside in the 'outer islands'. The Cook Islands' main industries are tourism and offshore banking and in common with other small island nation states the Cook Islands have little in the way of natural economic resources and arable agricultural land. As a consequence, the Cook Islands have a large diasporic community. Approximately 80,000 live abroad, the majority (around 58,000) of whom live in New Zealand, the former colonial administrator of the Cook Islands (Statistics New Zealand 2007). The islands have been self-governing in 'free association' with New Zealand since 1965. The associated state relationship means that Cook Islanders have local political autonomy as well as automatic entry to, and dual citizenship with, New Zealand. New Zealand supports the Cook Islands economy through the provision of aid and development assistance while, in a more informal but equally substantial economic network, diasporic Cook Islanders provide remittances for relatives living within the nation state. Cook Islanders are highly mobile. Familial and community networks are maintained across the diaspora through frequent visits home and abroad for weddings, funerals, family reunions, village and island events and Christmas celebrations. The transnational nature of Cook Islands' communities, in addition to the sizeable tourist industry and the large expatriate community on Rarotonga, means that most Cook Islanders have first-hand understandings of Western people and social norms.

Western notions of homosexuality are, at times, actively incorporated into local Cook Islands' cross-dressing performance contexts and within personal negotiations of homosexual identity. At other times, local homosexual practices and identities are actively defined in opposition to Western ones. Another key discourse in shaping ideas about homosexuality is Christianity. Religious belief and practice pervade many aspects of everyday life in the Cook Islands. All community events, staff meetings, dance group practice, even drag competitions begin and end with a prayer.[3] The newer evangelical denominations in particular target homosexuality as a perversion of Christian sexuality. Ideas about sex and gender are further shaped by other important categories of social distinction, familial and socio-economic status. In the Cook Islands, as in Polynesia generally, social status is largely ascribed by one's position in a hereditary, stratified system of chiefs, sub-chiefs and commoners. In contemporary Cook Islands society status can also be achieved through occupation (doctor, lawyer, pastor and politician are considered high-status professions) and economic wealth, but it is also usually high-ranking individuals who have opportunities to succeed in these areas. As I demonstrate below, status is considered key to social organisation, and far more central to individual identity than issues of sexual preference and desire. I begin by providing a brief overview of the culturally specific configuration of homosexuality and the ways it intersects with other aspects of Cook Islands social organisation.

Homosexuality in the Cook Islands

Cook Islanders identify people who behave like the opposite sex as *tutuvaine* (like a woman) and *tututane* (like a man); the prefix *tu* denotes likeness – in this case it refers to resemblance of comportment, appearance or conduct to biological men and women.[4] The colloquial term for men who act like women is *laelae*; it is this category that I focus on here. There is no female equivalent of *laelae*. Women who display male attributes are generally called 'tomboy'; however, they are less visible than *laelae*. On Rarotonga a small group of women self-identify as lesbians. Some of these women have spent time in New Zealand and define themselves more in terms of a Western gay identity, which involves not only openness about sexuality but also Western style of dress, demeanour and taste in music. Some *laelae* self-identify as 'queens', a term that plays with both Western homosexual nomenclature and the Cook Islands' chiefly system, in which female chiefs are often referred to as queens. For instance, one *laelae* on Rarotonga took great delight in referring to himself as 'the paramount queen of the island'.

In many ways the category *laelae* is fundamentally different from categories such as homosexual, transvestite or transsexual. The term *laelae* is used to describe a wide range of peoples and practices, as it does throughout Polynesia (Besnier 1994, 2004; Mageo 1996; Elliston 1999). Some *laelae* view themselves as women trapped in men's bodies, others see themselves as both women and men, as possessing the finer attributes of both sexes. Yet others view *laelae* as a distinct category of person – neither man nor woman, a category often jokingly referred to in English as 'shim', a combination of she and him. As Besnier (1994) has argued, one of the defining features of *laelae*, and their equivalent throughout Polynesia, is that they engage in women's work, such as cooking, cleaning and sewing. *Laelae* also tend to prefer to socialise with women, and tend to adopt female comportment, mannerisms and dress. *Laelae* are considered by their female friends to be highly entertaining company, excellent sources of gossip and information. Many are also skilled performers and have prominent positions as costume designers, singers and choreographers in the performing arts. Although *laelae* exist in all status levels, high-status *laelae*, those with important chiefly titles, will not engage in public performances, in keeping with expectations that those of high status are the dignified spectators rather than participants: as one female chief explained, 'I don't dance. Now I am *ariki* [chief], the people entertain me.'

Laelae is a term also used to describe men who are considered to be heterosexual but are effeminate in some regard. Men of slight stature, often those who engage in white-collar, intellectual work, not manual labour, who are friendly with women or are single past their mid-thirties are often referred to as *laelae*. Finally, actions that are considered unmanly may lead to categorisation as a *laelae* and frequently young boys are told they are acting like a *laelae* if they cry, show fear or express similar 'feminine' emotions.

One key area of difference between *laelae* and Western homosexuality is that *laelae* have little desire to have sex with other *laelae*. The object of their attention is usually 'straight' men, not 'girls like us', as one *laelae* remarked. During a description of his holiday in Australia, a *laelae* shuddered in horror as he recalled being propositioned by an Australian gay man: 'He was so girly! I think it is sickening how gays like each other in your country.'[5] 'Straight' men who have sex with *laelae* are not necessarily considered, nor consider themselves, to be homosexual. I have had women tell me that, if a man is drunk and there are no available women around, he may have sex with a *laelae*. Some young men have their first sexual relationships with an older *laelae*, who may also provide them with money, gifts of clothes and alcohol.[6]

While sexuality may not determine *laelae* identity, the subject of sex can be a central aspect of *laelae* everyday existence. In female company, *laelae* often engage in highly risqué and provocative stories of sexual desire (as women in general do) and liaisons (not usually their own). A few *laelae* I knew well would discuss their desire for a long-term relationship and the futility of such wishes, as men they have sex with often embark on heterosexual relationships at a later stage in their life. On one occasion when I was at Rangi's house admiring his recently finished *tivaevae*,[7] he commented, 'I make them for me and the man of my dreams, so they will keep us warm when we are together,' to which he added a moving rejoinder: 'Well, I guess he will be just a dream, that is all I have really.'

Laelae occupy a contradictory position in relation to the Cook Islands' mainstream. They are regarded with a mixture of acceptance and contempt. Both men and women are fascinated by *laelae* and will comment on their behaviour, report on their outfits and discuss with open admiration the skills of talented *laelae*, particularly when they cross-dress and perform. One of my clearest images of easy acceptance of *laelae* was seeing a purportedly straight man, his son and a *laelae* neighbour all under a blanket watching a video with other family members, including the man's wife, who was sitting on the couch behind them.

This hyper-visibility, relative tolerance and integration of *laelae* into mainstream Cook Islands life contrasts dramatically with the avoidance of *laelae* sexuality as a topic of discussion. The ambivalence surrounding *laelae* is, more often than not, to do with their private sexual behaviour rather than their public behaviour. Many Cook Islanders aim at complete disavowal of *laelae* sexuality.

The following examples are indicative. Early on in fieldwork, I commented on the camp demeanour of a prominent Cook Islands performer, who wore loud, brightly coloured, frilly shirts and whose flamboyant acts resembled those of Elton John or Peter Allen. My female companion replied with some hostility: 'No! He has a son. He's not gay. He's a *laelae*.' This comment was made despite the fact that the woman worked with the man's current partner and it appeared – to me at least – blatantly obvious that the two were sexually involved. When I asked what the difference was, she said that *laelae* 'just love the girls' (that is, they like socialising with women) whereas 'gays sleep with men'. On another occasion, as I pushed another woman on the topic of *laelae* and sex, I was firmly told, '*Laelae* sexuality is a non-issue; it is their way of life that people talk about, people always notice them and watch them, especially when they drink and get violent.'

Laelae private sexual behaviour is regarded by many as a 'non-issue' if it remains concealed from public view. It is the foregrounding of sexuality that leads to disquiet about *laelae*. A young *laelae* commented to me that he thought one of his *laelae* friends had become too influenced by 'gay' culture, as he wore skimpy Western-style outfits and was overtly sexual in public: 'If his Dad finds out he will be in big trouble, he'll get a hiding!', referring to the fact that *laelae* who are caught engaging in homosexual practices are often beaten up by male members of their family. Counter to ideas of tolerance towards *laelae*, this young man emphasised that having a *laelae* in the family was 'shameful'. His friend was gambling with his family's reputation and as such deserved to be punished.

The comments made above suggest three main forms of *laelae* categorisation: a fascination with *laelae* as an almost eroticised spectacle, the silencing of *laelae* sexuality in speech and the often violent prohibitions attached to the shameful revelation of *laelae* sexuality. This impossibly contradictory positioning of *laelae* evokes the open secret structure of homosexuality identified by Sedgwick (1990) in the *Epistemology of the Closet*. Drawing on the work of D.A. Miller (1988), Sedgwick argues that secrecy can establish the oppositions public/private, secrecy/disclosure, known/unknown among others. The 'open secret' does not, as one might expect, render these binaries inoperable but rather serves to confirm their efficacy. Put another way, secrets speak; they underline or prop up the primary term of conceptual categories. The 'open secret' of homosexuality functions as potent knowledge that maintains the supremacy of heterosexuality and propels the disciplinary surveillance of homophobia.

Public and private sex

While Sedgwick's notion of homosexuality as an open secret is highly evocative of the interrelationship between public compulsory heterosexuality and private homosexuality in the Cook Islands, it was developed with reference to Western understandings of sexuality and identity that are not wholly applicable to Cook Islanders' perceptions of this relationship. To put it more concretely, it does not help us to understand why non-*laelae* men who have sex with *laelae* avoid classification as *laelae*. The answer lies in the different understanding of identity composition in the Cook Islands.

From the nineteenth century, Western sexuality, in particular the heterosexual/ homosexual division, came to occupy a central role in the construction of individual identity. Sex, Foucault says, became an explanation for everything, 'our bodies, our minds, our individuality, our history' (Foucault 1978: 78). Similarly, Besnier argues that 'lesbian and gay identities arose in the West, particularly among the middle classes, in the context of recent historical evolutions in the notion of personhood as a holistic and atomistic entity, a trend closely tied to the elaboration of individualism as a foundational value of capitalism' (Besnier 1994: 300).

The non-emphasis of sexuality as a determinant of identity points to notions of personhood that differ from Western atomistic versions of the self. *Laelae* identity differs from homosexual identities in the West in another significant aspect alluded to in the previous section. The range of meanings attached to *laelae* centres less on gender as an essential identity tied to sexual orientation and more on gender as a series of performative practices (Besnier 1994, 2004; Alexeyeff 2000, 2008). In contrast to Western notions of homosexuality, where identity is based on sexual preference, *laelae*-ness tends to suggest behavioural style – speech, deportment, dress and labour – not primarily sexuality. To reiterate, sexuality does not necessarily determine *laelae* status. Non-*laelae* men who have sex with *laelae* are not categorised as *laelae* as they are men in terms of the work they engage in and their emotional and physical comportment. Unlike Western understandings of sexual identity, it is gender that is productive of sexuality rather than sexuality producing self-identity.

Besnier suggests that homosexuality in Polynesian societies must be contextualised through Polynesian notions of personhood. Sexuality, 'rather than being grounded in the individual in an essentialist fashion, is more crucially a characteristic of the relationship between the individual and the social context' (Besnier 1994: 313). That is, sexuality is found in the social space between people; it is not encoded in an individual's essence. These issues of personhood and social context, the de-emphasis of individuality and the focus on social accountability are crucial to understanding how sexuality is understood in public and private spheres of Cook Islands' social life. Many scholars have noted that Polynesian personhood is malleable and multifaceted, made up of relatively autonomous aspects, which can be foregrounded and backgrounded according to context (Shore 1981; Mageo 1992; Besnier 1994; Elliston 1999). Besnier (1994: 318) contrasts this notion of personhood with Goffman's (1964) understanding of stigmatised individuals (and 'stable' notions of personhood) in North America, 'whose persona may be "spoiled" in the eyes of society by a single trait (alcoholism, physical handicap, homosexuality, etc.)'. While I consider malleability an aspect of personhood regardless of cultural background, context-appropriate behaviour is highly significant for Cook Islanders. Personhood is not understood as an immutable, essential feature of a person but as a relationship between persons and social contexts.

The centrality of social context means that 'individuality' is viewed somewhat negatively by Cook Islanders. People who act in ways that overtly put their own interests before the interests of those around them are not seen as 'go-getters', possessing initiative and drive to succeed, but rather they are viewed as selfish, acting above themselves and inconsiderate. A criticism I frequently heard about a female chief who was not well liked was that 'she shows her individuality'; in pursuing her own moneymaking ventures she did not seem to have the interests of her villagers at heart. As mentioned earlier, familial status is central to social classification and organisation throughout Polynesia (Mageo 1992; Sua'ali'i 2001). Within this system, individuated notions of sex and gender are secondary to the more pivotal issues of familial status and its maintenance. Sex, as Wallace (2003: 151) says, 'needs to be understood in relation to kinship structures rather than a privatized sphere of sexual motivation'. In this configuration, individual desires and beliefs are required to be subsumed in, or at the very least concealed from, public display. The public sphere is where individuals not only present themselves but are viewed as representatives of their family and conduits for their reputation.

To return to the issue of sexuality, the separation between sexual desire and gender identity into private and public 'bits' makes sense in terms of Cook Islands notions of personhood, in particular the relationship between the person and the social context. Jackson (1997) makes a related point about homosexuality in Thailand. He says that there is 'comparatively little pressure for integrating one's public and private lives in Thailand' (Jackson 1997: 176). He goes on to say that in Western countries 'having sex with a man has at times been a crime, admitting homosexual feelings has rarely been so. In contrast, in Thailand private sexual practice evades cultural and legal sanction, but publicly proclaiming one's sexual preferences is regarded as highly inappropriate' (Jackson 1997: 178). In a similar vein, Rangi would often question me about attitudes towards gay men in Australia. When I explained that homophobia is common in mainstream Australia, he countered with a comment that reflected his rather different concern about public disclosure: 'Yes, but if Junior and I went there we could be together, *as no one would know us*.'[8]

The integration of private and public aspects of personhood is not a strong value in the Cook Islands. Far more important is to be seen as acting in a context-appropriate manner in public. The following case is an example of the expectation that individual desires are kept hidden and familial and social obligations to the fore. At the same time as the Lewinsky–Clinton affair was revealed in 1998, a Cook Islands politician was caught by police having sex with a woman who was not his wife in a public place (in a car parked on a back road). Comparisons were often drawn between the two incidents in daily discussion. It was generally agreed that the fuss surrounding Lewinsky and Clinton was ridiculous: 'If they were *publicly* displaying their affair, well that would be a scandal but in private, come on, it's two consenting adults.' In contrast, the dominant reaction to the Cook Islands politician was that he was negligent for being caught in the act: 'He has lots of money, he should have hired a place. Bill wasn't that stupid. Our politician, he must have rocks in his head!' This is not to say that people did not think extramarital sex was wrong, but rather what was seen as most objectionable was the public flaunting of private desires. Being seen to act in ways that fulfil familial and other community responsibilities, while also attending to individual needs behind the scenes, is the key to successful everyday negotiations with others.

It is this relationship between personhood and social context, in particular familial accountability, that configures the open secret of homosexuality in somewhat different ways from Western contexts. While sexuality may not be central to the categorisation of individuals in a society where ascribed status distinctions dominate, sexuality is still highly regulated through the social norms surrounding public and private behaviour. Tensions between personal desires and public conventions are constant components of everyday Cook Islands social life.

Telling secrets

So far I have argued that *laelae* are tolerated to the extent that they are not 'embodied sexual subjects' (Wallace 2003: 156) in the public sphere of Cook Islands social life. Yet the embargo on discussing homosexual acts contrasts starkly with explicit references made about homosexuality in performance contexts that are both public and mainstream. Cross-dressing performances are staged for religious and government events, and audiences comprise men and women of all age groups and social status, family members and friends. They are extremely popular, and are considered the most humorous form of entertainment in the Cook Islands, except perhaps by the most dour of religious ministers.

The Drag Queen Competition mentioned above was one such occasion where men performed sexuality (which often encompasses female, *laelae* and gay sexuality) through eroticised movement, dress and dance. For example, one contestant, Lady Posh, was introduced by the Master of Ceremonies as: 'Her measurements are 38, 21 [Lady Posh massaged her 'breasts' and slid her hands down to her waist], and 19 [she grabbed her penis], but 30 at her full potential [she slid her hands up and down her inner legs].' She went on to perform a lip-synced dance to 'River Deep Mountain High', which involved Western-style gyrating and lap dancing with male audience members, and combined this with Cook Islands *ura* – fast swaying hip dance movements.[9]

Other performances involving cross-dressing occur across all social contexts. At nightclubs a 'straight' man may do highly accurate imitations of Cook Islands' female dancing for his male friends' amusement; inevitably one of the latter dances in male Cook Islands' style, incorporating explicitly sexual movements that suggest intercourse. Women in all-female company will also take on male and female dance roles with each other and dance in humorously eroticised ways. This style of same-sex dancing contrasts with the often stilted quality of similar dancing between men and women. Church youth groups have an Easter sports day that includes female-only rugby and male-only netball. At one netball competition I attended, all the men were dressed in female netball skirts; the majority of men were 'straight' and a few *laelae* were also playing. Male members in the crowd wolf-whistled the 'straight' males, who responded by wiggling their bottoms and lifting their skirts on request. More official occasions such as Independence Day and Christmas celebrations involve Cook Islands dance competitions between different islands and villages. Rarely will one such event take place without some form of cross-dressing and performing. These may involve individual male audience members 'teasing' the performing team by dancing like women in front of them, to choreographed displays by participants. The point of this, I was told, was to make the performing team laugh so they would forget their choreographed moves and lose the competition. Other performances will include large groups of men in choreographed displays where half the men dance as women and half as men. In 'straight' versions of this style of dancing, men and women rarely make physical contact but perform in alternating lines of males and females. 'Drag' versions will deliberately violate these lines and end up with men and 'women' touching each other's breasts and penises and dancing suggestively in pairs (see Alexeyeff 2000).

Here we are in the territory of 'licensed transgression' (Bakhtin 1968; Turner 1969), where what are collectively referred to as 'rituals of reversal' enable the display of aspects of social life normally not shown. In the Pacific context, rituals of this kind often involve 'clowning', humorous performances based on the reversal of status hierarchies – commoners performing as chiefs, and men and women inverting gender roles and the norms governing sexuality (Mitchell 1992; Sinavaiana 1992; Hereniko 1995). As a space bracketed off from the everyday, the transgression of existing social inequalities and contradictions are tolerated as 'performance' or 'play'.

One little discussed aspect of rituals of reversal is that they often employ non-linguistic or extralinguistic realms of communication such as dance, movement, mime and music far more often than verbal communication. Isadora Duncan's famous quote 'If I could say it, I wouldn't have to dance it' captures the possibility that non-linguistic and verbal communication are different orders that cannot necessarily be translated into one another. The potent appeal of the 'unspoken' (MacDougall 1998, 1999) is that it enables the revelation of key social tensions and 'awkward cultural seams' (Mitchell 1992: 30) in ways that do not pose outright challenges to the hegemonic social order. Similarly, Cook Islands' cross-dressing productions act out contradictions that are embedded in the social structure, and, as such, 'mediate' between the realm of public and private sexuality.

Polynesian communities, often small and tight-knit, place enormous importance on the maintenance of social cohesion and harmony. As a consequence, the display of conflict is rarely direct and tends to occur in private 'background' settings (such as gossip) or situations of licence (rituals of reversal, and when people are drunk). Cross-dressing performances in the Cook Islands operate in this register. They perform the 'open secret' that men have sex with men. This is most obviously done in performances combining participants who are 'straight' and *laelae*, who often erotically dance sexual desire and the public prohibition of these relations. Equally, *laelae* performances activate the 'open secret' when they engage in interactions with straight male spectators. The contradiction revealed in cross-dressing performances is between the fact of male-to-male sexual relations as opposed to the fact of compulsory heterosexuality enforced in all aspects of Cook Islands' public life. *Laelae* sexuality exposes this lack of fit, as many often desire to belong in long-term relationships with 'straight' men, and presumably some 'straight' men have genuine attachment to *laelae*. The humour of these shows is that they make 'a submerged alternative momentarily apparent' (Barlow 1992: 60). In this case the alternative is that relationships between men could be publicly sanctioned, a highly improbable scenario within the existing moral order in which heterosexual masculinity and heteronormativity dominate.

What makes cross-dressing performances particularly compelling is that they also gesture to broader social contradictions about personal desires and public conventions. In the Cook Islands homosexuality is a powerful conduit for ideas about private and public. As discussed earlier, the tensions that exist between individual desires and hegemonic social norms feature prominently in individuals' everyday negotiations. The performance of *laelae* sexuality acts out the inherent ambiguity between these public and private aspects of social life, presenting the centrality of this lived tension in mainstream individuals as well as *laelae* lives. In blatantly foregrounding sexual desires that have nothing to do with the reproduction of the (heterosexual) social body, they distil the message that abandonment to individual desires poses a threat to group solidarity; a cornerstone of Polynesian society.

Conclusion

My reading of cross-dressing performances as a reiteration of the hegemonic ideology of compulsory heterosexuality is not meant to restrict them to a singular interpretation. Certainly, for audience members and performers who may not have an investment in the maintenance of heterosexuality, cross-dressing performances may act like an 'as if' type of performance. As rituals that reverse the dominant sexual order, their subversive potential lies in their exploration of alternative social forms and other ways of being (Bakhtin 1968; Mbembe 1992). But, while these performances cannot be reduced to a singular cohesive meaning, it is important to stress that these alternative possibilities are necessarily framed in relation to the heterosexual status quo.

My main intention here has been to show how the politics of sex in the Cook Islands is constituted alongside culturally specific notions of public and private, and the ways in which the boundary between public and private sexuality is rigorously policed. The display of homosexuality is one practice which clearly illustrates the tensions that operate between public and private spheres of everyday life. The public display of homosexuality, even talk about it, is considered extremely offensive by most Cook Islanders. As long as homosexuality remains silenced, *laelae* are constructed through other aspects of their identity; their familial status and their work rather than their sexuality, and are thus tolerated, even admired, members of the community. The relationship governing public and private is breached in performance contexts that flagrantly display homosexuality. But, while it is transgressive to talk about engaging in homosexual sex, it is not transgressive to dance it in certain staged arenas. Rather than being offensive, performances of this sort are extremely popular, the frequency with which they occur suggesting a compulsion to reiterate the porous boundary between public and private, homosexuality and heterosexuality. In sum, Cook Islands' cross-dressing performance spaces are the sanctioned and culturally appropriate sites of 'public' sexuality. In any other social context, sexuality is 'private'; its display is subject to often violent reinforcement of heterosexual rule.

For *laelae* and their male partners who violate these boundaries between public and private, the consequences can be severe. What remains to be seen is how increasing contact with Western gay identities will impact upon the way *laelae* locate themselves in Cook Islands society and influence the ways in which they are perceived.[10] The incorporation of Western ideas of gay identity, such as the emphasis on sexuality as central to identity, the importance placed on 'outing' sexual identity in gay politics, has been adopted by some *laelae*. It is this explicit sexualisation of what is seen as a private concern that disturbs many Cook Islanders. The connection made between the West, inappropriate sexuality and moral laxity, and the increasing onslaught of this nexus on the Cook Islands way of life may serve to reconfigure further the relationship between public and private, homosexual and heterosexual practices.

Notes

1. I have conducted fieldwork in the Cook Islands and with Cook Islands communities in New Zealand and Australia from 1996.
2. All the names used in this chapter are pseudonyms.
3. The majority of Cook Islanders (around 80 per cent) belong to the Cook Islands Christian Church, the descendant of London Missionary Society Protestantism. Around 20 per cent of the population belongs to Seventh Day Adventist and Catholic congregations. Evangelical churches are becoming increasingly popular, particularly Assemblies of God and the Apostolic Revival Fellowship.
4. Gender diversity including transgenderism is a well-researched topic in anthropology. Key texts include Wikan's (1977) work on *xanith* in Oman, Nanda's (1999, 2000) on Indian hijras and gender diversity more generally, Kulick's (1998) study of Brazilian *travesti*, and the edited collections of Herdt (1996) and Blackwood and Wieringa (1999). Transgendered men are also common throughout the Pacific region. See Besnier (1994, 1997, 2004) for Tongan *leiti*, Levy's (1973) and Elliston's (1999) work on Tahitian *mahu* and Shore's (1981) and Mageo's (1992, 1996) analyses of Samoan *fa'afafine*.
5. Transgendered men throughout the Pacific exhibit the same orientation towards 'straight' men.
6. I have very little information on 'straight' male perspectives on their relations with *laelae*. 'Straight' men do not speak about their sexuality to women, given the highly gender segregated nature of Cook Islands social life. My understanding is based on comments made by Cook Islands women *laelae* and my own observations, which presumably do not cover the whole gamut of these men's interactions with *laelae*.
7. *Tivaevae* are appliquéd quilts that depict local flowers and plants. They are highly prized items that are sewn by women as presents for important life-stage rituals such as weddings.
8. This kind of anonymity is often romanticised by Cook Islanders, particularly in relation to kin obligations. Like many communally oriented societies where reciprocal sharing is stressed, individuals imagine the benefits of living far away from kin, and the possibilities of accumulating wealth without having to share it with needy family.

9. In Alexeyeff (2008) I explore this Drag Queen competition in realtion to globalisation and the dynamics of cross-cultural exchange.
10. Obviously this exchange is not one-way as scholars of colonisation and globalisation remind us. In her book *Sexual Encounters: Pacific Texts, Modern Sexualities* Wallace (2003) argues for the mutually transformative effect of the colonial and postcolonial interactions between 'European' and 'Polynesian' in relation to ideas of homosexuality.

References

Alexeyeff, K. 2000. 'Dragging Drag: the Performance of Gender and Sexuality in the Cook Islands', in R. Henry, F. Magowan and D. Murray (eds) *The Politics of Dance*. Special Issue 12. *The Australian Journal of Anthropology* 11 (3): 253–60.

———. 2008. 'Globalizing Drag in the Cook Islands: Friction, Repulsion, and Abjection', in M. Jolly (ed.) *Re-membering Oceanic Masculinities*. Special Issue. *The Contemporary Pacific* 20 (1): 143–61.

Bakhtin, M. 1968. *Rabelais and his World*. Cambridge, MA.: MIT Press.

Barlow, K. 1992. 'Dance When I Die! Context and Role in the Clowning of Murik Women', in W. Mitchell (ed.) *Clowning as Critical Practice. Performance Humor in the South Pacific*. Pittsburgh: University of Pittsburgh Press, pp. 58–87.

Besnier, N. 1994. 'Polynesian Gender Liminality Through Time and Space', in G. Herdt (ed.) *Third Sex, Third Gender. Beyond Sexual Dimorphism in Culture and History.* New York: Zone Books: pp. 285–328.

———. 1997. 'Sluts and Superwomen: the Politics of Gender Liminality in Urban Tonga', *Ethnos* 62: 5–31.

———. 2004. 'The Social Production of Abjection. Desire and Silencing among Transgender Tongans', *Social Anthropology* 12: 301–23.

Blackwood, E. and S. Wieringa (eds). 1999. *Female Desires: Same-sex Relations and Transgender Practices Across Cultures*. New York: Columbia University Press.

Butler, J. 1990. *Gender Trouble. Feminism and the Subversion of Identity*. New York: Routledge.

Elliston, D. 1999. 'Negotiating Transnational Sexual Economies: Female *Mahu* and Same-sex Sexuality in "Tahiti and Her Islands"', in E. Blackwood and S.E. Wieringa (eds) *Female Desires: Same-sex Relations and Transgender Practices Across Cultures*. New York: Columbia University Press, pp. 232–52.

Foucault, M. 1978. *The History of Sexuality*, Vol. 1. An Introduction. New York: Vintage.

Garber, M. 1992. *Vested Interests: Cross-dressing and Cultural Anxiety.* New York: Penguin Books.

Goffman, E. 1964. *Stigma: Notes on the Management of Spoiled Identity*. Englewood Cliffs, NJ: Prentice-Hall.

Henry, R., F. Magowan and D. Murray. 2000. 'Introduction', *The Australian Journal of Anthropology*. Special Issue 12. *The Politics of Dance* 11 (3): 253–60.

Herdt, G. (ed.). 1996. *Third Sex, Third Gender: Beyond Sexual Dimorphism in Culture and History*. New York: Zone Books.

Hereniko, V. 1995. *Woven Gods. Female Clowns and Power in Rotuma*. Suva: Institute of Pacific Studies, University of the South Pacific.

Jackson, P. 1997. '*Kathoey*><Gay><Man: The Historical Emergence of Gay Male Identity in Thailand', in L. Manderson and M. Jolly (eds) *Sites of Desire, Economies of Pleasure: Sexualities in Asia and the Pacific*. Chicago and London: University of Chicago Press, pp. 166–90.

Kulick, D. 1998. *Travesti: Sex, Gender and Culture among Brazilian Transgendered Prostitutes*. Chicago: University of Chicago Press.

Levy, R. 1973. *The Tahitians. Mind and Experience in the Society Islands*. Chicago: University of Chicago Press.

MacDougall, D. 1998. *Transcultural Cinema*. Princeton: Princeton University Press.

———. 1999. 'Social Aesthetics and the Doon School', *Visual Anthropology Review* 15 (1): 3–20.

Mageo, J. 1992. 'Male transvestism and cultural change in Samoa', *American Ethnologist* 19 (3): 443–59.

———. 1996. 'Samoa, on the Wilde Side: Male Transvestism, Oscar Wilde, and Liminality in Making Gender', *Ethos* 24 (4): 588–627.

Mbembe, A. 1992. 'The Banality of Power and the Aesthetics of Vulgarity in the Post-colony', *Public Culture* 4 (2): 1–30.

Miller, D.A. 1988. *The Novel and the Police*. Berkeley: University of California Press.

Mitchell, W. (ed.). 1992. *Clowning as Critical Practice. Performance Humor in the South Pacific*. Pittsburgh: University of Pittsburgh Press.

Murray, D. 1998. 'Defiance or Defilement? Undressing Cross-dressing in Martinique's Carnival', *Sexualities* 1 (3): 343–54.

Nanda, S. 1999. *The Hijras of India: Neither Man nor Woman*, 2nd edn. Belmont, CA: Wadsworth.

———. 2000. *Gender Diversity: Crosscultural Variations*. Prospect Heights, IL: Waveland Press.

Sedgwick, E.K. 1990. *Epistemology of the Closet*. Berkeley and Los Angeles: University of California Press.

Shore, B. 1981. 'Sexuality and Gender in Samoa: Conceptions and Missed Conceptions', in S. Ortner and H. Whitehead (eds) *Sexual Meanings. The Cultural Construction of Gender and Sexuality*. Cambridge: Cambridge University Press, pp. 192–215.

Sinavaiana, C. 1992. 'Comic Theater in Samoa as Indigenous Media', *Pacific Studies*. Special Issue. *The Arts and the Politics* 15 (4): 199–210.

Statistics New Zealand. 2007. http://www.stats.govt.nz/2006-census-data/quickstats-about-culture-identity/quickstats-about-culture-and-identity.htm acessed 31 May 2007.

Sua'ali'i, T. 2001. 'Samoans and Gender: Some Reflections on Male, Female and Fa'afafine Gender Identities', in C. Macpherson, P. Spoonley and M. Anae (eds) Tangata O Te Moana Nui: *The Evolving Identities of Pacific Peoples in Aotearoa/New Zealand*. Palmerston North: Dunmore Press, pp. 160–80.

Turner, V. 1969. *The Ritual Process: Structure and Anti-structure*. Chicago: Adline.

Wallace, L. 2003. *Sexual Encounters: Pacific Texts, Modern Sexualities*. Ithaca and London: Cornell University Press.

Wikan, U. 1977. 'Man Becomes Woman: Transsexualism in Oman as a Key to Gender Roles', *Man* 12: 304–19.

CHAPTER 7

'LET THEM HEAR US!' THE POLITICS OF SAME-SEX TRANSGRESSION IN CONTEMPORARY POLAND

Monika Baer

In contemporary Poland, homosexuality is beginning to be debated in public, though mainly only in academic and socio-political circles. In the eyes of many, this exemplifies 'an initial emancipating stage' (Leszkowicz 2004: 97) and an encouraging development in the face of the homophobic voices that have long resisted attempts by gay rights activists to air gay issues more widely (Kitliński and Leszkowicz 2005). Anna Gruszczyńska (n.d.), a lesbian rights activist, concludes her essay on the invisibility of the lesbian movement in Poland with an appeal to 'Let them hear us!' The result of such calls is that homosexuality in Poland is gradually beginning to enter the public arena and to become a politicised space of possibility and practice.[1]

As Witkowski (2005) notes, homosexuality has recently created a field of struggle both for those who are 'for' and also for those who are 'against'.[2] In his view, this situation reflects a wider problem around the 'crisis of sexuality', which is characteristic of Catholic societies, where sex is perceived as a sort of profanation of rationality. The Roman Catholic Church declares homosexuality to be a sin and its catechism states that 'in their deepest nature homosexual relationships are disorderly'

(Katechizm Kościoła Katolickiego 1994: 2357). Witkowski believes that it is this socio-religious context which makes homosexuality in Poland particularly transgressive. According to him, it constitutes an important element of a socially rebellious world view: 'It is an alternative project because it subverts convention, and almost attacks social stereotypes ... Homosexuality appears to be a rebellion, a blow against social schemata' (Witkowski 2005: no page numbers in original).

Fuss (1991: 1–2) draws our attention to the fact that the opposition between 'heterosexual' and 'homosexual', like many other conventional binaries, has always been constructed on the foundations of another related opposition: 'inside' and 'outside'. The inside/outside dialectic has historically limited discussion on hetero/homo hierarchies of the symbolic order based on a logic of limits, margins, borders and boundaries. The distinction between inside and outside designates the structure of exclusion and oppression that is imposed on those subjects who are routinely relegated to the outside of systems of power, authority and cultural legitimacy. This is why gay and lesbian theories and politics usually begin with analysing 'outsiderness' and reflect on the processes by which sexual politics, borders and identities are formulated. However, as Fuss notes elsewhere, 'identity always contains the specter of non-identity within it, the subject is always divided and identity is always purchased at the price of exclusion of the Other, the repression or repudiation of non-identity' (Fuss 1989: 103).

Fuss stresses that heterosexuality finds homosexuality necessary in order to secure its self-identity and ontological boundaries by protecting itself from its contaminated outsider other:

> The homo in relation to the hetero ... operates an indispensable interior exclusion – an outside which is inside interiority making the articulation of the latter possible, a transgression of the border which is necessary to constitute the border ... But borders are notoriously unstable, and sexual identities rarely secure. Heterosexuality can never fully ignore the close physical proximity of its terrifying (homo)sexual other, any more than homosexuality can entirely escape equally insistent social pressures of (hetero)sexual conformity. (Fuss 1991: 3)

Fuss warns us that, if the inside/outside rhetoric remains undeconstructed, it prevents us from realising that most people are simultaneously inside and outside. It is constructing the outside as a privileged site of radicality, which gives it away, because the ability to idealise the outside is closely connected to the central position of the speaker. While due to its position at/as the border, homosexuality may seem capable of transgressing heterosexuality, it may at the same time (re)construct it: 'Homosexuality, read as a transgression against heterosexuality, succeeds not in undermining the authoritative position of heterosexuality so much as reconfirming heterosexuality's centrality precisely as that which must be resisted' (Fuss 1991: 6). With this in mind, in this chapter I shall analyse how gay and lesbian groups use 'homosexuality' to transgress 'heterosexuality' in Polish public space.

Homosexuality goes public

Compared with other European countries, Polish law has been relatively progressive and homosexuality was decriminalised as early as 1932. Nevertheless, this legal situation has not changed perceptions of homosexuality as deviant.[3] Attempts to establish a gay and lesbian movement in Poland emerged in the 1980s, but it was not until 1990, with democratisation that the first gay and lesbian organisations were able to register formally.[4] These organisations aimed to raise tolerance for homosexuals in society by building a positive identity of homosexual men and women; by campaigning for safer sex; and by cooperating with state and non-governmental organisations to prevent an AIDS pandemic. Economic development has resulted in a rapid increase of gay infrastructure, including clubs, dating services, publishing houses and erotic and socio-political magazines, whose interests were formerly published in the so-called 'third circulation' (as distinct from the 'second circulation' published by anti-communist opposition). Since the mid-1990s, improved Internet connections have given access to a broad range of erotic and socio-political websites, creating an extremely important new space for many gay men and lesbians in Poland (Adamska 1998: 129–59).

While economic development is commonly perceived as positively effecting gay and lesbian circles in Poland, primarily in terms of infrastructural changes (Majka-Rostek 2002: 197–204), other aspects of commercialisation are not viewed in this way. As a former activist said: 'Once, to organise a gay disco was a deeply political act. Now, while running a club, what counts is making money. Nothing else matters.'[5] Consequently, after an early period of relatively intense activity, the movement started to decline. But, since 2000, partly due to a generational shift, a revitalisation process has occurred. Additionally, the development of gender studies in academic circles and other feminist initiatives with their gay-friendly social spaces, as well as the country's accession to the European Union, has encouraged debates about the place of sexual minorities in contemporary Poland. Two national-level organisations registered in 2001.[6] As a result, the number of grass-roots groups aimed at helping gay people to accept their sexual orientation, to build a positive identity and to 'come out' has increased. However, this process is usually limited to cities, and such organisations are practically non-existent in the countryside (see Adamska 1998: 102–3).

The most recent revival of the movement has led to spectacular public displays which have brought the issue of gay and lesbian rights to public attention. Over the last four or five years, these displays have included the Parade of Equality (modelled on the international Christopher Street Day[7]); 'Let Them See Us', the first national campaign aimed at promoting tolerance towards groups other than heterosexuals; a series of Gay and Lesbian Days billed as 'Culture for Tolerance'; and parliamentary lobbies when, for example, a draft of the same-sex partnership act was submitted to the government. By 2005 most of these initiatives were supported morally and financially by a feminist-oriented Government Plenipotentiary for Equal Status of Women and Men.

All these initiatives faced dissent from the conservative public. In fact, 'sexual panic' was visible in Poland long before gay and lesbian activists had a chance to speak out, as for example when marriage was defined as a relationship between a man and a woman in the 1997 Polish Constitutional vote (see Mizielińska 2004). When lesbian and gay issues did enter public arenas, panic increased. The posters of the 'Let Them See Us' campaign were removed within a week following widespread protest by conservative opponents;[8] the 2004 March of Tolerance in Krakow was physically attacked by young fascist squads (All-Poles Youth); the then president of Warsaw (who was elected as President of Poland in 2005) illegally blocked attempts to organise the Parade of Equality both in 2004 and in 2005;[9] and voting on the same-sex partnership act was constantly obstructed until the parliamentary recess in autumn 2005. Numerous media announced that society faced 'homosexual conquest', 'homosexual revolution' and 'promotion of homosexuality'; that homosexuals 'waged a cultural war' or 'fought for a socially privileged position in society'.

These initiatives spawned a lively debate. Supportive voices finally began to appear in public discourse. Two main threads can be identified in these public discourses: the conservative and the liberal. Conservative discourse stresses the deviant character of homosexuality and shows open hostility towards any form of 'homosexual emancipation'. Public gay and lesbian movement initiatives are perceived as an aggressive propagation of their own sexual orientation. Liberal discourse does not simply accept homosexuality as just one among many forms that sexuality can assume, but it tolerates homosexuality in terms of personal freedom, which belongs to the private sphere. Discourses of 'limited' and 'full emancipation' have also emerged. 'Limited emancipation' is considered a strategy of cultural compromise. It echoes the liberal approach to an extent, but these are primarily gay men and lesbians who believe that introducing 'the homosexual question' as a distinct political issue does not provide an effective strategy for gay rights activism in contemporary Poland. Consequently, they stress that, in order to avoid direct threat, homosexual people should not claim marriage or adoption of children, but solely the opportunity to register civic unions of an economic character. Conversely, proponents of 'full emancipation' declare that 'homosexuality' should constitute a distinct political issue. They insist that, as fully fledged citizens, gay men and lesbians should actively fight for all civil rights enjoyed by the heterosexual majority (Gawlicz and Starnawski 2004; see also Sypniewski and Warkocki 2004b).

However, even though homosexual activism in Poland seems to be gaining acceptance in some quarters, the situation is far from encouraging. It is commonly claimed that only a few people are actively engaged in the gay and lesbian movement. Activists are still searching for a common identity and effective political and theoretical frameworks. They suggest that the problem of institutional and socio-political recognition is due to the lack of established (and powerful) organisational structures, disagreements regarding the specific meanings a common identity should assume and controversies over basic political aims and effective strategies. The debates on homosexuality also reveal a more pervasive condition of Polish society, reflecting non-participatory attitudes with no tradition of grass-roots initiatives. The weakness of the gay and lesbian movement is said to reflect the weakness of civil society in general and to highlight the passivity of groups that should be concerned with improving their own situation in society (Basiuk 2000).

Hann (1996) suggests that European intellectual debate on civil society is deeply embedded in a particular Western theory of autonomous individuals. Nevertheless, the apprehension of civil society that builds on pluralism and the liberal individualism of de Tocqueville is just a discourse of one type of regime: 'the late-twentieth-century linking of civil society with non-governmental organisations in a context of deregulated and increasingly globalised economies is but one highly specific instance' (Hann 1996: 21). Aware of this fact, anthropologists investigating the issue of civil society should not be circumscribed by modern Western models of liberal individualism, but should pay careful attention to a range of informal interpersonal practices that contribute to social cohesion, and that are overlooked by other disciplines (Hann 1996: 3).

The success of any political undertaking in the area of gay and lesbian rights depends partly on support from strong organisational structures and a politics of common identity. However, there is no easy answer to the question as to what political strategies would be most effective for sexual minorities' rights in the context of contemporary Poland. In analysing the Polish gay and lesbian movement, we should also look beyond formal structures to the everyday practice of gay and lesbian identities, and to the way in which they help to generate a sense of commonality that is so central to the political struggle for gay rights. In fact, 'homosexuality' can inform community action and interaction differently. It does not need to become a politicised space in the terms that mainstream activists who advocate the 'full emancipation' perspective suggest. Consequently, while 'homosexuality' frequently can be read as having transgressive potential in contemporary Poland, the meaning of transgression should not be taken for granted.

I focus below on the Lesbian/Gay/Bisexual/Transsexual or Transgender (LGBT) studies group at Wrocław University in south-western Poland, namely the Queer Studies Students' Association 'Nothing the Same'. I participated in the group's activities between 2002 and 2006, and carried out fieldwork among its members in spring and early summer 2003.

Homosexuality in grass-roots arenas

Griffin (2001: 16–24) observes that, in countries where women's studies and gender studies have been long established, academic debates are basically separated from grass-roots movements and scholars seem uninterested in activities aimed at women's advancement in society. By contrast, in countries where women's studies and gender studies have had a relatively short history, academic and political initiatives converge more strongly. This is the case in LGBT studies in Wrocław. Together with the more feminist-oriented Interdisciplinary Gender Studies Group (Gender Studies), the Queer Studies Students' Association 'Nothing the Same' (NTS) constitutes an important political forum for debates on homosexuality and gay rights in contemporary Poland.

NTS was established in February 2001 as an extension of Gender Studies (which was set up in September 1999) and brought together students, scholars and activists interested in non-normative sexuality-related issues. They decided to establish a separate group. One of NTS founders commented:

> At the outset we planned to have an association of gay men and lesbians at Wrocław University … We spread some placards around the university saying that we are establishing an association to promote student culture of homosexuals … But this provoked a homophobic reaction … [People] … were afraid of coming out; they thought it would make their lives difficult; would disturb their careers or whatever. And then Iza [a board member of Gender Studies] suggested we should set up a scientific students' association, particularly because the director of her Institute supported this idea.

NTS's activities were to include organising lectures, discussion groups and conferences, as well as cultural and social events. Even though they are separate organisations, NTS and Gender Studies cooperate closely, and the same people frequently attend both groups' meetings. Gender Studies is more established in terms of financial and human resources, and when NTS faced financial problems and both groups suffered from a lack of volunteers, their board members agreed to share each other's resources. This cooperation reflects a general trend in the relationship between feminist and gay and lesbian groups in contemporary Poland, on both academic and activist levels. It is a common perception that both groups wish to denaturalise gender and sexuality categories. Moreover, both groups experience similar modes of exclusion from public political space. Thus, in the eyes of many, feminist, gay and lesbian activists are natural allies (Basiuk 2000: 36). However, compared with gay and lesbian initiatives, feminist agendas are more widely recognised. This is why NTS, an obviously LGBT studies group, was called rather euphemistically, a *Gender* Studies Students' Association until 2006 and was only then changed to *Queer* Studies.

NTS brings people together who differ in terms of their structural position, such as students and scholars or mainstream and anarchist activists, as well as those who differ in terms of their personal world views. Participants have divergent ideas about gender and sexuality as the basis of a common identity; different visions of the relationship between privacy in sexuality and the publicity of socio-political sexualised acts; and different concepts of the permissible links between academic and political action, including what might constitute such action. Consequently, even though all of them have been in one way or another attracted by transgressive potentials, which homosexual aspects of the association offer, their actual expectations of NTS differ and result in clashes.

Different objectives

Some participants express the desire for a support group and to engage intellectually in sexual issues, while political activism is of minor importance. One of them said: 'It's a personal question, extremely personal. I think I needed support, because it works as a support group. Similar people who think similarly get together and it gives you such self-assurance ... I'm too shy for any real activism, but scientific aspects are really interesting to me.' Such participants thus seek 'limited emancipation', and use the group to widen personal social networks rather than to go public.

Another group within NTS comprises politically motivated academics. They have joined NTS mainly due to theoretical interests, but combined with political ones. A representative of this faction noted that the political significance of NTS membership was an opportunity to declare being 'a lesbian' and thereby to become a discursive being and to find others who share similar needs. In this case it is the transgression of private perspectives entering the public sphere (though limited to an academic space) which are particularly important, and the emotional and moral support offered by the group members is of only secondary importance.

A third faction represents a 'full emancipation' approach aimed at securing gay citizens' civil rights. Those who take this view openly admit that they joined NTS to consolidate gay and lesbian circles in Wrocław, and to proceed with mainstream political activism. Recalling the association's early days, one of them noted:

> We wanted to move towards social actions or even political ones. That is, we wanted to make gays visible in public life; to check that civil servants don't pursue discriminatory policies; not to let gay voices be excluded; to participate in conferences; to deliver our opinions on issues of importance; but most of all, we wanted to do something for the [gay] milieu of Wrocław.

Finally, a fourth faction within NTS comprises anarcho-feminist squatters, whose concerns for political activism are of a more radically transgressive character. They were encouraged to join NTS by a French separatist lesbian activist, who lived in their squat at the time and wanted to contact a lesbian activist circle in Wrocław. She is reported to be actively involved in raising the political consciousness of indigenous anarcho-feminists for whom (according to some academics) radical feminism was about drinking vodka in a female circle. In this group the 'full emancipation' project is to be implemented not by use of civil rights rhetoric, but as part of a radical critique of the heterosexist capitalist society.

The split between academics and activists in NTS led to the emergence of the informal feminist group Durga in January 2003. Durga was founded to coordinate the Women's Day celebration after one of the Gender Studies' organisers rejected the idea that a university unit could co-organise an openly political event. Durga brought together those participants (mostly women) who wanted to challenge the predominantly academic profile of both NTS and Gender Studies' activities. Furthermore, the founders of the group are reported to be keen on developing a space in which social relations would be of a more egalitarian character.

However, Durga has not managed to form an entirely safe space where all participants' needs could be met. When the Women's Day celebration was over, Durga's activities declined. The group's leaders, who were based in a feminist Gender Studies programme, were accused of sticking to mainstream political activism and of not paying due attention to specific lesbian issues. Consequently, anarchists, and particularly anarcho-feminist lesbians, felt they suffered the discrimination they had hoped to avoid. To address this problem, they proposed a more anarchic Lesbians, Gays and Friends Festival, aimed at making their artistic, social and political projects visible in a public space in Wrocław in order to transgress its hetero-normative character. The successful event included films, concerts, performances, exhibitions and socio-political debates. Nevertheless, these

problems show clearly that, even within an apparently united
group, what constitutes transgression for some is insufficiently
transgressive for others.

Different identities

The differing objectives of NTS participants are combined with
divergent ideas about gender and sexuality to form the basis of a
common identity. NTS discussions about a common identity
rooted in sexual orientation have been based on an essentialised
homosexual identity (lesbian or gay) and on a more fluid
(anti)identity connected to queer theory. Accordingly, some
participants stress that the group should be more openly defined
as a gay and lesbian space to distinguish it from Gender Studies.
The common identity is perceived not only as a political tool
aimed at transgressing hegemonic heterosexual discourses in
public, but also as the condition for safe, private homosexual
spaces of disclosure. It is the otherness of gay men and lesbians'
experience that cannot (and should not) be shared with the
heterosexual 'other', and which constitutes the group's unity and
its transgressive power.

Others resent such a narrow approach. As one of its founders
reports, NTS was not meant to be a gay and lesbian club, although
the consolidation of gay men and lesbians of Wrocław University
was its main goal:

> If someone comes to NTS meetings or marches in the
> Parade of Equality, it doesn't mean he or she wants to say
> 'I am a gay man, I am a lesbian,' but is just interested or
> supports the event … But some people believe that, if
> someone comes to an NTS meeting, he or she just must be
> gay. Such essentialist, binary thinking excludes many
> people, prevents them from speaking up. Certainly, if
> someone with no gay experience tries to impose
> something, it's paranoia. But, if someone comes and wants
> to say 'we', it's just great.

Representatives of this approach stress that 'To forge a positive
identity is important … and queer identity doesn't indicate an in-
between position; it's just against exclusions and stable categories,
because we are different.' Consequently, NTS members in this
faction believe that it is understandable that some gay men or
lesbians need to create various same-sex groups to feel comfortable,

but it should not be used as a weapon against all others. This anti-essentialist stance taken, alongside others, by the NTS board caused some to leave the association, because they expected it to be based on a more clearly defined homosexual identity.

NTS participants who were disappointed in the overarching identity politics felt more comfortable in Durga. As one said, 'Durga has a somewhat separatist character. It's "second wave" thinking. I like queer ideas on a theoretical, intellectual level, but within activism, somehow emotionally, I feel closer to the "second wave".'[10] In Durga, the problem of establishing a common identity was based primarily on gender issues. Some of its participants insisted it should be an exclusively women's space: 'Women need to feel they are together ... I don't need any guys to take my space ... Guys take space everywhere, they talk about everything everywhere, so, if we meet, I don't want any guys there.' But others argue that, if a man wants to act for women's advancement, he should be allowed to. Consequently, some pro-feminist men have been invited, although not all Durga participants support this situation.

Sexual identity was also negotiated within this group. Many participants perceived Durga as a lesbian space. As a lesbian-identified person stated, 'Only lesbians sit there. All Durgans are lesbians.' However, those women who do not identify as lesbians felt uncomfortable at times:

At the outset, wherever we went, Magda began almost every conversation with: 'she's got a boy-friend'. It's the same as I would say: 'she's a lesbian'. I've finally got pissed off and told her how I see it. I've even complained to the group, so now we're just joking about it. But now Magda says I belong to a lesbian continuum, because I want to be with women.[11] Everyone there has to identify oneself. Once, when I mentioned I had kissed a girl, they were so happy.

Different visibilities

The idea of sexuality as belonging to the private domain is underlined in Durga, which reflects a wider issue of the lack of lesbian public visibility. Although the situation has been changing gradually, there are still few lesbian activists demonstrating in public spaces, and Polish lesbians, in general, are reported to prefer staying in the closet (Gruszczyńska 2003). Consequently, they seem in much greater need of maintaining their social circle in terms of private safe space than of engaging in public political action. One of the lesbian activists in NTS states ironically:

> I think that most of us just want it to be nice, we don't want to redeem the world, we don't want to get involved in big things ... Obviously, it is nice to be among women, particularly those we like ... But the problem is that, when such a group is staying in a safe private closet, it cannot come into public being.

Some of the Durga participants noted the paradox in this situation during group meetings. One group of women debated political events, while a much bigger faction of women stayed in the kitchen joking and chatting in a lesbian circle. However, outside the group, invisibility is a strategy for lesbians to cope with a homophobic environment. An activist recalls a critical attitude among the lesbian community towards her political involvement: '"Why should we get involved? For what should we speak up? Why attract attention? You'll get yourself and others into trouble." These are women who think this way. They believe nobody thinks two women living together might be in an erotic relationship. Especially, when they behave themselves, and don't hold hands or kiss publicly.'

In contrast, lesbian activists report that they experience frequent discrimination, as their male colleagues in gay and lesbian organisations are not interested in lesbian problems. Indeed, a dominant image of the homosexual community in Poland is its androcentric character. The Lesbian Coalition (LBT) was formed in an effort to change this situation. Nonetheless, lesbian activists have complained that, while it was mostly women who organised the Parade of Equality in 2005, male leaders appropriated the results of their work. They dominated the interviews in the media, which referred to the event as 'a gay parade'. This provoked a strong feminist response within NTS space. A participant of 2005 Lesbians, Gays and Friends Festival remarked that 'women in Poland are still "the second sex" who are brought up to serve men. Thus, women work hardest, while the men star in the media.'

Divergent opinions about managing sexual orientation and politics are not limited to lesbian spaces. In NTS the more universally inclined view that 'private is political' clashes with the more individually oriented idea that 'private is private'. One of the leaders of the Campaign Against Homophobia (CAH, a national-level organisation fighting for the rights of sexual minorities in line with the 'full emancipation' approach) insisted that as gay people living in a homophobic society, they should show solidarity and create a positive common identity as a distinct social group to engage with an anti-discriminatory political agenda. Not all lesbian and gay members agreed. They claimed that society is not as homophobic as NGO reports show, because these reports are based on tendentious polling aimed at proving discrimination against sexual minorities. One member commented, 'When I meet any homophobic people and they see what a cool guy I am, they are not homophobic any more'. Thus, not all gay men and lesbians in Poland necessarily support the socio-political initiatives and/or identity politics of the mainstream gay and lesbian movement. A refusal to identify with a group of 'the oppressed others' may be one of the reasons why they do not become actively engaged, rather than apathy or a lack of civil consciousness as is commonly claimed.

Nevertheless, even those people in NTS who reject any possibility of a real common homosexual identity agree that, to proceed with the 'full emancipation' project, a sort of 'common identity' is necessary as a political weapon because it enables public visibility. According to them, to fight for gay men and lesbian civil rights, a distinct social group of citizens whose rights are threatened is indispensable. When CAH attempted to sue a Polish bishop for saying that homosexuality is like a plague and homosexuals should not be allowed to work as schoolteachers, the summons was dismissed because, according to the judge, there was no such social group as homosexuals whose rights had been violated. Attempts to legalise same-sex partnerships are intended to offer a platform for the recognition of homosexual identity:

> An essentialist identity would be necessary if gays and lesbians in Poland, not only in a course of a single action, but in a long-term process, wanted to act for a certain political aim, and the right to legalise the same-sex partnership is just such a main aim at the moment ... We cannot base our political claims on the lack of identity.

Different activities

NTS participants have different ideas about what academic and political actions should be taken to challenge the hetero-normative social order. Those who joined the association to pursue their intellectual aims believe the group's association with the university prevents it from becoming formally involved in political actions, unless they are legal: 'If the university gives us money, it helps us; there are people who believe that what we are doing is important ... and then, if we as a scientific association got involved in any illegal anarchic riot, they would feel we abused their trust.' But legal undertakings are accepted. Consequently, they decided to apply for university funding for NTS participation in the Parade of Equality in 2003. Nine people took part in the event and held the NTS banner. Furthermore, they stress that intellectual activity is political:

> When we deconstruct the dominant discourses on gender and sexuality at the state university, it's political, we transgress something, we enter symbolic public space ... Moreover, when a newspaper writes that 'Nothing the Same' is active in Wrocław, it means that someone noticed that such a group exists, that the group does something. I find it politically significant. And all those accusations that we are not involved in political activity seem not entirely fair to me.

Others who believe that the university is a proper arena in which to consolidate gay and lesbian agency and pursue political activism admit that they have not been able to establish a formal political organisation:

> All people in NTS believed that we need to establish a political association, because it gives us more options for political involvement. But no one wanted to support it officially for personal reasons [due to the danger of 'coming out'] ... And, in fact, it's not necessary. Different things are happening anyway, even if without legal authorisation. It appeared that formal institutionalisation is not indispensable to do something.

Consequently, despite NTS heterogeneity, thanks to the students' association of Wrocław University, events such as the annual Lesbians, Gays and Friends Festival and a major conference entitled 'Europe without Homophobia' have taken place in Wrocław. In addition, by 2005 the group cooperated with the Government Plenipotentiary for Equal Status of Women and Men and still cooperates with the Greens 2004 and other gay-friendly political parties and non-governmental organisations that work with sexual minorities. Thus, 'homosexuality' has become transgression against 'heterosexuality' in a politically oriented public. Furthermore, these activities bring measurable effects, such as increased funding from the university. The NTS leader reports, 'People complain about terrible homophobia in Poland, but a handful of disgusting fags and dykes, who organise sect meetings at the university, got much more money than, for instance, law-abiding Polish philology students.'

The shared festival

The most politically oriented public event in which NTS has been involved is the Lesbians, Gays and Friends Festival organised annually since 2003. The multiplicity of perspectives within the association is evident within the festival itself. The festival first arose out of anarcho-feminist lesbian disappointment with the overly academic character of NTS, on the one hand, and strong mainstream activism within Durga, on the other. What constitutes acceptable 'gay visibility' as a tool of political transgression has been at issue in the festival since the outset. In 2003, the mainstream activists stressed that at some point the festival ceased to have anything in common with a 'gay culture' and, in fact, became an entirely anarchist event: 'They invited rock bands which nobody knows, which have nothing to do with the gay culture. But the gay milieu of Wrocław is responsible as well.'[12] While a political debate organised by the NTS was attended mainly by academics and mainstream activists, anarchists appeared in greater numbers at an illegal gathering in the city market. In line with the famous slogan 'We're here, we're queer, get fucking used to it,' the main objective was to invade a public hetero-space, and same-sex couples walked around the market kissing and holding hands. Nevertheless, all participants found a common space at one of Wrocław's squats, where the 'Let Them See Us' exhibition was displayed.

Transgressive homosexuality?

The Wrocław case is a microcosm of all the internal problems that the gay and lesbian movement encounters in contemporary Poland. In fact, NTS leaders share the view that civil society is weak and passive, which makes it extremely difficult to proceed with any long-term gay and lesbian activities. However, they demonstrate that it is possible to mobilise an event in NTS spaces. Neither established organisational structures nor a common identity or consolidated aims and strategies are required to do so. Despite diverse opinions and ensuing conflicts among NTS participants, a sort of cultural capital, a set of shared values based on the belief that the fight against sexual discrimination is worthwhile, enables them to transcend all those differences and unite in common undertakings aimed at making the 'homosexual question' a part of public debate. Thus, it is a civic consciousness, allegedly lacking in Poland, that is at issue here.

Because of the NTS and other gay and lesbian groups in contemporary Poland, homosexuality has entered the public arena and become a socio-political issue. Given that until recently it was muted or mentioned solely as a 'distant and dangerous curiosity' (Sypniewski and Warkocki 2004a: 7), its current visibility constitutes a transgression against heterosexuality. However, this study shows that what is regarded as politically transgressive for particular people should not be taken for granted. A faction of academics in NTS believes that creating a space to discuss sexuality-related issues at the state university constitutes sufficient political involvement. While some perceive this activity in terms of a private safe space, others declare that within that space they have simultaneously managed to raise public awareness. Conversely, others within the group stress that political activism requires transgression of university boundaries and penetration of the wider public sphere. While the mainstream-oriented insist that gay rights should be implemented via cooperation with existing state structures, the anarchically inclined claim that real transgression involves a radical critique of the whole social, political and economic system.

Furthermore, the concept of homosexuality covers a number of different approaches. For some NTS members it is an identity based on common homosexual experience that should define the group boundaries and thereby constitute its privately safe and publicly transgressive character. Others claim that 'common homosexual experience' does not exist because of differences among homosexual people. Moreover, it is based on symbolic violence and exclusion of those who do not fit their ethos. In their view, queer theory that transgresses homo–hetero binary opposites provides NTS participants a safe space with politically subversive potential. Nevertheless, both factions believe that 'homosexual identity' should constitute a political weapon to transgress the hetero–normative social order. But what publicly visible facets 'homosexual identity' should comprise is not entirely clear. Besides, not all NTS members support the above stance and some suggest that there is no reason why homosexual people necessarily need to become the political subjects of public debates as 'the oppressed others'.

The variety of ideas on homosexual transgressions that are at play in NTS (and many other gay and lesbian groups) suggests that political struggle based on the homo/hetero binary, where the status and meaning of 'homosexuality' as 'heterosexuality's other' remain unquestioned, will not be able to create the sense of commonality necessary to raise wider support for the activists' political agenda. As Dunin (2004) notes, the image of homosexuality promoted by mainstream activism in Poland is rooted in politics of assimilation and is by no means rebellious against dominant cultural norms. All people who do not suit this image are automatically muted. Furthermore, dichotomously oriented debates limit sexual emancipation because they constantly reconstruct heterosexuality as a standard that needs to be transgressed. Thus, it seems that the next stage of political struggle should indicate a shift from the discourse and practice of homosexual unity to the discourse and practice of diversity (see Leszkowicz 2004). Returning to the call by lesbian and gay mainstream activists foregrounded at the start of this chapter, the exhortation to 'Let them hear us!' should not only propel gay and lesbian circles to become more dynamically involved in the identity politics of the 'full emancipation' project, but also encourage gay mainstream activist circles to pay more careful attention to the various identities that fuel the gay and lesbian projects that are pervasive in Polish life.

Notes

1. The term 'homosexuality' and its variations, as well as the term 'sexual minorities', can be misleading because of the emphasis they give to sexual orientation and/or preferences over other forms of identification (see Valentine 2002). Nevertheless, I retain both terms to indicate discursive groups in whose name many activists in Poland claim to speak.

2. Although contemporary public discourses on gay rights in Poland are predominantly built around liberal 'for' (homosexuality as an object of tolerance) versus conservative 'against' (homosexuality as an object of condemnation), most gay rights activists stress that it is principally the denaturalisation of heterosexuality that constitutes a fundamental step necessary for normalising homosexuality (see Sypniewski and Warkocki 2004b).

3. An opinion poll in 2005 showed that public acceptance of homosexuality is still extremely low in Poland. Thirty-four per cent of respondents believed that homosexuality is abnormal and should not be tolerated, and 55 per cent that, even if it is deviant, it should be tolerated. Only 4 per cent regarded homosexuality as normal. Seventy-eight per cent and 74 per cent respectively believed that same-sex couples should not be permitted to display their lifestyle publicly, and that gay and lesbian organisations should not have the right to organise public political demonstrations (CBOS 2005).

4. In popular usage 'gay and lesbian movement' can have a variety of referents and meanings. I use it here to refer to all organisations whose activities are aimed at generating social approval and legal recognition for non-normative sexual/gender identities and behaviours.

5. Unless indicated otherwise, unacknowledged quotations are from fieldwork conducted in Wrocław in 2003.

6. One is a Polish section of the International Lesbian and Gay Cultural Network and the other is the Campaign Against Homophobia. While a third organisation, the Lesbian Coalition (LBT), operates on both national and international levels, it remains an informal platform.

7. Christopher Street Day involves an annual gay pride parade held in a number of European cities. It takes its name from the location of a gay bar in New York that was raided by police in June 1969.

8. Posters by Karolina Breguła with thirty same-sex couples holding each others' hands were to be posted on billboards in major Polish cities for two months to show that homosexuals are as normal as the heterosexual majority.

9. Both parades took place anyway. Because of the spectacularly undemocratic nature of the ban, the event attracted widespread media attention.

10. Here 'second wave' (an abbreviation for 'second wave' feminism) suggests a sense of solidarity based on a more essentialised 'women's identity' constructed in opposition to an essentialised category of 'men'.

11. Rich (1993: 239) uses the term 'lesbian continuum' to refer to a range of woman-identified experiences distinct from 'the fact that a woman has had or consciously desired genital sexual experience with another woman'.

12. This refers to the refusal of Wrocław gay club owners to waive the admission charge for the festival party on Saturday night on the grounds that this is their busiest night of the week and when they make most money.

References

Adamska, K. 1998. *Ludzie obok. Lesbijki i geje w Polsce*. Toruń: Pracownia Duszycki and Graffiti BC.

Basiuk, T. 2000. '*Queerowanie* po polsku', *Furia Pierwsza. Zeszyty Gender Studies* 7 (1): 28–36.

CBOS. 2005. 'Akceptacja praw dla gejów i lesbijek i społeczny dystans wobec nich'. Komunikat no. 3377, Warsaw: CBOS. http://www.zigzag.pl/cbos/details.asp?q=a1&id=3377

Dunin, K. 2004. 'Fałszywi przyjaciele. Pożądana asymilacja czy asymilacja pożądania', in Z. Sypniewski and B. Warkocki (eds) *Homofobia po polsku*. Warsaw: Wydawnictwo Sic!, pp. 17–26.

Fuss, D. 1989. *Essentially Speaking. Feminism, Nature and Difference*. New York and London: Routledge.

———. 1991. 'Inside/Outside. Introduction', in D. Fuss (ed.) *Inside/Outside. Lesbian Theories, Gay Theories*. New York and London: Routledge, pp. 1–10.

Gawlicz, K. and M. Starnawski. 2004. 'Budzenie dyskursu. Analiza debaty o prawach gejów i lesbijek na internetowym forum "Gazety Wyborczej"', in Z. Sypniewski and B. Warkocki (eds) *Homofobia po polsku*. Warsaw: Wydawnictwo Sic!, pp. 27–51.

Griffin, G. 2001. 'Kooptacja czy Transformacja? *Women's* i *gender studies* na świecie', *Katedra* 3: 9–28.

Gruszczyńska, A. 2003. 'W poszukiwaniu lesbijek', *Zadra. Pismo feministyczne* 4/1 (13/14): 24–25.

———. n.d. 'Ślady ruchu lesbijskiego'. http://www.nic-tak-samo.uni.wroc.pl/tv.html.

Hann, C. 1996. 'Introduction. Political Society and Civil Anthropology', in C. Hann and E. Dunn (eds) *Civil Society. Challenging Western Models*. London and New York: Routledge, pp. 1–26.

Katechizm Kościoła Katolickiego. 1994. http://www.katechizm.diecezja.elk.pl.

Kitliński, T. and P. Leszkowicz. 2005. 'God and Gay Rights in Poland', *The Gay and Lesbian Review*, May-June: 26–28.

Leszkowicz, P. 2004. 'Przełamując hetero-matrix. Wojna seksualna w Polsce i kryzys praw człowieka', in Z. Sypniewski and B. Warkocki (eds) *Homofobia po polsku*. Warsaw: Wydawnictwo Sic!, pp. 85–112.

Majka-Rostek, D. 2002. *Mniejszość kulturowa w warunkach pluralizacji. Socjologiczna analiza sytuacji homoseksualistów polskich*. Wrocław: Wydawnictwo Uniwersytetu Wrocławskiego.

Mizielińska, J. 2004. 'Nasze życie, nasze rodziny, nasze wartości, czyli jak walczyć z moralna paniką w ponowoczesnych czasach', in Z. Sypniewski and B. Warkocki (eds) *Homofobia po polsku*. Warsaw: Wydawnictwo Sic!, pp. 113–36.

Rich, A. 1993. 'Compulsory Heterosexuality and Lesbian Existence', in H. Abelove, M.A. Barale and D.M. Halperin (eds) *The Lesbian and Gay Studies Reader*. New York and London: Routledge, pp. 227–54.

Sypniewski Z. and B. Warkocki. 2004a. 'Wstęp', in Z. Sypniewski and B. Warkocki (eds) *Homofobia po polsku*. Warsaw: Wydawnictwo Sic!, pp. 5–13.

Sypniewski Z. and B. Warkocki. (eds). 2004b. *Homofobia po polsku*. Warsaw: Wydawnictwo Sic!

Valentine, D. 2002. 'We're "Not about Gender". The Uses of "Transgender"', in E. Lewin and W.L. Leap (eds) *Out in Theory. The*

Emergence of Lesbian and Gay Anthropology. Urbana and Chicago: University of Illinois Press, pp. 222–45.

Witkowski, M. 2005. 'Wszyscy mężczyźni to pederaści. Refleksje na temat homoseksualizmu', *[fo:pa] kwartalnik literacko-filozoficzny* 2. http://www.fopa.pl/czytelnia/wszyscy_mezczyzni_to_pederasci.htm.

CHAPTER 8

TAMING THE BUSH: MORALITY, AIDS PREVENTION AND GAY SEX IN PUBLIC PLACES

Laurent Gaissad

This chapter explores the temporal and spatial dynamics of secret encounters between men who seek sexual partners in city neighbourhoods associated with male sex work and gay cruising. Focusing on sexualised public places in the south of France, it examines the interaction between gay men whose activities are shaped by urban planning, and the cyclical redesignation of such spaces according to the time of day or night (Gaissad 2005). In addition to the powerful influences of urban planning on the ecology of such 'moral spaces' within the cityscape, the chapter examines the impact of 'do-gooders' on these environments (Park, cited in Raushenbush 1979: 96). In particular, it focuses on AIDS prevention outreach teams, whose activities also influence the territorial patterns of seeking sex in public places and the risks that such sex entails. It situates this research in historico-geographical perspectives on public sex environments.[1]

Many researchers in the field of gay sex find it necessary to maintain a distinction between an honourable version of gay life and what takes place covertly in the bushes: they tend to emphasise the social and cultural dimensions of collective and individual gay identity based on sexual orientation, sometimes referred to as 'homosociability', as opposed to the clandestine aspect of anonymous sex in public places. While AIDS awareness campaigners define men cruising for sex as a 'target population' located in the distant and dangerous outskirts of emerging organised communities (such as gay commercial venues, activist groups and self-support networks), researchers often neglect the fact that volunteer field interventions or empirical surveys are not only biased by the aims and purposes of prevention programmes but can be perceived as intrusions, and can considerably affect local uses of space. This chapter will establish that hidden forms of sexuality between men persist and expand both temporally and geographically in the midst of ordinary, everyday urban life. In particular, it shows that public spaces can be used for secret sex at night or during the day, and that sexual conduct is very different in the two cases: men cruising for sex are more isolated and visible at night, while they organise themselves more discreetly in the daytime, when they must mix with people of other sexual preferences. The 'transgressions' entailed are consequently different in the two cases.

Contrasting interpretations have arisen around secret forms of men-to-men sexual interactions in public places. In America such interactions are mostly associated with psychological instability, while French surveys are more likely to explain them in relation to the privatisation of public space normally dedicated to the expression of citizenship. In this context, this chapter further considers how NGO volunteers seek to assist or offer health advice to men cruising for sex, and how this effort to educate them may constitute a transgression of local clandestine homosexual activities and norms. These volunteers' perceptions of their own roles are further examined with regard to the moral conception of the risks they associate with cruising for sex in public spaces.

Urban anthropology and the construction of gay sex in public spaces

An examination of the public spaces where men cruise and have sex together has been a growing focus in urban anthropology and the sociology of cities (Humphreys 1970; Troiden 1974; Corzine and Kirby 1977; Delph 1978; Chauncey 1994; Bell and Valentine 1995; Pickering et al. 1996). Drawing on such work, my own research has sought to explore the connections between sexualised public spaces and urban planning. Fieldwork in

Marseille and Toulouse, as well as in Barcelona, revealed that public locations dedicated to male cruising for sex, rather than being stable in time, were continually 'moving' throughout the city landscape. Pressures to move came from local planners, sometimes prompted by neighbourhood complaints and even petitions. Men who sought to have sex in city parks and squares were continually being moved on, usually because bright street lighting had been installed to discourage them, or because the street vegetation itself had deliberately been removed, a trend that some French urban sociologists have suggested may be linked to a strategy of state control over the use of public space (Cauquelin 1977; Sansot 1993). In fact, it is not difficult to document such objective transformations, and the research I have been conducting since 1998 provides many examples of situations where antagonistic moral positions clearly affect the design of urban neighbourhoods. Nevertheless, long-term fieldwork suggests that the situation cannot be understood in terms of a simple opposition between repression and transgression.

One must also consider the practical constraints that men face when they shift from conventional life to cruising in the bushes, such as a fear of losing their anonymity or of forever having to live with the consequences of their behaviour. Their participation in such clandestine forms of sexual activity could be considered transgressive in itself. However, I have chosen to focus on how men engaged in cruising limit the risk, harm and physical transgression that are often directed at them. To avoid the risk of verbal and physical abuse, many men stay away from the main cruising spots. For example, rather than cruising at exposed meeting places near the entrance or in the car park, they seek shelter further inside the park itself, until these havens themselves become too well known, and the action once again moves on. Such expansion can also reflect the relentless pursuit of new 'tricks' beyond one's existing network. In some cases, an area can become so busy that cruising for sex ends up occupying daytime hours as well. At first sight, it is as if the secret sexual night-time activities continue during the day, especially when the same places are used for cruising. However, the use of space is very different in daylight hours, when encounters must be more direct and more cautious to determine whether desire is mutual in the little time that the journey between home and work allows to confirm this. Transgressing the agenda to identify a sexual partner requires specific skills that are paradoxically highly normative in the cruising context. My data on local interaction rituals have shown, for example, that, as in most forms of sex work, it is acceptable not to kiss a partner and yet alright to touch his genitals without saying hello or without even knowing his name. In fact, requesting a telephone number or address can be considered tactless. Simmel (1908) postulated that engaging in activities outside general habits means an absence of normative support, and that a ritual's details compensate for this lack of precision, as in a sort of oversimplified 'counter-norm' that preserves human nature's equilibrium. In general, sexual desire relies on silent eye or body contact, and men follow or avoid one another without conflict. Sexual intercourse takes place in more isolated areas, yet partners sometimes expose themselves to perform group sex. In this case, newcomers may join in according to the couple's desire to welcome additional partners, although they might just as well be politely excluded: it would be a transgression to insist on joining in, to express frustration or to cause a scandal in such a situation, and it happens very rarely. Surprisingly, however, this moral aspect of local gay face-to-face interactions is not examined in the scholarly literature. To understand how sexual risks are handled in these contexts, this chapter considers specific patterns of physical intimacy and social distance amongst men cruising for sex in public places. It begins by situating transgressive sexual acts within the broader context of risk and its territorial dimensions in urban public places.

An island within the city

In Toulouse, the park of the Île du Ramier is located on an island whose recent history clearly illustrates how the role of a public space dedicated to cruising for sex can shift from night to day in response to a generally hostile environment and local constraints. The area is similar to the Donau Insel in Vienna, whose relatively secluded location has also encouraged cruising for sex. Isolated in the middle of the Garonne River, the Île du Ramier park is active night and day and is easily accessible from the city centre and from Toulouse's ring road.

The park brings together both the norms of established nightlife based on sexual encounters between men in close-knit groups and the general trends of casual city commuters during the day. On the one hand, young gay men predominate in the park once the bars and nightclubs have closed after 2 a.m., or in the early morning hours on weekends. On the other hand, the park is used discreetly by men for sex during the day, in the morning, over lunch break and in the early evening, as the men travel to and from their work.[2] Figure 8.1 shows, in grey, the spot in the woods where men meet and have sex (on the western

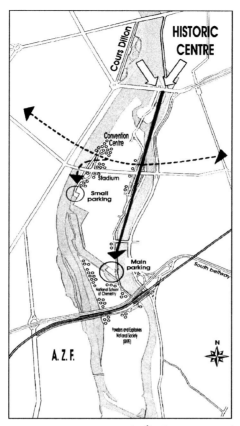

Figure 8.1 *Gay cruising areas in the Île du Ramier park, Toulouse*

bank of the middle of the island). There are car parks on both sides of the park. The cours Dillon is another public park closer to the city centre, along the left bank of the Garonne River to the north. This area was one of the first cruising sites, the predecessor of the cruising area on the Île du Ramier. A few decades ago, it was a suburban garden situated opposite Toulouse city centre on the eastern bank. The Garonne River has long been a frontier between the earlier provinces of Gascony and the Languedo.[3] On the Île du Ramier, the main car park is at the southern end, where it is difficult to find a place to park on Friday or Saturday after midnight, as many gay men head to this spot when the bars have closed. There are very few roads on the island and the road out of the city centre leads directly to this car park (indicated by the black arrow from north to south in Fig. 8.1). More secluded cruising areas (indicated by the small circles in Fig. 8.1) are either very close to the main car park, or directly linked to it. A second car park at the northern entrance is used when the first one is too crowded (as the dotted arrows running east to west by the stadium in Fig. 8.1 indicate). Wherever the men come from, they end up congregating in the middle of the woods, where the bushes are dense enough to hide them during the day and dark enough at night, even though they are only five minutes' drive from the crowded historic city centre. The men also meet in a row of small, derelict houses that skirt the main route crossing the park. In all these areas, sexual affairs are conducted consensually. Men already engaged in sexual activity may accept or reject a newcomer in quick and silent agreement. A few feet away, another group may be forming. In this way, a group may grow or decrease in number depending on who comes and goes; yet it is very rare that a refusal produces tension or conflict. A wall provides other opportunities for encounters, as does the entrance to one of the houses, which offers a good vantage point for those who choose to keep cruising outside among the trees. As already mentioned, insisting on being accepted by a sexual partner or a group already engaged in sex would contradict the local gay morality and transgress the consensus that underlies all such interactions. These local rules of the game, however, provide no protection from external threats, or even from violence, as men cruising for sex very rarely respond collectively to homophobic assaults. Such assaults occasionally occur on the parking lots rather than in the protective darkness of the woods and, in general, they involve groups of individuals who consider men-to-men sexuality itself a transgression of the general moral order. But it needs to be underlined that they are very rarely the result of the agreed norms of those who are there to cruise for sex.

The areas used for gay sex in the Île du Ramier are themselves marginal and liminal spaces in the urban landscape. The park has a volatile history. An explosives factory built in 1675 on the northern tip of the island was moved southwards following a series of accidental explosions and in response to the growth of Toulouse. The most recent explosion, which resulted in the loss of many lives and caused much damage, took place on 21 September 2001, just a few yards from the Île du Ramier park. The cours Dillon and the Île du Ramier are among the last districts in the city not to have protection from flooding, as the devastating figures over the past century have shown.[4] At the entrance to the park are a number of intimidating signposts. These official warnings on big, bright panels not only caution against the dangers of sudden flooding, but also refer to the presence of hydroelectric and chemical factories in the area, strictly forbidding entry to all but factory staff. The derelict houses frequented by gay men once belonged to the explosives factory but were destroyed by accidental explosions in the mid-nineteenth century.

Following the destruction of the neighbouring National Chemistry School in the most recent explosion, a group of Bulgarian Roma settled in what remained of the buildings, and their presence substantially changed the habits of the men cruising for sex in the area, particularly at night. Fear of these newcomers, who were expected to react aggressively to the visibility of sexual traffic, pushed the gay men northwards, away from the main car park and towards the stadium and wide pathways of the Convention Centre, and they only returned to the original site when the ruins of the factory were demolished and the Roma relocated. The cruising site then expanded out under the motorway bridge, occupying waste ground where even by day passers-by would never expect to see anyone. With the return of cruising gay men to the main car park, new conflicts are currently being played out at the entrance to the woods. Moralising graffiti have appeared on the gates. On the official sign of the city council's Atelier terre ('Earth Workshop'), someone dismayed at the condoms to be found everywhere has written: 'The Earth belongs to our children'. The same unofficial hand has added the exhortation to: 'Preserve the planet'.[5]

Figure 8.2 *Graffiti on city council signpost, Toulouse*

'Either bashers, the police or "them"'

The crux of the conflict for those trying to control or limit homosexuality in public places is education. The Île du Ramier park has become a kind of educational venue. The whole area was closed temporarily and reopened with new signage and visitor facilities that emphasised the preservation and enjoyment of the local flora and fauna. Families are invited to use the new picnic tables and playgrounds and to consult the information panels on the local wildlife. Providing information for visitors to the park is not a new phenomenon, although educational agendas may change, along with the educational issues themselves. For example, community AIDS organisations in Toulouse addressed the issue of men having sex together in the Île du Ramier park more than ten years ago. In 1990, colourful banners bearing the names of local AIDS victims were hung from the trees in the middle of the woods,[6] as a memorial and warning to its clandestine users, supposedly at a higher risk here than anywhere else in the city. Of course, AIDS activists have since developed a greater understanding of men cruising for sex in public places, but in the past the key strategies to fight HIV in the area were sometimes very intrusive and transgressed local rules of secrecy and consensual silence.

Volunteers play a central role in prevention programmes and they are confronted with moral and ethical issues when dealing with men cruising for sex. This is particularly the case for men who self-identify as gay, and who have difficulty with interpretations of men-to-men sex that see it as a 'problem'. Despite this, the volunteer 'must momentarily be sexually neutral, to make his presence as an HIV prevention agent legitimate' (Mendès-Leite and Proth 2002). Volunteers who are gay also make an official commitment not to go cruising for sex in the area just before and just after their team's intervention (Jäcklein 1998a).[7] Nevertheless, volunteers do make moral judgements. For example, the former prevention outreach project coordinator in Toulouse found it inconceivable that men would have sex with strangers in the park.

What happens when an awareness team interferes with cruising to promote AIDS prevention? A university report describes how volunteers continually seek out gay men in the park to talk to them:

> Friday night at 11 p.m. a number of men simply leave the
> parking lot as they see the NGO car arriving with four

people in it. Their coming is like a disturbance in local order: it's either bashers, the police or 'them'. Cruising comes to a halt, and most men think it's best to leave immediately. The ones who stay are called over one by one by the volunteers. Those who try to avoid talking to them are 'trapped': in the group coordinator's terms the strategy is to 'catch' as many men as possible. On the one hand, volunteers invest the place with a precise idea of what sexual intercourse should be; on the other hand, men are put in a position where they have to 'confess' their practices. The volunteers' intrusion on the cruising ground seems legitimate, and they seem excited over dealing with such an 'exotic' field, but they consider it from a distant and superior point of view. The NGO's ethics forbid men to cruise during the intervention, much as any health or social service would do, respecting 'proper' distance between intervener and user (Jäcklein 1998a: 6–7).

In fact, AIDS activist teams are often perceived as intruders, and their efforts to make themselves as visible and as distinct as possible from the men who cruise obviously create a general feeling of distrust. On Sebastopol Square in Marseille, for example, regular cruisers mention the volunteers' 'impressive white tee-shirts with the NGO logo', and the fact that some of them seem to take pleasure in saying words like 'prick', 'anus' or 'sperm'.[8] Men who come to cruise for sex know when NGO activists in Marseille will visit the area and they schedule their own movements to avoid them, as in Toulouse, where the NGO volunteers follow a well-known routine. The volunteers in both places are thus in contact with similar sorts of 'clients', namely those who do not mind having a chat about AIDS and generally do so in gay bars or in their networks of friends. In their attempts to develop strategies to 'trap' what they call their 'target population' and to heighten AIDS awareness, the routine practices of volunteers thus change the landscape of cruising spaces for at least a short time. Not only are they responsible for mass departures from an area, but also for the sudden flow of men to be observed in other parts of the city.

There has been little discussion in the literature of volunteers and processes of intervention by NGO volunteers. This may be because it is as difficult to assess gay NGOs' perceptions of their own roles and their impact upon the cruising scene as it is to assess the cruisers' views of NGO volunteers. Research shows that some NGOs take certain aspects of cruising for sex for granted:

what happens in the bushes is a precarious and primitive form of sexuality, considered to be promiscuous, secret, silent and lonely, all of which are interpreted as risk factors, a view with which at least some social researchers concur (see Somlai et al. 2001). Somlai et al. (2001: 512–13) consider that some men are able to cruise for sex on 'the strength of their risk behaviour choices and the fragility of their personal psychological and physical safety'. However, they do not provide empirical data on the men's concrete risk-taking. American scholars argue that 'cruising' is often an activity engaged in by men as a form of release and escapism from their problems (Vicioso et al. 2005: 14): 'The physical and social characteristics of public and commercial sex environments ... frequented by men who have sex with men may provide the heightened emotional experiences that enable cognitive escape by amplifying sexual arousal.'

This cognitive escape model (McKirnan et al. 1996) is based on a subsample of the Seropositive Urban Men's Study.[9] It posits that multiple psychosocial stressors – homophobia, depression, substance abuse, sexual risk behaviour, HIV infection – contribute to driving individuals to these venues, where 'they seek release from distress and vulnerability through immersion in sexuality' (McKirnan et al. 1996: 655). Perceptions of 'sexual compulsion' are then cited as factors that should be integrated into health and social services training programmes (Reece and Dodge 2004). Unfortunately, the moral dimension of such a framework of analysis grounded on 'sexual addiction or compulsion' remains unquestioned.

In France, research on sexual activities has been greatly influenced by a demographer who was involved in the last extensive telephone survey on French sexual behaviour conducted in the country (Spira and Bajos 1993). Bozon (1995: 48) initially declared that one of the main problems of researching sexual activity was that it was 'inaccessible to observation', and that 'no hope could be grounded on the methods of anthropology'. Very few social researchers have responded to this criticism, although Beylot (2000) has suggested that observing sexual activity is possible, and might be approached through a reflexive process of 'seeing oneself seeing'. Others have argued that the collective dimension of intimacy in gay back rooms (i.e. dark rooms for direct sexual interactions generally located at the back or in the basement of gay venues) or sex clubs could include the observer (Jäcklein 1998b).

At the same time, the activities of NGOs, which are always in need of legitimising their research to maintain funding, have found many opportunities for collaborating with social scientists. As a result, a number of institutional reports expose the hegemonic nature of the NGO volunteers' responsibility in displacing men from those areas where secret sex occurs. These reports reveal that a growing fringe of 'civilised' and sympathetic volunteers hand out condoms along with questionnaires to the usually unreachable element of the gay community.

Paying closer attention to the information gathered in surveys proves to be especially revealing. In one survey conducted in the Marseille metropolitan region (Mendès-Leite and Proth 1998), it turned out that, not only was the typical interviewee male, homosexual, relatively young, a single city-dweller with a good level of education and a decent profession, but that he was also *français de souche* (Mendès-Leite and Proth 1998: 6). This expression, which translates as 'French-born', created considerable debate at the Institut National d'Études Démographiques (INED) (National Institute of Demographic Studies) and ended up in court in the same year. As the expression discriminates between a foreign minority and a sovereign majority, dispute raged over the use of the term, and the INED reproached Hervé Lebras, a social scientist, over his argument that demography in France was becoming a way to express racism.[10] Based on a qualitative study conducted in the late 1990s, an article published in 2002 also used ambiguous expressions to distinguish localised practices that were found in peripheral public spaces (Mendès-Leite and Proth 2002). It stated that: 'It is important to understand the way a minority appropriates a marginal place, to perform "natural" acts since they are perceived as traditional by those who share them as customs' (Mendès-Leite and Proth 2002: 38).

For several years, this team of researchers has focused on interactive rituals that characterise what they call 'anonymous' sexuality. Their 1997 study of two Parisian back rooms (Mendès-Leite and De Busscher 1997) identifies considerable differences between the city centre and the outskirts of Paris as regards the spatial organisation of gay bars and the practices of the gay scene within them. It also indicates major differences between the two locations in the relationship between sociability and sexuality, and how this results in the specialisation of different areas inside the bars. Rather than separating the social from the sexual aspects of these relationships, my research has sought to elicit qualitative data from which comparative models of cruising-for-sex encounters can be explored. Instead of creating an illogical separation between the two spheres of experience, this approach is important to explain how sociability and sexuality can be linked or connected in a relationship where proximity and distance are key to sexual engagement.

Recent studies based on a distinction between public and private space have come to similar conclusions: not only does the private nature of men cruising for sex create a subcultural atmosphere, it also 'hijacks' the public space normally used by all citizens, turning it into a restricted area, at least temporarily (Proth 2002: 387–88). The idea is similar to that of an area beyond the rule of law (a *zone de non-droit*), where preventive actions are required to restore the normative status and relative safety of the public space. In the French context, a parallel may be drawn with the representation of dangerous suburbs inhabited by Muslims who supposedly disregard secular law and republican order forbidding religious (i.e. private) expression in the public domain. Amidst the shadow of the bushes, then, the NGO volunteer becomes the 'master of the game' (*maître du jeu*) in his dealings with men who cruise for sex, and he is said 'to impose a spatial and symbolic shift' on the men who inhabit these zones (Proth 2002: 279, 285). Following such an interpretation, it is expected that a volunteer's message on AIDS will change isolated, silent and shameful homosexuality – reduced to a strict physical desire – into a public, collective and civil expression of homosociability as the only way towards integration and respect.

Drawing on Mauss's classic essay on the gift (1923–24), Proth (2002: 302) refers to the NGO volunteer as giving of himself and his time for the sake of the community: he hands out condoms as a kind of token given away, as a 'confessional' object. Such a 'gift' automatically creates an obligation to return in the recipient, as does the 'good' advice: in many gay venues and community organisations, gays are warned about the dangers of cruising in public places, compared to the safety of mixing in an established, sociable and clean atmosphere. Choosing public spaces for homosexual activities and face-to-face encounters is asking for trouble. In this context, many gay men – NGO leaders and gay club owners in particular – tend to consider it as a form of transgression. As the general public has recently become more aware of instances of homophobic attacks in France, especially due to the demand for new legislation to prevent them, gay sex in public places is being presented as particularly unsafe and risky. In a country where the public expression of racism and other forms of discrimination are strictly prohibited, even though the National Front party leader reached the second ballot in the 2002 presidential election,[11] the problem of violence has to be addressed within the broadest institutional framework, especially the violence inherent in value systems that promote sameness and assimilation, or when identity is under question as a stable value in a complex cultural or sexual environment. Violence in public places used for cruising for sex is not a new phenomenon in France, nor has it particularly increased over the past few years according to my research in southern France. What is changing, though, is the way a growing number of seemingly unruly, partially secret activities are being considered in the public debate. In this context, it may become even more difficult to identify the emerging norms of former marginal categories of the population, and to reveal the way they define new boundaries for transgression in space and time.

Notes

1. I am grateful to my colleagues in the Centre d'Études des Rationalités et des Savoirs in Toulouse for inspiring many of the research questions addressed in this chapter. I also wish to thank Joël Coyo and Eve Lanchantin for their help with the English translation.

2. Around the motorway rest areas near Montpellier in southern France, cruising is organised according to a similar pattern, as earlier surveys have shown:

> In the middle of the night, especially on weekends, certain picnic areas are used exclusively by young self-identified gay men from the Montpellier gay scene, transferring codes of interaction from the bars and discos there, and often gathering in small groups of acquaintances which makes it very difficult to remain anonymous. Cruising is both very visible and normative, as it is nearly the only activity. Conversely, during daytime rush hour, cruising is almost invisible, and the population of men cruising and having sex is more mixed in terms of class, ethnicity, age and professional activity as it is influenced by inter-city travel. In fact, various categories of people can be observed in all of the motorway picnic areas along the Mediterranean coast between Montpellier and Nîmes. The increase in traffic during peak travel times generally results in an increase in the number of men cruising for sex, as well as in a greater diversity of age, status, and origin, including tourists (especially during holidays), truck drivers, businessmen, commuters, and gay men wanting to cruise 'outside the ghetto'. This heterogeneous composition of men cruising seems to be limited to the daytime (Gaissad 2005: 23).

3. The river also marked the east/west linguistic frontier between the two Occitan dialects.

4. The worst flooding in Toulouse was in June 1875, when the water level rose to 8.32 metres above normal, far exceeding the 2.50 metres at which a public alert is declared.
5. The word 'planet' is misspelt, and in the left-hand corner someone else has advised 'Go learn to spell'.
6. Though badly weathered, the memorial was still visible in 1997.
7. The literature on these issues is very limited, even that on the so-called 'relapse' in gay men's behaviour. The latest survey in France indicates that unprotected sexual relations among gay men has increased by 70 per cent since 1997. See 'Les relations sexuelles non protégées ont augmenté de 70% depuis 1997 chez les homosexuels', *Le Monde*, 20 June 2005.
8. Comments of men interviewed by me in Marseille in 1998.
9. The SUMS project, funded by the Centre for Disease Control and Prevention (see Parsons et al. 2003; Wolitski et al. 2004), comprises 250 men from New York City and San Francisco.
10. See U. Gauthier, 'Des dérapages racistes à l'INED? La guerre des démographes', *Le Nouvel Observateur* 1776, 19–25 Novembre 1998: 116–18.
11. On the first ballot in the presidential election of 21 April 2002, National Front leader Jean-Marie Le Pen took second place after Jacques Chirac, with nearly 17 per cent of the votes.

References

Bell, D. and G. Valentine (eds). 1995. *Mapping Desire: Geographies of Sexualities*. Routledge: New York.

Beylot, J.M. 2000. 'Comment épouser son terrain? L'accès à autrui dans l'imaginaire des rencontres', *Journal des Anthropologues* 82–83: 215–33.

Bozon, M. 1995. 'Observer l'inobservable: la description et l'analyse de l'activité sexuelle', in *Sexualité et sida. Recherches en sciences sociales*. Paris: ANRS, pp. 39–56.

Cauquelin, A. 1977. *La Ville la nuit*. Paris: Presses Universitaires de France.

Chauncey, G. 1994. *Gay New York: Gender, Urban Culture and the Making of the Gay Male World, 1890–1940*. New York: Basic Books.

Corzine, J. and R. Kirby. 1977. 'Cruising the Truckers: Sexual Encounter in Highway Rest Area', *Urban Life* 6 (2): 171–92.

Delph, E. 1978. *The Silent Community: Public Homosexual Encounters*. London: Sage.

Gaissad, L. 2005. 'From Nightlife Conventions to Daytime Hidden Agendas: Dynamics of Urban Sexual Territories in the South of France', *Journal of Sex Research* 42 (1): 20–27.

Gauthier, U. 1998. 'Des dérapages racistes à l'INED? La guerre des démographes', in *Le Nouvel Observateur* 1776, 19–25 Novembre 1998: 116–18.

Humphreys, L. 1970. *Tea Room Trade: Impersonal Sex in Public Places*. New York: Aldine.

Jäcklein, W. 1998a. 'Enjeux et rationalités des acteurs de prévention contre le sida en milieu gai à AIDES Toulouse'. Unpublished manuscript, Université de Toulouse le Mirail.

———. 1998b. 'Les modulations de l'intimité dans les établissements commerciaux à prestation sexuelle'. Unpublished manuscript, sociology PhD project (DEA), Université de Toulouse-le-Mirail.

Mauss, M. 1923–24. 'Essai sur le don. Forme et raison de l'échange dans les sociétés archaïques', in *L'Année Sociologique*, 2e série I: 145–279. Also published in 1950, in *Sociologie et anthropologie*. Paris: Presses Universitaires de France.

McKirnan, D., D. Ostrow and B. Hope. 1996. 'Sex, Drugs and Escape: a Psychological Model of HIV Risk Behaviours', *AIDS Care* 17: 655–69.

Mendès-Leite, R. and P.O. De Busscher. 1997. *Back-rooms: Microgéographie sexographique de deux back-rooms*. Lille: Gay-Kitsch-Camp.

Mendès-Leite, R. and B. Proth. 1998. *Sexualité et gestion des risques de transmission du VIH dans le milieu homo-bisexuel masculin de la région Provence-Alpes-Côte d'Azur*. Paris: AIDES-Provence and GREH, DDASS des Bouches-du-Rhône.

Mendès-Leite, R. and B. Proth. 2002. 'Pratiques discrètes entre hommes'. *Ethnologie Française* 32 (1): 31–40.

Parsons, J.T., P.N. Halkitis, R.J. Wolitski and C.A. Gomez (The Seropositive Urban Men's Study (SUMS) Team). 2003. 'Correlates of Sexual Risk Behaviours among HIV+ Men Who Have Sex with Men', *AIDS Education and Prevention* 15: 383–400.

Pickering, H., M. Okongo, K. Bwanika, B. N'nalusiba and J. Whitworth. 1996. 'Sexual Mixing Patterns in Uganda: Small Time Urban/Rural Traders', *AIDS* 10: 533–36.

Proth, B. 2002. *Lieux de drague. Scènes et coulisses d'une sexualité masculine*. Toulouse: Octares.

Raushenbush, W. 1979. *Robert E. Park: Biography of a Sociologist*. Durham, NC: Duke University Press.

Reece, M. and B. Dodge. 2004. 'Exploring Indicators of Sexual Compulsivity among Men who Cruise for Sex on Campus', *Sexual Addiction and Compulsivity* 11 (3): 87–113.

Sansot, J. 1993. *Jardins publics*. Paris: Payot.

Simmel, G. 1908. 'Das Geheimnis und die geheime Gesellschaft', in *Soziologie. Untersuchungen über die formen der Vergesellschaftung*. Leipzig: Verlag Duncker & Humbolt, 256–304.

Somlai, A.M., S.C. Kalichman and A. Bagnal. 2001. 'HIV Risk Behaviour among Men who have Sex with Men in Public Sex Environments: an Ecological Evaluation', *AIDS Care* 13 (4): 503–14.

Spira, A. and N. Bajos (Groupe ACSF). 1993. *Le Comportement sexuel des français*. Paris: La Documentation Française.

Troiden, R. 1974. 'Homosexual Encounters in a Highway Rest Stop', in E. Goodes and R. Troiden (eds) *Sexual Deviance and Sexual Deviants*. New York: William Morrow, 211–28.

Vicioso, K.J., J.T. Parsons, J.E. Nanin, D.W. Purcell and W.J. Woods. 2005. 'Experiencing Release: Sex Environments and Escapism for

HIV-positive Men who have Sex with Men', *Journal of Sex Research* 42 (1): 13–19.

Wolitski, R.J., J.T. Parsons and C.A. Gomez. 2004. 'Prevention with HIV-seropositive Men who have Sex with Men: Lessons from the Seropositive Urban Men's Study (SUMS)', *Journal of Acquired Immune Deficiency Syndrome* 37 (2): 101–9.

CHAPTER 9

TRANSGRESSION AND THE MAKING OF
'WESTERN' SEXUAL SCIENCES

Mark Johnson

This chapter explores some of the connections between the
contemporary anthropology of gender and sexual diversity and
nineteenth- and early twentieth- century sexology. As others have
suggested, present-day anthropological work on gender and sexual
diversity tends to suffer from genealogical and historical amnesia
(Roscoe 1995; Weston 1998: 1–28; Lyons and Lyons 2004). The
important question is: what are the effects of this amnesia? Here I
want to suggest two. First, the distinction between 'Western' and
'non-Western' discourses of sexuality and erotic practice have not
been sufficiently interrogated. Secondly, there is an assumption that
a distinct epistemological and ethical gulf separates the recent
anthropological study of gender and sexual diversity from the work of
the early sexologists and earlier ethnographic imaginings and
representations of the gender and sexuality of the 'Other'. This
chapter challenges such straightforward assumptions and distinctions.

First, I draw on recent historical work to show how imaginings
of and encounters with, as well as deliberate conscriptions of,
non-Western 'others' were inextricably linked with and a
formative part of the making of Western sexualities (e.g. Said
1978; Stoler 1992, 1995; McClintock 1995; Nagel 2003; Lyons
and Lyons 2004). This work has clearly demonstrated how the
boundaries of Western categories of normative gender and

sexuality were established and resisted not simply in relation to the deviant within, but also in relation to the transgressive gender and sexuality of the racialised other without. More specifically, as I shall outline below, central to the changing terms and shifting ground of homosexual transgression in the West has been the figure of the gender-variant other, a recurrent and repeated leitmotiv of both ethnological and sexological imaginings, at least since the Enlightenment (Bleys 1996).

Secondly, I argue that what nineteenth-century sexology and present-day anthropology have in common is that both are involved in normalising transgression, by which I mean the attempt not only to render difference intelligible, but also to establish gender and sexual variation as a fundamental condition and effect of human likeness and similarity (Argyrou 2002). What has most often been emphasised in our historical reconstruction of nineteenth-century sexology is the pathologisation of the homosexual as a sexual intermediate. However, in the most radical of sexological accounts, sexual intermediacy was considered to be not just the property of an anomalous body, the homosexual, but rather an essential characteristic of every human individual. As I demonstrate, such a view in many respects resonates with the insights of recent queer-insppired anthropology, where, in contemporary parlance, the 'transgendered' other emerges not as evidence of sexual intermediacy, but rather of the indeterminacy of all subjectivities.[1]

However, there are other more problematic continuities between nineteenth-century sexology and twenty-first-century queer anthropology than the continued preoccupation with the 'transgendered' other as the key site of and metaphor for sexual transgression and/or sexual variability. More specifically, I suggest that, for all the liberating effects and possibilities of both radical nineteenth-century discourse on sexual intermediacy and twenty-first-century postmodern discourse on subjective indeterminacy, each is nonetheless laden with the weight of a universalising morality that ultimately reinscribes social difference and distinction between those people and societies who have an enlightened approach to perceived sexual transgressions and those who do not. For the radical sexologists, the key distinction to be made was between people who were aware of the biological basis and foundation of sexual intermediacy and who advocated social justice and equality on that basis and people who held unscientific beliefs about sexual variation that led them either naively to tolerate or stigmatise sexually intermediate persons. For queer anthropology, which eschews positivistic biological explanations in favour of a postmodern epistemology that upholds the indeterminacy of all subjectivities, the key distinction is between those who, mistakenly, claim certain knowledge about gender and sexuality and those who know that claims to certain knowledge are always exclusionary and inevitably produce transgressions. The irony is that, in attempting to move away from the moralising tone and tenor of earlier Western discourses, in which the perceived gender and sexual transgressions of the other were linked and mapped on to a presumed inferior cultural or racial status, both radical nineteenth-century sexology and contemporary queer anthropology reinscribe gender and sexual transgression as a key site for and index of cultural and moral hierarchies.

Transgressive sex/transgendered others: colonial encounters and the making of the modern homosexual

Up until the beginning of the eighteenth century, the various sodomitic practices of people – both among men and between men and women – in the Old World and the New were primarily inflected by Western observers in terms of moral degeneracy and heretical religion, rather than in terms of racial difference (Bleys 1996: 31–36; see also Roscoe 1995). However, in what was to become a recurrent theme that in certain respects continues up until the present day, European representations increasingly focused particular attention on male-bodied persons among peoples of the New World whose dress and social role was that of women and who, according to most of the European observers, engaged in and sought out 'passive' sodomy with other men. The increasing attention paid to people described as 'sodomites' in the New World, coincided, Bleys (1996: 44) suggests, with a shift in European discourse from sodomy as a transgressive sexual activity to the sodomite as a distinct kind of sexual transgressor: persons defined both by femininity and by being the presumed penetrated partner in anal intercourse.

Though cross-dressing was not unknown in Europe, it was found in relatively restricted spheres of activity: certainly it was not visibly present both in everyday mundane contexts and in important ritual contexts, as it was in different parts of the New World. The point is that among many groups in the New World this was not an unusual practice and as such was not, we might presume, anything out of the ordinary. However, for male

European observers, for whom, Bleys suggests following others (e.g. Stone 1979; Trumbach 1989a, b), there were growing anxieties about maintaining and ensuring gender difference; the fact that genitally male bodies were dressing in women's clothing and engaging in women's occupations made such individuals remarkable and a source of consternation. Explanation for this gender variation was to be found in what was assumed to be their sexual transgressions, i.e. sodomy. As Bleys (1996: 81) summarises it:

> The actual or presumed coincidence of cross-gender roles with same-sex praxis [in the New World] made the former instrumental to new sexual theory in Europe that locked sodomy inexorably into the corset of femininity. Passivity, more particularly, as located in the receptive use of the anus, became quintessential to the 'sodomite' identity – a different idea, altogether, from previous notions of sodomy, which included the active partner as well as the passive one, men as well as women.

The shift from sodomy to the sodomite during the latter part of the eighteenth and early part of the nineteenth century corresponds with several other transformations that were under way at this time. These changes included the increasing development of distinctive and visible subcultural communities of effeminate sodomites in European cities, who at least among the middle classes may have been drawing on ethnographic reportage about what were presumed to be similar groups of people in other parts of the world (Bleys 1996: 98). The shift from sodomy to the sodomite also corresponded with the emergence of biological theories of sexual difference between males and females, the naturalisation of (hetero)sexual attraction and the development of racial theories of human diversity.

In sum, what emerged out of Enlightenment, brought about both by various social changes in Europe and by colonial entanglements and encounters, was the establishment of an increasingly secular and scientific view of sexual and racial difference, linked together through various forms of analogous reasoning (see, for example, Laqueur 1990; McClintock 1995; Nagel 2003). Sodomy was still seen, by some, as part of the endemic immorality of other peoples. However, it was increasingly identified with the sodomite, an individual whose sexual proclivities were seen as linked to some kind of seen or unseen or as yet undiscovered physical abnormality. Moreover, the perceived gender-anomalous status of the sodomite – their effeminised status – metonymically stood not just for the moral turpitude of primitives or cultural decay among the civilised but rather both for the racial inferiority of non-Western peoples and a sign of biological degeneracy among a Western minority.

If the eighteenth and early nineteenth centuries were marked by the emergence of the sodomite, the key change that emerged during the nineteenth century, consolidated by the sexologists, was a shift from an emphasis on anatomy to that of the internal nervous system and psychopathology: a shift, as we know, that was central to the making of the homosexual. While both the sodomite and the homosexual were associated with femininity, previously the sodomite's femininity was thought to be rooted primarily in anatomical abnormality or bodily hermaphroditism. The homosexual's femininity was to be found in the mind, a hermaphroditism of the soul (Foucault 1990).

What was the source of this psychopathology? Some nineteenth-century sexologists argued that it was the product of mental disorientation brought about by the excessive strains of civilisation (neurasthenia), while others argued it was the product of a congenital condition. These questions were premised on the distinction between the 'real' homosexual and the 'circumstantial' or 'acquired' homosexuality of others. They were also posed in terms of evolutionary and racial theorising, which posited an original sexually undifferentiated 'hermaphroditic' primitive state. Hence, whatever perspectives argued for, the answer given by many, though by no means all, of the sexologists (see below) was that homosexuality, at least among the civilised, was posited both as primitive 'remnant' that might disrupt normal species development and/or as biological degeneracy and a 'relapse' into a less advanced state (Bleys 1996: 144; see also Storr 1997, 2002).

Science and social justice: sexual intermediaries and the transformation of the socially stigmatised body

In the preceding section I have drawn on the work of Bleys to show how encounters with and imaginings of the racial and cultural 'other' were inextricably linked with the development of Western sexual sciences, and more specifically the discursive shift from sodomy and the sodomite to the homosexual 'other'. The relation between 'ethnographic imaginings' and Western discourses on sexuality was not simply one of conscription, i.e. of drawing on various representations of 'the other' to support one or other Western theories (e.g. Lyons and Lyons 2004). Rather, these encounters with the other themselves shaped, as they were in turn shaped by, changing discourses about the nature of same-sex sexuality and the nature of race and sex/gender: in particular, the visibility of the gender-crossing other informed the development of what was to become the dominant model of homosexuality, which persisted well into the twentieth century. In this sense, and notwithstanding Foucault's (1990) distinction between Western sexual sciences and the erotic arts of the East, one cannot speak of a history of Western sexuality as if this were a singular and geographically bounded process. The importance of considering the role of the non-Western 'other' in shaping Western discourses is not simply to complicate a certain kind of historical narrative and show how 'they' figure in discourses of 'our' sexuality, but also, and perhaps more importantly, because Western discourses of sexuality and gender are, as they have always been or aspired to be, universalising in their scope and imaginings.

In what follows, I want to pick up on some of the cross-currents within this process in order to demonstrate that at the heart of the sexual sciences was the normalisation of sexual difference and transgression. That nineteenth century sexology was also about normalising difference may at first glance appear ludicrous, since sexology has routinely been described as a pathologising science. Sexologists certainly normalised the reproductive heterosexual, a normalisation that, as Foucault (1990) demonstrated, fundamentally depended upon its identification of the pathological 'other' and the homosexual in particular. But the pathologisation of the homosexual 'other' was already the first move towards its normalisation, in so far as it rendered it intelligible and gave a name and status to it.

Perhaps no better example can be given than Richard Frieherr von Krafft-Ebing whose most well-known work, *Psychopathia Sexualis* (1918 [1886]), was written for lawyers and doctors involved in 'sex crime' trials. Although Krafft-Ebing's work presents one of the clearest articulations of the creation and medicalisation of deviant sexual subjects, it was also considered liberating and progressive in its time because of its insistence that sexual perversion was not a sin or a crime, but a disease. Moreover, as Oosterhuis (1997) points out, many of the individuals who read and contributed to Krafft-Ebing's work saw it not as confirming their degenerate heredity, but as demonstrating the naturalness of their ascribed and perceived difference.

In fact, the pathologising discourse set up the preconditions for early homosexual emancipation in so far as it naturalised homosexuality in terms of biological predispositions that were posited in terms of a broader pattern of sexual variance understood as encompassing sexual orientation, bodily gender and psychosexual identity. One of the most important sexologists and advocates of homosexual emancipation of the late nineteenth and early twentieth centuries who developed this perspective most systematically was Magnus Hirschfeld (1868–1935). Trained in medicine and schooled in the emerging evolutionary theory, Hirschfeld (2000 [1914]) drew together the Darwinian insistence on natural variation, with the original 'third sex' view of the *Urning* (male homosexual), first postulated by an earlier sexologist Karl Heinrich Ulrich (1825–95), to elaborate a view of the 'geno-genetic' laws of sexual intermediacy (Kennedy 1997; Steakley 1997: 143). Like Ulrich, Hirschfeld sees homosexuality as the outcome of sexual intermediacy, itself the product of natural and continually unfolding evolutionary processes, rather than as either simply the vestiges of primitive bisexuality or of moral or biological degeneracy or disease. Demonstrating this natural and normal 'biological' basis for homosexuality is seen as a key component in the fight for social justice and social reform.

Both Ulrich's and Hirschfeld's views were challenged (both by some of their contemporaries and colleagues and by present-day observers, including Bleys 1996: 214–15) on the basis of their overemphasis on the 'third sex' model of homosexuality, and a presumed downplaying of forms of male homoeroticism between men who were otherwise regarded – by themselves and others – to be absolutely 'masculine'. However, Hirschfeld's view was far more complex than a narrow reading might at first suggest. As Steakley (1997: 143) suggests, Hirschfeld's thinking about and development of ideas on sexual indeterminacy leads him, if not to drop completely, certainly to downplay the 'third sex' terminology because he came to 'regard it as both scientifically inaccurate and tactically counterproductive to minoritise homosexuals in a world populated entirely, as he ultimately saw it, by sexual intermediaries'. In other words, Hirschfeld can be read as suggesting that there are no 'pure' or 'originary' sexes; rather, there is infinite variation across and within individuals categorised as women and men. This variation was not imagined as falling along a simple linear continuum between male and female, but rather as forming a closed circle (Hirschfeld 2000: 420). In such a situation, Hirschfeld 'declared sexual unambiguity itself to be a fiction' (Steakley 1997: 145).

Moreover, while other sexologists assumed that homosexuality was indicative or constitutive of more general neuroses and psychopathologies, Hirschfeld held that any psychological problems experienced by homosexuals were the product of their socially stigmatised status, and not an inherent part of who or what they were (Steakley 1997: 138). Hence, while the first part of Hirschfeld's *magnum opus* is concerned with outlining his theory of the homosexuality of men and women, the remaining part of his work is devoted to a comparative sociological and ethnographic account of homosexuality focused, in particular, on the degree to which diverse sexualities were criminalised, tolerated or accepted in different cultures and societies.

Summarising his ethnographic overview, Hirschfeld (2000: 712–14) enumerates eight general principles with respect to homosexuality. His central contention is that there is no substantial difference in the incidence or occurrence of homosexuality: in all countries there exist women and men who 'sometimes exclusively, sometimes occasionally' feel attracted to their own sex. This suggests, he argues, that homosexuality cannot but be the product of 'natural law'. What I wish particularly to take up here is his sixth principle, namely that, 'Ethnographically, the assessment of homosexuality can be recognized in three stages' (Hirschfeld 2000: 712). The first stage, Hirschfeld suggests, is the 'naïve toleration and usefulness of homosexuality' in that homosexual members are 'acknowledged and related to certain social functions'. He then goes on to specify that in some cases they may be masculine-identified, 'virile ones', who may be associated with martial or pedagogic roles; the feminine-identified, who are associated with the 'service sector in the widest sense'; and finally those in the middle, neither masculine nor feminine but both, who have roles as 'priests, magicians, physicians, sages, seers, poets, singers, and artists'. His celebratory account of the 'intermediate sex' during the 'naïve stage' is very much akin to that of the English socialist reformer and advocate of sexual emancipation, Edward Carpenter, who viewed the intermediate sex as being, when accepted and embraced, always and everywhere among the heroic figures in the vanguard of culture (Lyons and Lyons 2004: 128–29).

The second stage is the 'instinctive opposition to same-sex sexuality by the majority' (Hirschfeld 2000: 713). For Hirschfeld, this stage clearly corresponds with the rise and spread of Christianity, and, drawing on both Westermarck and Carpenter, he suggests, as have subsequent historians, that the 'heavy sentence and punishment of homosexuality had its actual origin more in public opinion which predominantly associated it with heresy than in a direct aversion to the thing itself' (2000: 925). The second stage Hirschfeld suggests will only be overcome when it is replaced by the 'third stage' of 'intellectual penetration and scientific research into homosexuality and related natural phenomena' (2000: 925). Although suggesting that the third stage 'occasionally' connects with the first 'naïve' state of grace, these are exceptions that have previously not had penetrating force.

In sum, Hirschfeld's ideas may be seen as among those of the most radical of all the sexologists not only in his insistence on the sexual intermediacy of all individuals, but also as bringing together and articulating a moral discourse based on the irreducibility and universality of human biological sameness and difference, i.e. the idea that everyone everywhere is the same in their individual biological uniqueness. That is to say, just as the notion of distinct biological races was to be systematically challenged in the twentieth century, Hirschfeld undermines the notion of there being any fixed or absolute distinction between male and female or between homosexual and heterosexual. Nevertheless, at the heart of Hirschfeld's thinking is an unresolved paradox. That is, while ultimately Hirschfeld sees sexual purity to be a mirage, he nevertheless persists in his belief that a properly trained scientist can distinguish and identify a real homosexual in terms of their underlying sexual intermediacy. This paradox is inflected in the very ambiguity of the title of his work, *The Homosexuality of Men and Women*, which may be alternatively read as referencing the sameness of all or referring more particularly to the homosexual.

Sameness and difference reconfigured: the moral universes of cultural relativism, social constructionism and queer theory

Hirschfeld's crusade for sexual emancipation was premised on the biological unity of sexual diversity. Hence, in one respect, society, culture and history were seen as largely incidental except in so far as they confirmed homosexuality to be a universal and natural variant. However, in another respect, society, culture and history were regarded as of primary importance in determining the relative social status or stigma of the homosexual, the legal sanctions enacted against same-sex sexuality and the relative form and visibility of some kinds of homosexuals and not others. In this way of viewing things, the respective moral and intellectual status, i.e. the relative enlightenment, of any society and culture was in effect measured both by their acceptance or not of sexual variation and by their understanding (or not) of the fundamental nature of sexual diversity as an expression of human sameness.

In what follows, I wish to explore, from the perspective of an anthropologist writing at the beginning of the twenty-first century, how far and to what extent our thinking about sexual diversity has changed as a result of cultural relativism and social constructionist approaches. The first contrast to be drawn between the sexologists and modern anthropology is between the explicit evolutionary ways of thinking about cultures and civilisations versus the cultural relativism of anthropology, a shift that took place in anthropological thinking at around the time when Hirschfeld was writing (see Argyrou 2002: 23–25).

Put in terms of sex, the fundamental difference between the cultural relativist anthropological perspective and that of the sexologists was that, while both recognised to a greater or lesser extent that culture shaped the particular form sex took and the different kinds of moral judgements attached to particular kinds of sexual practices, the cultural relativists argued that there was no absolute measure either of what constituted good or bad sex or of how these were variously understood or construed. Nevertheless, despite this apparent theoretical commitment to cultural relativism, early twentieth-century anthropologists drew more on the hetero-normative sexology of Havelock Ellis and Sigmund Freud rather than on the more radical ideas of Magnus Hirschfeld or Edward Carpenter, and still worked within a conceptualisation of basic biological distinction between male and female, and of normal opposite-sex attraction between them. In fact, early twentieth-century anthropological work on sexuality was decidedly heterosexual in focus, informed as much by previous Victorian debates about primitive promiscuity and marriage as by specifically sexological work focused on homosexuality.

This is not to say that same-sex sexualities were not on the agenda of anthropologists at all. Views of homosexuality were varied, with some anthropologists, like Malinowski, seeing in what he perceived to be the complete lack of homosexual relations among the Trobriand Islanders, evidence that homosexuality only arose in certain kinds of situations, especially those where there was greater restriction of heterosexual freedom among the young (see Lyons and Lyons 2004: 165). Mead similarly reported some intense but temporary same-sexual affairs among both young women and men in Samoa. She noted, for example, that 'native theory and vocabulary' recognised the 'real pervert' although the only evidence of perversion she found was an effeminate man and some 'mixed types' of females, though she doubted the latter were really genuine (Mead 1965 [1928]: 121–22). For both Malinowski and Mead, the lack or relative lack of the 'real pervert' was in effect the result of the general sexual freedom of the young, and more particularly, for Mead, a result of the fact that heterosexual practices encompassed 'secondary variations of sex activity which loom as primary in homosexual relations' (Mead 1965: 122). As Lyons and Lyons note (2004: 196–97), Mead closes down a potentially more radical view of sexual variation, however, by positing Samoan heterosexual freedom as a kind of inoculation against the development of 'real' perversity.

The 'inoculation' theory of sexuality is extended in different ways and forms by various anthropologists, among them George Devereux, who is perhaps best known for his account of the Mohave 'berdache' or *alyhas* and *hwame*, both of whom he refers to mainly as respectively male and female transvestite homosexuals (Devereux 1937). Devereux does note that same-sex practices were not solely the preserve of transvestites. However, as with observers in prior times, cross-dressing and the adoption of the sex roles and occupations of the genitally opposite sex were seen by him as intimately linked to and ultimately an identifying mark of the 'real' homosexual. For Devereux, moreover, the social confirmation and public acknowledgement of the homosexual were the means whereby the Mohave ensured that this abnormality was regulated and prevented from corrupting the mainstream through its institutionalisation.

In sum, the main message to emerge from anthropologists in the first part of the twentieth century with respect to same-sex sexuality is twofold. First is the persistence of the idea of 'real perverts', increasingly understood in Freud's (1938) terms as psychosexual 'inverts' whose sexual deviance is seen to be rooted not, as with sexologists, in biology but in an abnormal development, resulting in the simultaneous misidentification with the opposite sex and sexual desire for the same sex. Secondly, non-Western societies and cultures deal with the perceived problem of homosexuality either by encouraging or enabling a much broader range of heterosexual experimentation, particularly among the young, or by according the homosexual some measure of legitimation or tolerance, thereby reaffirming and protecting normative heterosexual identities and desires.

Seen from the perspective of social constructionist accounts of sexuality that emerged in the second half of the twentieth century, the more radical potential of some early cultural relativist approaches was compromised both because of a persistent and as yet un-interrogated biological essentialism with respect to sex and sexuality and more specifically because of the persistence of a discourse that viewed homosexuality as a fundamentally abnormal condition of a particular kind of deviant personality type. In fact, as Weston (1993) notes, discussions of homosexuality in anthropology generally remained sub rosa until the late 1960s. Its re-emergence and gradual institutionalisation as a proper field of enquiry coincided with, and were successively informed by, the rise of second-wave feminism, lesbian and gay political movements, social constructionism and queer theory.

The lesbian and gay movement challenged the pathologising discourse of homosexuality even as it further stabilised the homosexual as a political and cultural identity, moves that were in some sense paralleled by a new 'ethnocartography' (Weston 1993: 341) that in many respects was not unlike the encyclopedic compendiums produced by nineteenth-century sexological/anthropological researchers, and that sought to document the presence and relative status of homosexuals in other societies (see, for example, Greenberg 1988). Meanwhile, feminists both inside and outside anthropology and social constructivist sociologists and historians were establishing the basis not only for deconstructing homosexuality and the homosexual as a universal and invariant 'it entity' (Herdt 1991), but also the Western heterosexist 'correspondence model of gender/sexuality that assigns anatomical sex a constant gender and prescribed object of sexual desire' (Weston 1993: 348).

Another important component of both feminist and social constructivist analysis was that each, if in different ways and with different emphasis, began to see in sex and gender 'a dense transfer point of power' (Foucault 1990). Within anthropology, as Lyons and Lyons (2004: 285) note, Ortner and Whitehead's (1981) *Sexual Meanings: the Cultural Construction of Gender and Sexuality* was something of a 'benchmark' in this regard. Emphasising the importance of seeing 'sex' (understood as both gender and sexuality) as a symbolic system, they sought in the volume both to challenge naturalistic assumptions and foreground the inherent political nature of cultural constructions of gender and sexuality while simultaneously being attentive to the individual experience and articulations of these. More concretely in ethnographic terms, Whitehead's (1981) essay 'The Bow and the Burden Strap' was, if not the first, certainly one of the most important in challenging a view of the Native American 'berdache' (a widely used term that has only recently become critically interrogated and replaced by 'two-spirit') as being fundamentally about deviant or abnormal sexuality. For Whitehead, in a system that differentially defined male and female access to and achievement of prestige and status, 'the berdache' was primarily about the pursuit of status through occupations defined as female.

While calling attention to the social dimension of the 'berdache' status that located them as a normative part of the sex/gender system, Whitehead's account still remains wedded to an originary male-bodied individual who in some sense is merely masquerading as a woman, because he is unable or unwilling to adopt or pursue masculine pursuits. In this respect, Whitehead's work demonstrated both the potential and the limitations of the sexual meanings approach, which effectively separated out gender and sexuality as it simultaneously reinscribed and reinstated the sexed body. The challenge to an underlying and originary sexed body was to come through the queering of anthropology that systematically challenged (Western) 'hegemonic ideologies of gender and sexuality' (Weston 1993: 348).[2]

Central to the queering of anthropology was the deconstruction of the sex/gender divide by showing the way in which the sexed body is not prior to, but is itself an effect of gender (Butler 1990, 1993; see also Laqueur 1990). To put it another way, the new politics of queer was 'to make apparent that what had been taken to be a limit set by the natural body is no such thing' (Alsop et al. 2002: 170). Just as the work of earlier relativist anthropologists, such as Mead, had previously been influential in showing the enormous variability of masculinity and femininity and in challenging dominant Western assumptions about men and women, one of the major contributions of anthropology to the development of a 'queer' perspective has been to show that a two-gender system 'imposes an arbitrary dichotomy upon a reality capable of supporting multiple categories, if not a continuum' (Lyons and Lyons 2004: 297). Work within the 'third sex/gender' (see Herdt 1994) was in particular concerned with situations where, it was argued, there was not simply gender-crossing, but culturally recognised and institutionalised multi-gender systems and, once again, the Native American 'two-spirit' was one of the key exemplars in this regard (see, for example, Roscoe 1991).

However useful a notion of multiple genders was and is for deconstructing Western binaries premised on the natural coherence between sex/gender/sexuality, the 'third sex/third gender' model may be criticised, among other things, for its assumptions about discrete gender categories and fixed gender identities, and for its unintended re-naturalisation of the 'sexed' body, which appears to be a throwback to earlier nineteenth-century categorisations of the homosexual as a 'third sex' (Weston 1993: 354). Thus, for example, while recent work on biological sex has seemingly arrived again at the conclusions that Hirschfeld articulated a century ago about the enormous variability of the body, concentration is generally focused on those whose bodily gender provokes the most cultural anxiety, namely the intersexed (Fausto-Stirling 2000). Much of this work has been useful in showing the way in which ambiguity is constructed in relation to perceived normal bodies and the changing ways these ambiguities have been dealt with. In the process, however, these variously reconstructed bodies become evidence of a distinct 'third sex' that simultaneously reaffirms two originary sexes even as they are meant to register the perceived limitations of the dual sex/gender system.[3]

For these and other reasons, as I discuss below, the term 'transgender' has now largely come to supersede, although not entirely replace, the 'third sex/ third gender' concept and discourse. Like the 'third sex' or multi-gender system, the term transgender is sometimes employed in situations where one or more alternative gender categories are culturally recognised, though the term 'transgender' is used both to flag the possibility for an even broader range of gender categories (Jackson 2000) and to problematise the notion of fixed and stable identities (Johnson 1997; Blackwood and Weiringa 1999). More broadly, it is used to describe people and situations that variously supplement and/or transgress dominant or mainstream understandings of gender, while not necessarily occupying a discrete gender category. Kulick's (1998) work on the *travesti* is a good example of the latter. *Travesti*, Kulick argues, are positioned within a dual gender system that defines them as lesser men, because they are seen to place themselves sexually as women in relation to other men as the penetrated partner in homosexual intercourse. At the same time, they variously transgress and redefine both masculinity and femininity, in so far as they not only reaffirm their bodily gender as male and may sexually act as penetrators of other men, but they also claim and aspire to be, despite or more precisely because of their male bodies, superior to women.

Kulick's work on the transgender *travesti* is one of the best examples of the new anthropology of gender and sexual diversity informed by and engaged with recent queer theory. First, it is concerned with reconnecting and interrogating the discursive linkages between gender and sexuality. Secondly, it affirms a view of gender as constituted through repeated bodily acts of identification within a culturally given and normatively enforced gender hierarchy that privileges some bodies over others. Thirdly, it essays a view of transgender people as situated within but at the margins of the norm. In other words, what makes the transgender individual significant is that, as with Newton's (1979) rediscovered ethnographic account of female impersonators in North America, they reveal both the limitations and exclusions affected by hegemonic gender categories and the artifices through which dominant and mainstream identities are naturalised. As marginal figures they also 'play' with, through parody and mimicry, gender and sexuality in ways that consciously and unconsciously challenge and potentially refigure, if never completely escape, the dominant.

It is perhaps unsurprising, moreover, that analogies are drawn between transgender people and people who occupy the margins and boundaries of ethnic, racial and national identities (Alsop et al. 2002: 213–14). Ethnographic accounts of transgendering are in fact at the forefront of anthropological discussions of the way in which globalising Western discourses of sexuality have been variously appropriated and reimagined in translocal spaces (see, for example, Johnson 1998; Elliston 1999; Jackson 2000; Besnier 2002; Manalansan 2003). Indeed, in many respects, the transgendered, as others have noted, emerge as 'queer heroes' not because they represent simply a literary or symbolic 'third space' (Garber 1992), or because they represent a definite institutionalised alternative gender identity in a multi-gender system (à la Roscoe 1991), and still less because they provide conclusive evidence of a distinctive 'third' or 'intermediary sex' (Hirschfeld 2000; see also Fausto-Stirling 2000). Rather, they are celebrated because they make clear what is said to be the general situation pertaining to all: namely, that any and all identity categories are problematic, since they provide the terms whereby the subject is formed and made intelligible and close down possibilities and enact violent exclusions that inevitably fail to 'make sense of the specific subjectivities of us all' (Alsop et al. 2002: 214); in this sense, as Halberstram (1994, cited in Alsop et al. 2002: 206) suggests, we are all 'trans', simultaneously caught up and constituted within the dominant categories, but always already exceeding and transgressing them in both deliberate and unconscious ways.

It is at this point that it is worth returning to consider the question of how far we have 'advanced' in our thinking since the advent of cultural relativism and social constructionism and the emergence of queer theory in the late twentieth century from the vantage point of Hirschfeld some one hundred years ago. Although not articulated in the same way, Hirschfeld's radical ideas about the infinitely variable body are nevertheless echoed in statements by gender theorists at the beginning of the twenty-first century: 'Whatever the bodily conditions may be, they exceed any account which can be provided of them, leaving open the possibility of alternative understandings' (Alsop et al. 2002: 171). The difference, of course, is that, whereas the former started with the necessity and possibility of comprehending the human body as the font of both human sameness and difference, the latter starts from the incomprehensibility and irreducibility of the human body and consciousness as the font of both sameness and difference: in each case, however, the 'intermediate sex' or 'transgender queer' becomes not the marginal figure, but, like the migrant and exile, the carrier of a new cultural truth.

From sexual intermediacy to subjective indeterminacy: the logic and morality of sameness and difference

In the conclusion to his book, Bleys (1996) notes that homosexuality has frequently been repressed in postcolonial discourses, which often stress the alienness of same-sex sexuality. He suggests that in this context homophobia may be seen as a reply to ways in which non-Western sexualities were constructed by the West in colonial and imperialist contexts as the site and repository of the deviant. The irony of the situation, as Bleys (1996: 266) suggests, is that they effectively reproduce the dominant hetero/sexist tropes of the coloniser, 'forgetting the toleration, if not inclusion of sexual variance' within traditional cultures.

In a similar manner, Peletz (2006) usefully reconstructs and attempts to recuperate for the South-East Asia region a more pluralist past where, he suggests, a variety of different gender categories and sexual practices were not only acknowledged but accorded social legitimacy. He also shows the ways in which this pluralism has become subject to various modernist discourses of state and nation, and demonstrates how Western discourses of sexuality are variously internalised, reproduced and replayed as 'Asian' values, the consequence of which is that transgendered individuals have come to be redefined 'as contaminating (rather than sacred) mediators who are perversely if not treasonously muddling and enmiring the increasingly dichotomous terms of sex/gender systems long marked by pluralism' (Peletz 2006: 310).

Neither Peletz nor Bleys subscribes to a naive romantic view of the past lives of exotic natives. Nevertheless, they do see sexual diversity and gender variation, and, for Peletz in particular, the legitimacy accorded transgendering as a marker and index of cultural pluralism more generally. As Peletz (2006: 324) suggests at the end of his paper: 'One can perhaps be more optimistic about the long term, hopeful that political and religious elites in the Philippines, Indonesia and other countries in Southeast Asia negotiate their present crises and variously defined projects of modernity in ways that build on and enhance rather than constrict the pluralistic traditions that long characterized the region.'[4]

The irony in what Peletz has to say is neither simply that Western colonial discourses that privileged heterosex/genders are now the source of the revaluing of transgender people in South-East Asia, nor that transgendering and same-sex sexuality are attributed by political and religious leaders in South-East Asia to the corrupting influence of the West. Rather, as I suggested at the outset, the real irony is that while contemporary anthropology has sought to distance itself from previous Western discourses in which gender variation was a marker of the sodomite and metonymic symbol of the general moral degeneracy and sexual transgression of the 'other', it paradoxically ends up reinscribing gender and sexual diversity as a measure or standard of the relative enlightenment of both our own and other societies. Thus, for example, concluding a critical review of anthropological writing on 'third sex/gender', Holmes (2004: no page numbers in the original) writes: 'It seems then, that until a society does away with a stratified sex/gender system, those things residing outside the accepted and central terms will continue to be perceived as impure states. Perhaps, therefore, the measure of a society's civil liberties comes partly through the measure of its sex/gender system.'

The above examples illustrate well the central contention of this chapter. I suggested at the outset that my aim was to rearticulate some of the historical connections and continuities between contemporary anthropological accounts of gender and sexual diversity and those of the past. I have, following others, sought to extend the history of sexuality by foregrounding the ways that the gendered and cultural 'other' is and always has been implicated in 'Western' discourses of sex. I have also sought to complicate the history of sexuality by suggesting that the

Foucauldian-inspired social constructionist break from the previous biological determinist view may not be such a radical break after all. More specifically, I have focused on the recurrent re-presentations of the 'transgendered' other and the various discursive shifts that have alternatively construed transgender either as the site of and index for moral degeneracy and/or sexual pathology or the site of and index for the universal variability and/or indeterminacy of the sexual subject. The overall point is about the way in which the refiguring of the 'transgendered' from essentially different to essentially the same in their irreducible and incomprehensible difference articulates what Argyrou (2002) has referred to as the logic and morality of the same.

For the radical sexologists at the end of the nineteenth and early twentieth century, the sexual intermediacy of the homosexual was grounded in, and iconic of, the underlying biological variability and hence fundamental sameness of every body. In sexological accounts, society was important in terms of the status and stigmatisation or not of the culturally acknowledged intermediate sex, and relative differences between societies and cultures were made and measured in these terms. Similarly, for queer theory and anthropology at the end of the twentieth and beginning of the twenty-first century, the indeterminacy of the transgender subject is grounded in, and is iconic of, the irreducibility and hence fundamental sameness of every body.

Whereas the former is premised on a positivist epistemology, the latter postmodern epistemology suggests that nothing can be said with certainty about the body except that the body inevitably exceeds any attempt to comprehend and contain it. In queer theory, society is important in so far as it is said to provide the terms and regulatory regimes within which different kinds of social bodies are culturally materialised and relative differences between societies and cultures are made and measured in terms of the various exclusions and exclusionary effects through which legitimate and illegitimate subjects are constituted in particular historical situations.

Notwithstanding their different epistemological starting points, both of these positions are, as Argyrou (2002) has argued with respect to anthropology in general, moral statements that are premised on a shared metaphysical belief in the ultimate unity and sameness of human beings. As such, they each in their respective ways, offer important means for combating racist, sexist and homophobic discourses. However, as Argyrou points out, the problem with the logic of sameness is that it inevitably engenders and reproduces difference and otherness.

On the one hand, the fundamental difference enacted in radical sexology was between those who had obtained true scientific knowledge about the unity and diversity of all and those who had not. Like Tylor, who eschewed biological racism and instead propounded a view of the psychic unity of mankind, this was not a question of any innate inability of the other to comprehend, but rather a question of instruction and development leading inevitably, for the natives, from naive acceptance to enlightenment and social justice (Argyrou 2002: 23–25). On the other hand, the fundamental difference enacted in queer anthropology is between those who claim certain knowledge about self and other – whether essentialised in terms of biology or in terms of identity – and those who claim no certainty at all either about self or other, since we are all, it is suggested, in the same uncertain boat together. While the former is inevitably exclusionary, the latter embraces transgression and transformation.

The problem, of course, with the latter is that it posits some people as having a certain moral and epistemological vantage point from outside the boat, with the majority of people apparently holding on to false and exclusionary truths about their own and others' identities, bodies and desires. Indeed, it is only from this morally certain and seemingly unassailable vantage point that one can view and penetrate the apparent naturalising conceits and exclusions that privilege some bodies over others. Moreover, it is not clear whether or not, or to what extent, the transgender individuals and other marginal figures whose transgressions are normatively sanctioned and who putatively make clear the indeterminacy of all subjectivities are actually aware of their privileged position in illuminating the operations and limitations of power. In which case it is perhaps not too much to suggest that, like Hirschfeld's or indeed Carpenter's naive natives, who celebrate the 'mix' without knowing about the biological basis of their – which is also ours and everyone else's – intermediacy, so too queer theory celebrates the transgendered as those who revel in, play with and immerse themselves in the 'trans', even if they never really completely know about the epistemological basis of their – which is also ours and everyone else's – indeterminacy. Whether or not we are able to think our way out of these ethical and epistemological conundrums is a question that remains to be answered. The first step, as Argyrou suggests, is to acknowledge the intellectual and moral conceits that engender difference in the pursuit of the logic and morality of the same.

Notes

1. The use of the term 'transgender' by anthropologists outside the specific historical context of Western sexual politics in which it was first used has been the subject of some critique (Valentine 2007). Though not unrelated, my concern here is with the broader intellectual shifts signalled by the now widespread use of the term 'transgender' in anthropology. It is also important to note that various 'trans'-identified people in the West continue to 'conscript' various ethnographic and popular representations of 'third gender' or 'transgender' people in other parts of the world in formulating their versions of what transgendering means (Towle and Morgan 2002).

2. Queer anthropology grows out of lesbian and gay studies. It reflects both important theoretical moves that followed Judith Butler's (1990) seminal text, *Gender Trouble*, and calls from within and outside of the lesbian and gay movements to recognise a much broader diversity of gender identities and sexual subjectivities that did not neatly fit within the male/female, masculine/feminine, gay/straight binaries. A recent review of queer studies in anthropology is provided by Boellstorff (2007), who also discusses some of the problems of defining and labelling what might be identified as 'queer' anthropology.

3. While some anthropologists maintain that it is possible analytically to separate sex, gender and sexuality without necessarily resorting to biological essentialism (e.g. Errington 1990; Shaw 2005), queer theorists such as Butler (1990, 1993) are insistent that one cannot speak of sex (however one might define it) without recourse to gender.

4. Peletz (2009) makes it clear that while he is writing as an advocate of gender pluralism, he also questions the stories of progress we in the patatively pluralist West tell ourselves. Butler (2008), too, has recently raised questions about the way that sexual minority rights are co-opted by Western states to legitimate violence in the name of freedom and democracy, though she does not reflect on the moral and ethical assumptions that underpin her own work.

References

Alsop, R., A. Fitzsimons and K. Lennon. 2002. *Theorizing Gender*. Cambridge: Polity Press.

Argyrou, V. 2002. *Anthropology and the Will to Meaning: a Postcolonial Critique*. London: Pluto Press.

Besnier, N. 2002. 'Transgenderism, Locality, and the Miss Galaxy Beauty Pageant in Tonga', *American Ethnologist* 29: 534–66.

Blackwood, E. and S. Weiringa. 1999. *Female Desires: Same-sex Relations and Transgender Practices across Cultures*. New York: Columbia University Press.

Bleys, R. 1996. *The Geography of Perversion: Male to Male Sexual Behaviour Outside the West and the Ethnographic Imagination, 1750 – 1918*. London: Cassell.

Boellstorff, T. 2007. 'Queer Studies in the House of Anthropology', *Annual Review of Anthropology* 36: 2.1–2.19.

Butler, J. 1990. *Gender Trouble: Feminism and the Subversion of Identity.* London: Routledge.

———. 1993. *Bodies that Matter: On the Discursive Limits of 'Sex'.* New York: Routledge.

———. 2008. 'Sexual politics, torture, and secular time', *The British Jounral of Sociology* 59 (1): 1–23.

Devereux, G. 1937. 'Institutionalized Homosexuality of the Mohave Indians', *Human Biology* 9: 498–527.

Elliston, D. 1999. 'Negotiating Transnational Sexual Economies: Female Mahu and Same-sex Sexuality in "Tahiti and her Islands"', in E. Blackwood and S. Wieringa (eds) *Female Desires: Same-sex Relations and Transgender Practices across Cultures.* New York: Columbia University Press, pp. 230–54.

Errington, S. 1990. 'Recasting Sex, Gender and Power: Theoretical Introduction and Regional Overview', in J. Atkinson and S. Errington (eds) *Power and Difference: Gender in Island Southeast Asia.* Stanford: Stanford University Press, pp. 1–58.

Fausto-Stirling, A. 2000. *Sexing the Body: Gender Politics and the Construction of Sexuality.* New York, NY: Basic Books.

Foucault, M. 1990 [1978]. *The History of Sexuality.* Vol 1. *An Introduction,* trans. R. Hurley. New York: Random House.

Freud, S. 1938. 'Three Contributions to the Theory of Sex', in *The Basic Writings of Sigmund Freud,* trans. A.A. Brill. New York: Random House, pp. 53–632.

Garber, M. 1992. *Vested Interests: Cross-dressing and Cultural Anxiety.* London: Routledge.

Greenberg, D. 1988. *The Construction of Homosexuality.* London: University of Chicago Press.

Halberstram, J. 1994. 'F2M: the Making of Female Masculinity', in L. Doan (ed.) *The Lesbian Postmodern.* New York: Columbia University Press, pp. 210–28.

Herdt, G. 1991. 'Representations of Homosexuality: an Essay on Cultural Ontology and Historical Comparison, part I', *Journal of the History of Sexuality* 1 (3): 481–504.

———. (ed.). 1994. *Third Sex, Third Gender: Beyond Sexual Dimorphism in Culture and History.* New York: Zone Books.

Hirschfeld, M. 2000 [1914]. *The Homosexuality of Men and Women,* trans. M. Lombardi-Nash. Amherst, NY: Prometheus Books.

Holmes, M. 2004. 'Locating Third Sexes', *Transformation: Online Journal of Region, Culture and Societies* 8. Available from: http://transformations. cqu.edu.au/journal/issue_08/article_03.shtml (accessed 2 March 2006).

Jackson, P. 2000. 'An Explosion of Thai Identities', *Culture, Health and Sexuality* 2 (4): 405–24.

Johnson, M. 1997. *Beauty and Power: Transgendering and Cultural Transformation in the Southern Philippines.* Oxford: Berg.

———. 1998. 'Global Desirings and Translocal Loves: Transgendering and Same-sex Sexualities in the Southern Philippines', *American Ethnologist* 25 (4): 695–711.

Kennedy, H. 1997. 'Karl Heinrich Ulrichs: First Theorist of Homosexuality', in V.A. Rosario (ed.) *Science and Homosexualities*. London: Routledge, pp. 26–45.

Krafft-Ebing, R.F. von. 1918 [1886]. *Psychopathia Sexualis*, trans. C. Chaddock. Philadelphia: F.A. Davis.

Kulick, D. 1998. *Travesti: Sex, Gender and Culture Among Brazilian Transgendered Prostitutes*. Chicago: University of Chicago Press.

Laqueur, T. 1990. *Making Sex: Body and Gender from the Greeks to Freud*. Cambridge, MA: Harvard University Press.

Lyons, A. and H. Lyons. 2004. *Irregular Connections: a History of Anthropology and Sexuality*. Lincoln: University of Nebraska Press.

Manalansan, M.F. 2003. *Global Divas: Filipino Gay Men in the Diaspora*. London: Duke University Press.

McClintock, A. 1995. *Imperial Leather: Race, Gender and Sexuality in the Colonial Contest*. New York: Routledge.

Mead, M. 1965 [1928]. *Coming of Age in Samoa*. Harmondsworth, Middlesex: Penguin Books.

Nagel, J. 2003. *Race, Ethnicity and Sexuality: Intimate Intersections, Forbidden Frontiers*. Oxford: Oxford University Press.

Newton, E. 1979. *Mother Camp: Female Impersonators in America*. Chicago: University of Chicago Press.

Oosterhuis, H. 1997. 'Richard von Krafft-Ebbing's "Step-Children of Nature": Psychiatry and the Making of Homosexual Identity', in V.A. Rosario (ed.) *Science and Homosexualities*. London: Routledge, pp. 67–88.

Ortner, S. and H. Whitehead. (eds). 1981. *Sexual Meanings: the Cultural Construction of Gender and Sexuality*. Cambridge: Cambridge University Press.

Peletz, M. 2006. 'Transgenderism and Gender Pluralism in Southeast Asia Since Early Modern Times', *Current Anthropology* 47 (2): 309–40.

———. 2009. *Gender Pluralism: Southeast Asia Since Early Modern Times*. London: Routledge.

Roscoe, W. 1991. *The Zuni Man-Woman*. Albuqerque: University of New Mexico Press.

———. 1995. 'Strange Craft, Strange History, Strange Folks: Cultural Amnesia and the Case for Lesbian and Gay Studies', *American Anthropologist* NS 97 (3): 448–53.

Said, E. 1978. *Orientalism*. London: Penguin.

Shaw, A. 2005. 'Changing Sex and Bending Gender: an Introduction', in A. Shaw and S. Ardener (eds) *Changing Sex and Bending Gender*. Oxford: Berghahn, pp. 1–19.

Steakley, J. 1997. 'Per Scientiam ad Justitiam: Magnus Hirschfeld and the Sexual Politics of Innate Homosexuality', in V.A. Rosario (ed.) *Science and Homosexualities*. London: Routledge, pp. 133–54.

Stoler, A. 1992. 'Sexual Affronts and Racial Frontiers: European Identities and the Cultural Politics of Exclusion in Colonial Southeast Asia', *Comparative Studies in Society and History* 24: 514–51.

————. 1995. *Race and the Education of Desire: Foucault's History of Sexuality and the Colonial Order of Things*. Durham: Duke University Press.

Stone, L. 1979. *The Family, Sex and Marriage in England, 1500–1800*. London: Penguin.

Storr, M. 1997. 'The Sexual Reproduction of "Race": Bisexuality, History and Racialization', in P. Davidson, J. Eadie, C. Hemmings, A. Kaloski and M. Storr (eds) *The Bisexual Imaginary: Representation, Identity and Desire*. London: Cassell, pp. 73– 88.

————. 2002. 'Transformations: Subjects, Categories and Cures in Krafft-Ebing's Sexology', in L. Bland and L. Doan (eds) *Sexology in Culture: Labelling Bodies and Desires*. Chicago: University of Chicago Press, pp. 12–25.

Towle, E. and L. Morgan. 2002. 'Romancing the Transgender Native: Rethinking the Use of the "Third Gender" Concept', *GLQ: A Journal of Lesbian and Gay Studies* 8 (4): 469–97.

Trumbach, R. 1989a. 'Gender and the Homosexual Role in Modern Western Culture: the 18th and 19th Centuries Compared', in D. Altman, C. Vance, M. Vicinus and J. Weeks (eds) *Homosexuality, Which Homosexuality?* London: Millivres-Prowler Group, pp. 149–69.

————. 1989b. 'The Birth of the Queen: Sodomy and the Emergence of Gender Equality in Modern Culture, 1660–1750', in M.B. Duberman, M. Vicinus and G. Chauncey (eds) *Hidden From History: Reclaiming the Gay and Lesbian Past*. New York: NAL Books, pp. 129–40.

Valentine, D. 2007. *Imagining Transgender: An Ethnography of a Category*. London: Duke University Press.

Weston, K. 1993. 'Lesbian/Gay Studies in the House of Anthropology', *Annual Review of Anthropology* 22: 339–67.

————. 1998. *Long Slow Burn: Sexuality and Social Science*. London: Routledge.

Whitehead, H. 1981. 'The Bow and the Burden Strap', in S. Ortner and H. Whitehead (eds) *Sexual Meanings: the Cultural Construction of Gender and Sexuality*. Cambridge: Cambridge University Press, pp. 80–115.

CHAPTER 10

WHAT CONSTITUTES TRANSGRESSIVE SEX? THE CASE OF CHILD PROSTITUTION IN THAILAND

Heather Montgomery

In the West, sex between an adult and child is one of the most transgressive forms of behaviour imaginable. Fear of paedophiles is widespread and adults who have sex with children are vilified. When adult/child sex is overlaid with a commercial aspect and children are paid for sex, it creates even greater social anxiety. In the 1990s, the commercial sexual exploitation of children, especially that involving Western men buying sex from children overseas, became an issue of particular concern, and pressure from non-governmental agencies forced changes in international law and practice, so that, for the first time, men could be prosecuted in their home countries for crimes committed against children abroad. In many respects, the campaigns against the commercial sexual exploitation of children were extremely straightforward, uniting women's groups, children's rights supporters, anti-tourism groups and anti-globalisation activists in a battle against Western men who wanted to have sex with children and feel immune from any consequences. Within this debate, there was little room for dissenting viewpoints; there could be no justification for these men, and the children's own voices were largely irrelevant. The commercial sexual exploitation of children became almost synonymous with transgressive sex, and national governments pledged to do their best to end it. In the 1990s, much of the concern about this issue focused on Thailand, presented by activists, the media and governments as one of the main destinations for foreign male tourists seeking sex with children and the place in which the problem was the most acute and where most needed to be done.

Western men who travel to poorer Asian countries to engage in paid sex with those under the age of sixteen are exploiting vast disparities in wealth, class, gender and ethnicity, and all the structural power these factors give them. There can be no defence for them, and the few that have been caught in places such as Thailand, Cambodia and the Philippines have been, quite rightly, harshly dealt with by the authorities. Despite this, however, the debate around the commercial sexual exploitation of children has cast only some forms of child prostitution as transgressive sex, while ignoring or glossing over other forms, so that the indigenous market for child prostitutes is routinely ignored or underplayed, despite estimates that many more children work in local Thai brothels than with Western clients. Activists against child prostitution deploy the language of women's rights and children's rights, but also use the image of the child prostitute as part of a larger agenda. Transgressive sex (in this case defined as the use by Western men of child prostitutes) symbolises other fears and social anxieties, which are less easy to articulate, so that child prostitutes are seen as a symptom of the wider problem of foreign (often Western) influence.

Writing this chapter in 2008 means that it is, in some ways, a historical piece. The economic crash in 1997 had profound effects on Thailand and, in the aftermath, issues such as child prostitution received much less prominence. However, it is no coincidence that child prostitution received so much attention in Thailand in the early to mid-1990s and it is difficult to understand it without looking at it within its social context and as a focus of anxiety about the social changes taking place in Thailand. The campaigns against child prostitution that I describe in this chapter occurred against a particular backdrop and took on a symbolic aspect above and beyond the suffering of individual children. Child prostitutes became a symbol for all that was wrong with Thailand's relationship to the West. Images of rape, penetration and deflowering used to discuss child prostitutes took on other metaphorical meanings, and attempts to talk about transgressive child sex revealed much deeper social anxieties about national identity.

The story of child prostitution

The accepted narrative of child prostitution in Thailand in the 1990s was that it was caused by corrupt and perverse foreigners coming to Thailand in order to fulfil desires for which they would be punished at home. The threat from these paedophiles was presented as urgent, ever-growing and necessitating eternal vigilance. The influx of child-sex tourists was described as an epidemic threatening to overwhelm all Thai children and the language of the Thai media and campaigning groups always suggested crisis and imminent chaos. Numbers were always said to be increasing (although the same figures were repeated year after year), until the number of one million child prostitutes in Asia came to be accepted as a fact, even though it had little basis in reality (Black 1994; Montgomery 2001). Transgressive sex in Thailand was represented by a clearly defined stereotype and a preset narrative. Both Western and Thai journalists and activists had a set story in mind, in which the child's life, circumstances and eventual fate had already been decided. Both NGOs and the media used very similar stories to attract attention, that of innocent rural girls tricked into brothels by unscrupulous middlemen and women, racking up huge debts they could never afford to repay and then being forced to have sex with at least ten foreign clients a night. These stories usually ended with a rescue by a local organisation and attempts to rehabilitate the child, only to find that the child was already dying from HIV/AIDS. It was common to draw attention to the price paid for sex, which was often described as equivalent to 'a loaf of bread' or 'a television', thereby insinuating that it was the small amount of money paid, not the abuse itself, that was so demeaning and also suggesting the root problem to be the unchecked materialism of greedy parents rather than the socio-economic pressures and structural inequalities faced by poor or marginalised families in Thailand.

The following three extracts are taken from articles that appeared within a year of each other during one of several peaks of media interest in the problem. They have been chosen out of a collection of hundreds, simply because they are so typical. The names of the children are different, as are their home towns and even the nationalities of the clients of these girls, but these are old stories with a set pattern and an inevitable consequence. As with folk tales or fairy stories, there is even a certain satisfaction in knowing how they will turn out. The first is the lead paragraph from the Australian newspaper the *Sunday Age*, published on 18 April 1993. Under the headline 'Bo, 12, Taken to a Hotel and Forced to have Sex', it tells the girl's harrowing story.

At 10, Bo was tricked into prostitution after the death of
her mother and father had substantially left her without
family. For five years in a brothel resort in the southern
Thai resort town of Songkhla, Bo endured countless Thai
and Western men, including many Australians, whom the
brothel owner called 'kangaroos'. The euphoria of escape
has been short-lived. Bo has been diagnosed HIV positive.
She is not expected to celebrate her 25th birthday. She
thinks she is now 17 or 18.

The second extract comes from the *New York Times* of January
1994, entitled 'The Littlest Prostitutes'. The child prostitute in this
instance is called Nit.

Nit, a peasant girl from the north, was sold for the price of
a television. In the Bangkok shelter where we met, she sat
politely on the edge of a sofa, fidgeting with her hair. At 13,
she still looked small and guileless enough to play with
dolls. And she talked only in whispers. Five months ago, an
agent paid her father 8,000 baht (about $320). The agent,
a soldier, told her she would wash dishes; instead he took
her to a house with 15 other girls.

Nit showed no emotion over what happened next. She
kept looking at the ceiling. She whispered that she was
very frightened when she faced her first client, an
American. She was also impressed: he had to pay 8,000
baht because she was a virgin. It did not occur to Nit that
this settled her debt.

Since her deflowering, Nit has seen her price drop like
bad stocks. Her second and third clients – from Hong Kong
– had to pay her boss 4,000 baht. Number five and six paid
only 1,500. After that she lost count and went down to the
'normal' price of 200 baht – $8 for an hour. Her boss kept
all the money. Nit seemed oddly resigned to her plight,
perhaps because it was her father's decision. But now, she
whispered, she wanted to go home.

Abuse and disease are rampant. The harm to their
bodies is easier to record: cigarette burns, self-inflicted cuts,
syphilis and gonorrhea, and increasingly the virus that
causes AIDS. Social workers worry also about the less
visible and harder part – the interrupted childhoods,
depression and distrust, the grim prediction that abused
children will themselves become perpetrators.

The final article, entitled 'Impoverished Thai Parents Sell Girls into Prostitution', is from the Sunday edition of the *Dallas Morning Star* of 21 March 1993. It is a longer article, which gives the name and addresses of an organisation at the end of it so its readers can find out more information or send a donation if they wish. Like the previous story, it is based on an interview the child gave the journalist in her home village after returning from a brothel.

At an age when many American teens are trying to talk Dad out of the car keys, she sits on the floor of a shabby cottage, trying to talk her frail, gaunt father out of sending her back to a brothel. At 17, she has already worked in three brothels, because of the need to help support her ailing parents. In the dim interior of the cottage purchased with her prostitute's wages, her father argues with social workers who want her to live and study at their shelter. The thatched cottage holds a few possessions: a charcoal brazier, a water jug, two battered tin cups and, on the room's one table, a television set. She is their only child, the father says. The brothel agent owns the land on which the house sits, and that day he has threatened to evict them. The father has borrowed money from the agent, with his daughter's work as collateral. What will happen to them if they lose her wages? He does not understand that, soon enough, he may lose her anyway. She has the AIDS virus.

An hour's drive north of Mae Chan, teacher Jandraem Sirikhampoo calls a group of students to her side. These little girls, she says, were sold as babies by their parents. The buyers are raising them, like livestock, to be sold into prostitution...

These girls and thousands like them are the clouded future of Thailand. A generation of girls is being turned into commerce: They are traded by their families or kidnappers for houses, water buffalo, land, cash, food – and televisions. Many girls now accept prostitution as their fate, the only way to support families, whose rural ways of life are disappearing.

Thailand has become the red-light district to much of the world. In a country of 56 million people, relief agencies estimate that there are 2 million prostitutes up to 800,000 of them children. Perhaps one in 12 women and older children may be involved, and up to 80 percent of the girls in some tribal villages.

Bo, Nit and the anonymous child in the third article have familiar stories. Abandoned by their parents into brothel life, they are rescued by good outsiders for a brief period of happiness before dying. In countless other articles, the pattern is repeated: betrayal, abuse, rescue, death. There is a neatness and coherence to this story which is compelling: no loose ends and a predictable outcome. The reader is invited to be outraged at the story, and to pity the victims but, ultimately, there is no escape from the plot and nothing that can be done to help these children. Once the story begins, it can only end, unhappily ever after, with the child's death. Yet these passages conceal more than they reveal. These stories are neat, self-contained and depressingly similar but they leave out certain key pieces of information. What happened to the children who did not contract HIV? Where did other girls go after they had been prostitutes? Did they marry, have their own children? What about girls who had local, rather than foreign, clients? Did they experience prostitution in the same way?

In contrast, much of the academic literature on child prostitution in Thailand paints a different picture. While not denying the levels of abuse that do go on, ethnographic studies of child prostitutes have consistently given different accounts of young prostitutes' lives and the after-effects of prostitution. Some academics, such as Phongpaichit (1982), Truong (1982, 1986, 1990), Hantrakul (1983), Muecke (1992) and Montgomery (2001), have examined the sociocultural background of young Thai prostitutes, arguing that particular religious and societal norms, in conjunction with economic circumstances can be predisposing factors in encouraging or discouraging children to become prostitutes (Thitsa 1980). They have focused in particular on the apparent religious sanction given to prostitution by Buddhist values, which stress models of duty and sacrifice for children, especially for girls. One argument is that by supporting her family through prostitution a girl gains merit rather than bringing shame on herself and her family. Although the role of Buddhism in supporting prostitution has been much disputed (see, for example, the debate between Thitsa 1980; Kirsch 1982, 1985; Keyes 1984), ethnographic evidence has shown the importance of filial duty and children's sense of obligation as factors that encourage them to enter and stay in prostitution (Phongpaichit 1982; Montgomery 2001). Other research suggested that while Western clients are the most visible users of child prostitutes, numerically they are in the minority (Black 1994). Indeed, the majority of young prostitutes are not found in the tourist bars of Bangkok, Pattaya or Phuket but in the brothels of rural Thailand or the backstreets of Bangkok. Another stereotype of child prostitution is for a very high price to be paid by a client for the child's virginity, this being particularly prized by Chinese men or others who believe that sex with a virgin cures AIDS (Lee-Wright 1990; Muntabhorn 1992; O'Grady 1992a, 1994). Despite the ubiquity of these myths, there is no ethnographic evidence, and no studies of male sexual behaviour, that have offered any support to the idea that some men believe sex with a virgin can cure disease. Indeed, even before the AIDS pandemic, the literature on child prostitution from other parts of the world claimed that child prostitutes were sought after because of a belief that penetrative sex with a virgin cured sexually transmitted diseases. Thus historical studies of child prostitution in Victorian London have claimed that men sought out sex with virgins in order to cure themselves of syphilis and gonorrhoea (Gorman 1978). For the majority of children, however, child prostitution is not about their virginity being bought for huge sums of money by foreigners, but is more to do with selling sex to whoever will buy it from them, often very cheaply. As Judith Ennew (1986: 83) has cogently argued:

> Children are not necessarily at the high price range of prostitution as something exotic and hard to find. Often they are the cheapest ... they are sought out by the most poor and marginalised as something they can have power over. They do not know the price of their own sexuality and will sell themselves for a cigarette ... The attraction of children [for the very poor] may be simply that they are social failures and that the child's social status and small size provides a means of exercising power which is otherwise not available to them.

Transgressive sex and social policy

In the 1980s and 1990s, successive Thai governments pushed for rapid industrialisation and modernisation of the country, and one of the key components of that strategy was the promotion of tourism so that, by 1998, seven and a half million tourists visited Thailand every year compared with two million in 1981. Thailand was promoted as an exotic country, where attitudes and behaviours were different and where Western values did not necessarily apply. At the forefront of these campaigns were Thai women, represented as docile, subservient and available, whether as air stewardesses on Thai Airways or as prostitutes in Bangkok and resort towns such as Pattaya. Among some government ministers, prostitution and sex tourism were seen as the necessary price of economic development. In 1980, the Deputy Prime Minister of Thailand justified sex tourism because it encouraged tourists and created jobs. In a speech to provincial governors, he acknowledged that there were 'some forms of entertainment that some of you might consider disgusting and shameful because they are forms of sexual entertainment that attract tourists [but] ... we must do this because we have to consider the jobs that will be created' (quoted in Ennew 1986: 99). The Thai authorities actively encouraged sex tourism, playing on orientalist images of subservient, sexualised women. In many ways, this was not a new departure for the Thai government. During the Vietnam War, they had allowed American servicemen to build bases in their country to prevent the war in Indochina from spilling over the borders. Alongside these bases an entire industry had grown up, based on providing 'R&R' ('rest and recreation') services to the servicemen, and these invariably included sexual services. At the end of the war in 1975, with most of the Americans gone, the infrastructure of bars, brothels and nightclubs was still in place and the image of Thailand as a paradise for cheap available sex with willing, docile women had become well established. Turning this over to the tourism industry was the obvious next step.

The increase in long-haul world travel meant that by the late 1980s and early 1990s tourism had become Thailand's highest source of foreign currency revenue (Lewis and Kapur 1990). Thailand became notorious as a country in which prostitution flourished and even the most uninformed tourist could buy sex very easily. The red-light districts of the major cities were overt and aggressively sexual. Signs up outside certain bars indicated in graphic detail what the women inside would do and these areas had become, at night, no-go areas for anyone not involved in the sex trade (Odzer 1990). Such activities were deeply resented by many, especially by the growing numbers of Thais involved in NGOs and social activism, who saw sex tourism as symptomatic of the way that Westerners treated Thais, and regarded tourists as the most visible symbols of the threat of Westernisation to Thai culture.

In the late 1980s, various anti-tourism NGOs sprang up, concerned not only with sex tourism but with the effects of tourism on the environment and on Thai society more generally. They began to protest against certain forms of tourism, for example, launching a No Golf Day to protest at land being bought up to build golf courses for Japanese tourists. Women's groups began to picket flights they believed were carrying sex tourists from Korea and Japan, carrying banners that read 'Thai-land not Sex-Land'. For the activists, tourism was beginning to take on a symbolic value, epitomising all that was wrong with Thailand's relationship with the West, and the issue of deviant and transgressive sexuality lay at its core. Prostitution was perhaps the most visible form of deviant sexuality supposedly imported from the West, but it was not the only one. Homosexuality was also increasingly condemned and represented as a dangerous Western threat: a vector of disease in terms of HIV and also a transgressive foreign import that had no place in Thai society (Jackson 1989; Fordham 1995). The former Deputy Minister of Education, Prasoet Bunsom, for example, was quoted as claiming that homosexuality and promiscuity in general were Western phenomena that had no relevance to Thailand. Speaking of these, he said, 'Overseas they have "free sex", as in America, where this type of behaviour might be such an ordinary thing that no-one takes much interest in it. But in Thailand, it may be seen as something detestable and a social abnormality' (Jackson 1989: 33). Again, despite a widespread and long-standing tolerance of homosexual acts in Thailand, if not an understanding of homosexuality as a sexual or personal identity (see Jackson 1989), homosexuality, like prostitution, was becoming perceived as a result of too much Westernisation and as an attack on the Thai social fabric.

The analogy between the bodies of Thai women and the country as a whole was increasingly used as part of the activists' rhetoric. In 1983, Nelson Graburn, one of the most vehement critics of the tourist industry, claimed that all tourism was analogous to prostitution and the latter was a simple extension of the former. He wrote:

> As host nations, they may have little to sell but their 'beauty' which is often desecrated by (sacrificed to) mass tourism. The men of such countries are forced into pimp roles... At a psychological level [poor] nations are forced into the 'female' role of servitude, of being 'penetrated' for money, often against their will: whereas the outgoing, pleasure seeking 'penetrating' tourists of powerful nations are cast in the 'male' role. (Graburn 1983: 441)

This line of thinking was extremely influential among Thai activists who saw tourism and prostitution as interchangeable. For activists, tourism caused and promoted prostitution, as their literature stated quite explicitly: 'The cause of the increase of prostitution is tourists. Third World countries of Asia promote their tourism industry to earn foreign currencies. One of the tourist attractions is sexual service' (Srisang and Srisang n.d.). Others went still further and some of the most vocal opponents of the spread of tourism in Thailand put it quite bluntly when they wrote in 1990: 'tourism is the rape of culture, the environment, women and children' (Srisang and Srisang n.d.: 11). A clear divide thus opened up between activists and the government over what constituted transgressive sex, and about whose body was being violated by tourism. On the one hand the government was promoting tourism and implicitly condoning the sexual use of Thai women in the promotion of the general economic health of the Thai state. On the other hand the activists were condemning the promotion of tourism as a violation of the Thai nation itself. While transgressive sex was being normalised by government officials as a necessary form of tourism, tourism itself was being recast as a form of transgressive sex by the activists and had become both a symptom of and a metaphor for the unequal power relationships between Thailand and the West.

Such a viewpoint, despite being passionately felt, ignored many of the realities of the prostitution situation in Thailand and reduced the social, political, economic and even historical contexts that allowed prostitution to flourish to a single issue: the problem of the foreigner. In 1991, this viewpoint was summarised most succinctly by the Foundation for Women, a Thai NGO, in their report on prostitution in Thailand for the UN. It began:

> Although prostitution as an organised business in Thailand only started in the 1930s with the import of Chinese prostitutes into the country to cater for Chinese immigrants, prostitution became a big problem in the 1960s with the presence of the United States military bases during the Vietnam war. It was taken over by local demand, and spurred on by the promotion of tourism. (United Nations 1991: 45)

In this narrative, prostitution is viewed entirely as an imported problem, caused first by the Chinese, then the Americans and now by Western tourists. Thais appear only as the innocent victims of foreign lusts. Despite the historical evidence of a long-standing culture of prostitution in Thailand (see, for instance, League of Nations 1933; Landon 1939; Fox 1960; Hantrakul 1983; Havanon et al. 1992; Boonchalaksi and Guest 1994), and studies of contemporary Thai male sexuality that show the high numbers of Thai men who visit brothels (Sittitrai and Brown 1994; Fordham 1995, 1998), prostitution is still understood as a function of Western imperialism and as both a cause and a symptom of the cultural crisis in Thailand.

By the early 1990s, the idea that Thai society was in crisis was widespread among the educated middle classes. The English-language Thai press ran a series of articles with titles like 'Culture in Crisis' (*Bangkok Post*, 24 January 1994), 'Observations on Thailand's Cultural Dilemma' (*Nation*, 18 March 1993), 'Lost in the Urban Jungle' (*Bangkok Post*, 19 May 1994) and 'Northern Villagers Put their Heritage up for Sale' (*Sunday Post*, 3 October 1993), all expressing the same fears that Thailand was losing its identity and becoming 'Westernised', and making explicit links between cultural decline, tourism and prostitution. The latter article expressed the sentiment that 'Art, tradition and culture are the root of society. Once the root is severed, people lose their knowledge of their own roots and rapidly accept a new culture, usually from the West, aggravating social problems such as prostitution' (*Sunday Post*, 3 October 1993). This sense of crisis came to a head in mid 1993 when two scandals generated extensive newspaper coverage and debate about the state of Thai culture and the perception of Thailand overseas. The first was the publication of an article in *Time Magazine* (21 June 1993) about adult and child prostitution throughout the world. The global problem was summed up by a picture on the cover of a Thai prostitute and her Western client. Many were indignant that Thailand and prostitution had become synonymous. Then, a few weeks later, there was more outrage following the revelation that the publisher Longman's newly issued *English Dictionary* described Bangkok as 'the capital city of Thailand. It is famous for its temples and other beautiful buildings, and is also often mentioned as a place where there are a lot of prostitutes.' The description caused great offence and led to protests as well as to much soul-searching about the nature of modern Thai identity.

In the face of this sense of crisis, 1994 was designated Thai Cultural Promotion Year, and there was a self-conscious attempt to promote a different image of Thailand, one that emphasised displays of Thai dancing, historical plays and events focusing on the historical Thai centres. That these events were traditionally elite pursuits emanating from the royal court was largely overlooked and, instead, all were enthusiastically promoted as the 'real' Thailand and the authentic face of Thai culture. Activities such as dancing and handicrafts were recognisable and concrete activities that could be claimed as authentic. It is these aspects of culture that could be saved from the creeping cultural imperialism of the West as something recognisably Thai to protect. Yet even these aspects of culture were threatened, and along with them, the integrity of Thai society. The threat, as ever, came from outside and it was the West that was to blame for the decline. Professor of Archaeology Srisak Wallipodom complained that he was 'deeply hurt when the younger generation feels indifferent whenever there is an insult to past sacred rituals, which have been circumvented into commercialised tools to attract tourists' (*Nation*, 18 March 1993).

Interestingly, all these articles were published in English, a language not widely spoken outside the educated middle classes, and published in metropolitan English-language newspapers. They reflected a very particular viewpoint, therefore, and it is unclear how widespread this anti-Western and anti-tourist stance was. Indeed, the impact of all of the campaigns against tourism and Westernisation was minimal. The Thai economy was booming and many were prepared to turn a blind eye to prostitution of whatever sort. The mayor of Pattaya, one of the most overt destinations for sex tourists, claimed that, 'Every morsel eaten by Pattaya's population of 200,000 is provided by tourists' (*Pattaya Mail*, 12 November 1993) and refused to see a problem with tourism, even if it included prostitution, as long as it brought in money. Although some of the anti-tourist protests were picked up by the overseas media, there was little interest in Thailand itself. It was only in 1991, with the formation of ECPAT – an NGO whose acronym stands for End Child Prostitution in Asian Tourism – that sex tourism began to be of wider concern and the anti-tourist lobby finally found an issue that allowed it some influence and a platform to campaign on. Trying to promote an understanding that tourism had caused an explosion of deviant sexuality, and, worse than that, that it was, in itself, a form of rape and abuse had proved unsuccessful. Focusing on the most extreme and repugnant end of the unequal and exploitative relationship between Thailand and the West proved much more effective in raising the profile of these issues, since it identified the one form of transgressive sex that could not be condoned or implicitly supported by the government. From the beginning of their campaigns, however, ending child prostitution was not an end in itself, but the start of a wider campaign to end what they saw as Western exploitation, a position made clear in ECPAT's founding statement, which declared that: 'The issue of child prostitution is a symptom of the broader oppression which faces people in developing countries but it may be a starting point for this wider debate' (1991: 1).

Child prostitution in Thailand

In uncovering the existence of Western men who travelled to Thailand to have sex with children, ECPAT – an offshoot of one of the original anti-tourist groups – had found an emotive and unchallengeable issue. There could be no justification for the behaviour of these men and stopping them, and campaigning against them, could alienate no one. It did not challenge government policy, it absolved Thailand of any guilt in allowing or encouraging certain forms of prostitution, and, by tapping into Western fears about paedophilia and child abuse (as well as a desire to read about such abuses), it ensured a willing audience in the West. As Black (1994: 13) argues:

> no society wants to admit that it practises 'child prostitution'. And where the evidence is undeniable, it is more bearable to blame the 'unclean other' – decadent foreigners with their incomprehensible tastes and misbehaviours. Where there is an overlay of North-South exploitation – the Western tourist ruining innocent paradise with his credit card and unleashed libido – this version plays easily in certain well-meaning ears.

Stories began to emerge of Westerners being arrested for molesting children and jumping bail or being let off on technicalities. A Swedish man, Benk Bolin, was caught with a naked boy in his bed, but claimed that he had been led to believe that the boy was over fifteen and therefore of legal age. Before he could be prosecuted, he applied for a new Swedish passport and left the country. The following year, an Australian, Bradley Pendragon, was arrested in Chiang Mai after trying to develop photographs clearly depicting the sexual abuse of a young girl. Thai newspapers ran a steady stream of articles about child prostitution documenting many cases of child abuse by foreigners (for example, 'German Engineer Arrested on Perverted Sex Charge', *Nation*, 3 March 1994; 'Child Molester Flees Thailand', *Bangkok Post*, 31 January 1995; 'German Couple Recruiting Kids for Sex Photos', *Pattaya Mail*, 4 January 1993: 'Swiss Caught with Small Boy', *Pattaya Mail*, 23 March 1994). The fact that many of these men did manage to leave the country or bribe police to drop charges created justifiable outrage and groups such as ECPAT bravely campaigned not only against these abuses but against the corruption and incompetence that allowed these men to escape punishment.

The campaigns they ran were highly personalised and emotive, giving quite horrific accounts of the abuse of individual children, describing exactly what had been done to them and appealing for help to end such abuses. One campaigner told the *Bangkok Post*, 'I still remember vividly the tears in the eyes of the child rescued from a Bangkok brothel who told me how she begged a customer not to harm her, only to have her pleas mercilessly rejected' (6 October 1993). Yet there were no actual help available to these children and no structures in place to remove children from brothels or to take them out of dangerous situations; there were no medical or psychological help available for them, no training for the future and no practical solutions. As one of the founders of ECPAT wrote, 'When boys and girls have been forced to receive several customers a night seven days a week, they will be so traumatized that very little can be done to help them resume anything like a normal life' (O'Grady 1992b: 1). The stories told, as suggested in the first section of this chapter, quickly became repetitive, containing the same ingredients and the same horrific images and stories until it seemed that every child prostitute had exactly the same background, the same route into prostitution, the same way out and the same terrible fate.

I should make clear that I am not treating the commercial sexual exploitation of children by foreigners as a myth. I spent fifteen months on the outskirts of a major tourist resort in Thailand working in a small community that survived through the prostitution of its children. There were over thirty children ranging in age from six to fourteen who worked as prostitutes and had exclusively Western clients, some of whom inflicted very serious injuries on them. Child prostitution and child exploitation by Westerners was, and is, a fact. However, the vast majority of child prostitutes in Thailand do not have sex with Westerners but are to be found in brothels used exclusively by local men. They are the worst paid and have the least freedom of any children working in the sex trade; these are the children most likely to be debt-bonded, tricked or kidnapped, or from ethnic minorities without papers and vulnerable to police harassment on these grounds. These are also the children who have provoked much less outcry and attention and who often seem to be the forgotten children of the international campaigns. Without foreign clients, they become invisible.

It is perhaps not surprising that there has been a reluctance to confront the issue of indigenous commercial sexual exploitation of children. It is much easier to raise sympathy and outrage about outsiders coming in to abuse children and harder to stand up to the enemy within. As in other 'sex tourism' countries, this mechanism parallels the distancing mechanism in the West that places the emphasis on 'stranger danger', so that sexual abuse within the family is played down in favour of fear of child rape by unknown, asocial men. By focusing exclusively on Thai children with foreign clients, the activists found an issue that put them beyond the criticism of the state, which had tacitly condoned the sex trade. The commercial sexual abuse of Thai children by foreigners was so transgressive, so taboo, that to campaign against it was a moral imperative that could not be ignored or disagreed with. Furthermore, it allowed other, more problematic issues to be sidelined in the face of this 'overwhelming' and 'ever-increasing' threat to Thai children. As child rescuers and avengers of betrayed childhood innocence, the activists who ran ECPAT and similar groups presented themselves as the saviours, not only of individual children, but of the next generation of Thai children, and by extension as the custodians and guardians of Thai culture. While there were serious issues with the Thai authorities in their promotion or condoning of adult prostitution, they could not be seen to allow child prostitution. As the clients were foreign, they could be easily and uncontroversially targeted. What had once been a political campaign against tourism and Westernisation had been transformed into a moral crusade that left no room for debate.

It was not coincidental that the rise in concern about child prostitution happened at the same time as concerns about Thai identity and Thai society were raised. The two were intimately linked, and one of the reasons that the ECPAT campaign succeeded where previous anti-tourism campaigns did not was that it avoided wider issues of foreign involvement in Thailand and concentrated instead on one where unrestrained resentment of foreigners was acceptable and encouraged. The perfect symbol for this resentment was the child-sex tourist, 'a potent symbol of touristic excess' (Black 1995: 20). Child prostitution, like so many 'moral' problems, was not the straightforward issue of good and evil, standing above politics and economics, that some campaigners claimed. Focusing on it was a conscious political decision, with a particular agenda and subtext. Muecke (1992: 986) writes:

[The Thai middle classes] interpret prostitution as a function of both the low education and poverty in Thailand

as a Third World country and as a function of the greed of
the individuals who sell, procure or buy girls for labour in
the prostitution industry. These views implicitly discount
class responsibility for prostitution by globalising it to the
scale of the Third World, and by individualising it to
detestable characters. This stance also safeguards the
women's groups members' relationships to their male
partners and peers. By championing the cause of child
victims of prostitution, the elite activists protect the
disadvantaged children of the nation and protect the
ideology of women – and themselves as nurturing mothers.
And by restricting their activism to child prostitution, they
avoid impugning male friends and relatives, that is those of
their own class, and elitist systems (such as police,
government officials surreptitiously involved in the sex
entertainment trade) for supporting adult prostitution.

In a society where public expression of anger and confrontation
are considered unacceptable, the success of the anti-child-
prostitution campaigns was in finding the one issue where such
anger was justifiable. They successfully harnessed the fear and
resentment of foreigners by focusing on the individual men
involved in exploitation of Thai children. This is not to accuse the
campaigners of cynicism or opportunism. There was a real
problem of child prostitution in Thailand and Thais had every right
to get angry about the foreign paedophiles who came to their
country and indulged in behaviour that would not be tolerated in
their home countries. Equally, Thailand's rapid industrialisation
caused divisive and long-term social problems. However, it is
extremely difficult for NGOs to generate interest about an issue on
an international level, especially if it is seen as a national or local
concern. Raising protests about cultural identity being distorted
tend to fall on deaf ears, as do pleas to help certain other exploited
groups, no matter how severe the exploitation.

Commercial child sexual exploitation by foreigners had thus
become the defining image of transgressive sex in Thailand. Yet,
at the same time, other forms of sexual abuse, sometimes
involving children, also occurred but received much less
attention. Chief among these was the treatment of Burmese
children and young women found in brothels on the Thai side of
the Thai–Burmese border. In 1993, Asia Watch, an American
human rights group, reported on the widespread collusion of Thai
officials in the indigenous sex trade and, in particular, their
treatment of Burmese girls in Thailand. They discussed at length

a raid on a brothel in Ranong (near the Burmese border) where 148 underage Burmese girls were rescued and then arrested. They claimed to have been forced or tricked into the brothels, and yet, rather than being treated as trafficking victims, they were arrested by the Thai police as illegal immigrants. No clients were charged and the police chief excused it on the grounds that 'In my opinion it is disgraceful to let Burmese men frequent Thai prostitutes. Therefore, I have been flexible in allowing Burmese prostitutes to work here. Most of their clients are Burmese men' (Pol. Lt. Gen. Sudjai Yanrat quoted in *Nation*, 16 July 1993). Although this case attracted some attention in the Western press, the treatment of these girls suggested that some forms of commercial sex with children were seen as transgressive in ways others were not. The police chief's comments reflected a view that what would have been transgressive in this case would have been if Thai children and women had had sex with Burmese men and that, by allowing Burmese girls to work in the brothels, he had avoided this deviancy. The age of the women involved, the dismal conditions in which they were kept and the fact that they were then treated as criminals who had entered the country illegally were irrelevant. Commercial child sex in this instance was not transgressive because it involved poor Burmese children having cheap sex with poor Burmese men rather than depraved Westerners indulging their tastes at a high price. It also involved issues of immigration and Thai national government policies, which made it extremely hard for local campaigning groups to get involved. Doing so would have meant abandoning their stance that the issue of child prostitution was a simple issue of good and evil and acknowledging that it was both intensely political and a way of raising other fears that could not be so easily articulated.

Conclusion

It would be wrong to claim that anti-child-prostitution groups did not have the very best of intentions. However, it is important to understand the ways in which child prostitution was used in the 1990s as a vehicle for raising other fears and for discussing other social anxieties. It is unsurprising that battles about tourism and Westernisation were fought over images of the unpolluted body of a child or that activists used the image of a violated child to fight a wider social battle against foreign values and outside influence. The child prostitute, raped and deflowered by the Western male, took on the symbolic role of Thailand itself and the images of violation were used, by association, to refer to the defilement of Thailand in general. For ECPAT, ending child prostitution was never an end in itself, but the start of a movement to re-evaluate relationships between Thailand and the West. The anti-child-prostitution lobby was successful because it managed to tap into the concern felt in the West about paedophilia, as well as presenting the issue in a way that encouraged the view that child prostitution was the inevitable result of mass tourism, and indeed Westernisation, and that the former could not be stopped without curbs on the latter. By focusing on one of the most repugnant and condemned forms of transgressive sex, ECPAT and groups like it found a platform to talk about other forms of transgression, about what they saw as the rape of their country, the dilution of their values and the damage to their society. Stories of transgressive sex often do read like morality or fairy tales, with the same figures of evil, the same elements of tragedy and the same unhappy-ever-after ending. Beneath this format, however, is another story, in which the transgressive sex is not only the defilement of individual children, but rather, the rape of culture and of Thailand itself.

References

Black, M. 1994. 'Home Truths', *New Internationalist* 252: 11–14.
————. 1995. *In the Twilight Zone, Child Workers in the Hotel, Tourism and Catering Industry*. Geneva: ILO.
Boonchalaksi, W. and P. Guest. 1994. *Prostitution in Thailand*. Bangkok: Institute for Population and Social Research, Mahidol University.
ECPAT. 1991. *Newsletter.* Bangkok: ECPAT.
Ennew, J. 1986. *Sexual Exploitation of Children*. Cambridge: Polity Press.
Fordham, G. 1995. 'Women, Whiskey, and Song: Men, Alcohol and AIDS in Northern Thailand', *The Australian Journal of Anthropology* 6 (3): 154–76.
————. 1998. 'Northern Thai Male Culture and the Assessment of HIV Risk: Toward a New Approach'. *Crossroads*, 12 (1): 77–164.
Fox, M. 1960. *Problems of Prostitution in Thailand*. Bangkok: Department of Public Welfare.
Gorman, D. 1978. 'The Maiden Tribute of Modern Babylon Re-examined. Child Prostitution and the Idea of Childhood in Late-Victorian England', *Victorian Studies* 21: 353–79.
Graburn, N.H. 1983. 'Tourism and Prostitution', *Annals of Tourism Research* 10 (3): 437–42.
Hantrakul, S. 1983. 'Prostitution in Thailand'. Paper presented to the Women in Asia Workshop, Monash University, Melbourne.
Havanon, N., J. Knodel and T. Bennett 1992. *Sexual Networking in a Provincial Thai Setting*. Bangkok: AIDS Prevention Monographs.
Keyes, C.F. 1984. 'Mother or Mistress but Never a Monk', *American Ethnologist* 11 (2): 223–41.

Kirsch, A.T. 1982. 'Buddhism, Sex Roles and the Thai Economy', in P. van Esterik (ed.) *Women of South East Asia*. Occasional Paper No. 9, Centre for South Asian Studies, De Kalb, Illinois: Northern Illinois University.
———. 1985. 'Text and Context: Buddhist Sex Roles/the Culture of Gender Revisited', *American Ethnologist* 12 (2): 302–20.

Jackson, P. 1989. *Male Homosexuality in Thailand – an Interpretation of Contemporary Thai Sources*. New York: Global Academic Publishers.

Landon, K. 1939. *Siam in Transition. A Brief Survey of Cultural Trends in the Five Years since the Revolution of 1932*. Oxford: Oxford University Press.

League of Nations 1933. *Commission of Enquiry into Traffic in Women and Children in the East*. Report to the Council, New York: League of Nations.

Lee-Wright, P. 1990. *Child Slaves*. London: Earthscan Publications.

Lewis, J. and D. Kapur. 1990. 'An Updating Country Study – Thailand Needs and Prospects in the 1990's', *World Development* 18 (10): 1363–78.

Montgomery, H. 2001. *Modern Babylon? Prostituting Children in Thailand*. Oxford: Berghahn.

Muecke, M.A. 1992. 'Mother Sold Food, Daughter Sells Her Body – The Cultural Continuity of Prostitution', *Social Science and Medicine* 35 (7): 891–901.

Muntabhorn, V. 1992. *Sale of Children*. Report submitted by the Special Rapporteur. E/CN.4/1992/55. New York: United Nations.

Odzer, C. 1990. 'Patpong Prostitution: Its Relationship to, and Effect on, the Position of Women in Thai Society'. Unpublished PhD thesis, New School for Social Research, New York.

O'Grady, R. 1992a. *The Child and the Tourist*. Bangkok: ECPAT.
———. 1992b. *Address to the Summit Conference on Child Prostitution of the Vatican Pontifical Council for the Family*. Bangkok: ECPAT.
———. 1994. *The Rape of the Innocent*. Bangkok: ECPAT.

Phongpaichit, P. 1982. *From Peasant Girls to Bangkok Masseuses*. Geneva: ILO.

Sittitrai, W. and T. Brown. 1994. *The Impact of HIV on Children in Thailand*. Bangkok: Thai Red Cross Society.

Srisang, S. and K. Srisang. n.d. 'Prostitution in Thailand: Products of Power Manipulation and Spiritual Bankruptcy'. Unpublished manuscript, Bangkok.

Thitsa, K. 1980. *Providence and Prostitution: Women in Buddhist Thailand*. Women in Society, Series No. 2. London: Change International.

Truong, T.D. 1982. 'The Dynamics of Sex Tourism', *Development and Change* 14 (4): 533–553.
———. 1986. *Virtue, Order, Health and Money: Towards a Comprehensive Perspective on Female Prostitution in Asia*. Bangkok: United Nations.
———. 1990. *Sex, Money and Morality*. London: Zed Books.

United Nations. 1991. *Promotion of Community Awareness of the Prevention of Prostitution*. Bangkok: United Nations.

CHAPTER 11

COURTING TRANSGRESSION: CUSTOMARY LAW AND SEXUAL VIOLENCE IN ABORIGINAL AUSTRALIA

Fiona Magowan

Women are falling down the cracks where the white systems and customary law meet. (Sex Discrimination Commissioner 2003: 97)

Managing sexual transgression in Aboriginal Australia is particularly complex as, in some regions, appeals for justice may be made via two realms of jurisdiction, either customary law or the courts. This chapter assesses how the courts have responded to the significant rise in rape, domestic violence and sexual abuse cases amongst Aboriginal people in the Northern Territory. It considers how sexual taboos have been shaped by Aboriginal customary laws and impacted by colonial intervention as well as by postcolonial changes to kinship structures. Taking Yolngu of north-east Arnhem Land as a case study, I argue that kinship is central to the control of sexual transgression, as sexual practices are regulated through communal surveillance by the social body over sexual bodies in family and ritual contexts. I discuss some of the dilemmas faced by the courts over sentencing when ruling on ritual punishment and show how the content and use of customary laws have adapted over time to accommodate social change. I focus in particular on the implementation of customary law on Galiwin'ku, an island lying 6 km off the north-east Arnhem Land coast, with approximately 2,000 Yolngu inhabitants. First, I begin by comparing two case studies of sexual transgression in the Northern Territory.

Courting transgression

In 2002, a fifty-year old Aboriginal man from Maningrida in western Arnhem Land was sentenced to thirteen months' jail for having unlawful intercourse with his promised fifteen-year-old wife. Since the girl's birth in 1986, the man had been paying her parents with customary gifts of spears, food and cash to fulfil the arrangement. The girl resisted his advances so he punched and raped her and 'put his foot onto her neck' according to her statement (Shah 2002: 1). When relatives stopped by they were unable to help when the man produced a shotgun and fired it in the air. When the police arrived they charged him with having unlawful sexual intercourse with a minor and discharging a firearm. He said, 'She is my promised wife. I have rights to touch her body. Yes, I know. It's called carnal knowledge, but it's Aboriginal custom – my culture.' After sentencing, an appeal was lodged and the man was released on bail. He complained of being humiliated at having to explain his customary law in the context of white law. The anthropologist in the appeal noted that 'sexual relations with a promised wife under the age of 16 were not considered aberrant in Arnhem Land society'.[1] The appeal judge then revoked the magistrate's decision and instead gave the man one day's prison sentence for having fired a shotgun to prevent his wife from leaving him. However, these rules of 'private' family intervention according to customary law came under criticism as the court learned that his relatives had been unable to act in accordance with custom to assist the young wife in this case and that the offender had been convicted in 1995 for the manslaughter of his former wife.

The second case I consider here took place in August 2005, when the Court of Appeal in Darwin overturned a one-month jail sentence given to a fifty-five-year old Yarralin elder who held a fourteen-year old girl 'against her will for four days, beat her with a boomerang and forced her to undergo anal intercourse' (Barker 2005: 1). The one-month sentence had been given by Chief Justice Brian Martin who had expressed sympathy for the offender as he believed his actions were permissible under customary law. However, on appeal, Justice Dean Mildren and two other judges increased the sentence from two years to almost four years and the non-parole period from one month to a year and a half, arguing that customary law does not excuse such behaviour and violence will not be tolerated whether it is under customary law or not. This case led to dissent between lawyers at the North Australian Aboriginal Justice Agency, who considered an appeal to the High Court to uphold the right to apply customary law in sentencing. Meanwhile others in Parliament, the law and the Indigenous community condemned the use of customary law as an excuse for violence (Barker 2005: 2).

In both these cases transgression has the potential to extend laws and define alternative rules (see Lashgari 1995). In the first case, the magistrate considered that the Maningrida husband showed a lack of control and reason, and his actions should be punished as his bride rights were not sufficient grounds for violence. Yet, on appeal, a judge considered customary law should take precedence and minimised the sentence by only punishing the firing of the rifle. In the second case, the Yarralin man equally claimed his rights to his promised bride through customary law but, in contrast, the Chief Justice handed down a lenient sentence in the first instance only to be increased afterwards by the Court of Appeal. So how can two such different judgments have been given for two such similar transgressions?

In order to understand how slippage occurs between perceptions of acceptable and unacceptable sexual behaviour between these two laws, we need to look at how the limits of sexual taboos are socially legitimated in Aboriginal society and interrogated under the legal system which may either reject or affirm them. Furthermore, these rulings have various implications for the victims, who are generally women and children. These cases raise two major issues: First, what counts as sexual transgression under customary law in Aboriginal Australia? And, secondly, how have anthropologists and the legal system engaged Aboriginal women's calls for assistance in relation to transgressive sexual acts?

Transgression may be understood as violating rules, principles of law, religious authority or social conventions. It generally entails crossing boundaries, subverting acceptable norms and inverting behavioural principles. Dubious acts that violate accepted codes of behaviour evoke negative feelings and disrupt social harmony and stability. How individuals perceive transgressive behaviours and how society evaluates them may conflict. So, ambiguities are embodied in how transgressive desires, states, acts and rules are experienced and categorised.

While each region of Australia has its own specific rules and practices around customary laws there are some general principles that may be identified in relation to the concept of transgression.

In Anglo-American cultures, Harvey and Gow (1994: 2) note that transgression is 'that aspect of self that emerges through lack of control that exists and finds expression against reason enabling the momentary transcendence of individuating boundaries'. At one level, the purpose of sexual taboos under any law is to maintain social order, although the very existence of taboos enables the possibility of violence and violation within the tabooed domain. Thus, sexual subversions and inversions are emotional violations towards the self and society. At another level, sexual transgression is transcendent of its breach because it refutes socially sanctioned boundaries. It involves self-sacrifice in the attainment of a sense of being that is beyond the regulation of self. Foucault (1977: 35) explains this idea of enlargement as opening up social norms. He notes that 'transgression is not related to the limit as black to white, the prohibited to the lawful, the outside to the inside ... Transgression contains nothing negative, but affirms the limitlessness into which it leaps as it opens this zone to existence for the first time.'

Transgression offers new limits, new possibilities for action and behaviour. So, when transgressive sexual acts take place, their taboos are paradoxically transcended and affirmed. Taboos are not subverted by transgressive acts, they are reinforced and completed by them (Bataille 1986), legitimated by the fear of their transgression.

Kinship and sexual taboos

Sexual violence and abuse are among the major social issues being addressed by the Northern Territory Aboriginal Family Violence Strategy. In the east Arnhem Land region, a holistic approach to integrated government and non-government sources began in 2005 with the recognition that the Yolngu are in a 'state of crisis' and communities need to be involved in projects to manage and sustain change (O'Meally and Barr 2005: 21).

Approximately 5,000 Yolngu live in north-east Arnhem Land. The thirty-two clans in the region are related to one another through their cosmology, based on the division of all things in the world into two patrilineal exogamous halves or moieties, known as Dhuwa and Yirritja. Customary law is a consubstantial local law of responsibility for the land and for the people expressed through the stories of the two moieties, which tell of the actions of ancestral beings who made the landscape and left exogamous marriage laws at places along the way. Customary laws are the moral and social principles of interaction that Yolngu must abide by derived from the ancestral law as told in stories and performed in ritual song and dance. An incongruity has persisted between Australian law and customary law in that the former is seen to be official and written, the latter informal and oral (Williams 2001: 5). Thus, until recently, Yolngu customary law has lacked formal status in the eyes of the courts. It has been argued by the Committee of Inquiry into Aboriginal Customary Law (2003: 11) that 'to write it would be to lose it', because formalising customary laws would jeopardise their existence by allowing Aboriginal interpretations to be subsumed within a legal framework. However, in contrast, Djiniyini Gondarra, who is a political leader of the Golumala clan on Galiwin'ku and former chairman of ARDS (Aboriginal Resource Development Services), has stressed that Yolngu ancestral law is not customary law, but is equivalent to the legal system as it has its own legal sanctions (ARDS 2006).

In a culture in which each individual is related to all others through kinship, the boundaries between kin behaviour, sexual interest and friendship are not always clearly defined (Allan 1989: 3). Unlike the rules of kin behaviour, friendship is not institutionalised, and, while correct sexual relations are prescribed, kinship ideals cannot prevent illicit affairs (Hess 1979; Matthews 1986). Social roles entail obligations and reciprocities, and establish a baseline for the feelings that arise in domestic situations. But, when roles change (and the taboos that order them are transgressed), so too do the rules for how to feel and interpret events (Hochschild 1983: 74).

Proper relations are conducted through discipline and rules that curtail transgressive behaviour. From an early age, small children are given the freedom to indulge in erotic play (see Berndt and Berndt 1946: 69) and sexual topics are aired in front of them as long as there are no kin present to whom sexual restrictions apply. In the 1970s, Berndt (1976: 6) reported that boys and girls who played together might tease each other by calling one another 'long vagina' and 'long penis', although they had to exercise constraint as they got older. These days on Galiwin'ku, sexual liaisons take place amongst teenagers at night-time when the island comes alive to the sound of whistling as boys hang out in the shadows of trees waiting for their girlfriends to reply with their own distinctive calls. As the whistles become less frequent, so the couples pair off and disappear into the darkness. Families tend to turn a blind eye to these relationships as long they do not result in wrong marriages or unwanted pregnancies.

Despite these freedoms, controlling sexual relationships is an important aspect of controlling social relations. By day, the behaviour of boys and girls who relate to one another as potential spouses is strictly observed and any visible form of sexual contact is frowned upon. The temporary absence of unmarried sweethearts from communal activities is seen as a form of sexual impropriety and on their return they may be embarrassed by public joking or shamed by being publicly reprimanded.

Colonisation has brought many challenges to Yolngu bodily and sexual practices through Western ideas of propriety. Certain ritual customs as well as ritual adornment have been viewed as sexually transgressive through non-Aboriginal eyes. Traditional material coverings were not full pieces of clothing but aesthetic artefacts that were not necessarily intended to cover the genitals (see Berndt and Berndt 1964: 103–4). As nudity was the norm, the naked body was not thought to be erotic in and of itself but its performance could effect a change in the way it was perceived. However, with the arrival of the Methodist mission to Arnhem Land in the 1920s, and the introduction of dresses for women and shorts for men, another mode of modesty grew up around the sexualisation of the body. Yolngu now expect the body to be covered to avoid being shamed by their relatives, the only exception to this is during certain rituals when women may paint their breasts and go topless although the younger ones will wear bras. The ideals that pertain to modesty have been challenged recently by some Yolngu actors. Robert de Heer's acclaimed 2006 film *Ten Canoes* tells the story of ten men, their families and lifestyles as the older men teach the younger men the origins of the laws that govern sexual behaviour. When an elder brother discovers his younger brother fancies his third wife, the elder brother decides to relate a story of wife-raiding in order to deter him from breaking the law and bringing disaster upon the camp. In his story a stranger appears in the camp and some time later a young woman vanishes. Believing the stranger has taken her, the men form a war-party to find her but kill the wrong man. They must face payback, a revenge spearing to be carried out by the aggrieved stranger's group. The film depicts traditional Indigenous lifestyles in which both the male and female actors are naked (see De Heer 2006). During its screening at the 2006 Garma festival, some Yolngu Christian women did not wish to view the production as they said they would be embarrassed to see their relatives naked on film. These attitudes of shame and embarrassment have been instilled over time as a result of colonial paranoia about the naked body being a sexually sinful body. The colonisers viewed clothing as next to godliness and sanity, while they saw nakedness as a paradoxical relationship between the innocence of Eden and the sinfulness of sexual desire (see Barcan 2004). Thus, the colonisers viewed Indigenous people as lacking morally, mentally and culturally due to their nakedness and instead they considered that clothes would civilise them (Thomas 1994: 72). The Aboriginal scholar Irene Watson has viewed colonisation as a form of enforced covering as colonisers violated the law, its peoples and lands by concealing their legal system and disposing of nakedness (Watson 1998: 2).

In February 2004, Aboriginal women from Papunya in Central Australia were preparing a group of girls to perform a traditional dance topless in an Alice Springs park which was to be showcased at a conference in Sydney. However, the women were told to move on by two white police officers because the law did not permit nudity in public places. The Aboriginal and Torres Strait Islanders' central zone commissioner was outraged. She commented, 'These people hold our lore and hand it down from generation to generation. This is the kind of thing we should be encouraging in a town like Alice so the tourists can see the good side of Aboriginal people' (quoted in Anon. 2004).

Just as nudity in ritual entails respect for Aboriginal kin and law, so touching between same-sex friends is not necessarily sexually suggestive. Women often lie together, one with her head on another's thigh having her hair groomed for lice. These more intimate acts of bodily contact reinforce friendships and affirm the right to touch. Touch is heightened when women tell jokes of a sexual nature. One afternoon, during fieldwork whilst I was sitting with my (fictive) Yolngu mother and grandmother, the conversation turned to a couple who had recently been seen together who were not of the right marriage skin.[2] Soon, my mother joked about my single status. The women laughed and my mother told me, winking, that I wasn't hunting for my yams properly, at which she firmly tweaked my nipple. The conversation continued in this vein with comments increasing in hilarity until she grabbed at my groin at another sexual innuendo. This nipple tweaking and groin grabbing was a sign of friendship and shared intimacy about sexual matters.

Ritualised sex

In Arnhem Land, ritual has always been central to enforcing the law as rituals consolidate social relations. In the past, normative sexual relations were affirmed by ritual sexual transgression. Amongst the major initiation, funerary and commemorative ceremonies in Arnhem Land, the Gunapipi ritual stood out for the exchange of wives between distant clan brothers. Over a period of several days the pair would dance and exchange gifts before engaging in a night of ceremonial intercourse (Warner 1937: 296). However, this sexual activity was highly conventionalised and not permitted until the final evening (Berndt 1976: 95), when a woman might have sex with several men if insufficient women were present for all the men attending. It was only in this context that women could take more than one sexual partner. So sexual licence under ritual law was an act of conformity rather than transgression (Malinowski 1913: 123; Berndt 1976: 13). If young men and women refused to participate in the ritual, they were breaking a taboo, even though the taboo stood contrary to normative sexual practices. Thus, the normative status of ritual sex meant that resisting involvement was a transgressive defiance. It held the potential to bring illness on a husband and the woman's ceremonial partner (Warner 1937: 224, 297). Sexual transgression could still occur within the ritual context if clandestine meetings between the couple took place before the final night. On one occasion, Warner (1937: 224) reported that two men were caught in illicit sexual relations with two women whilst ancestral emblems were present in the ritual ground. This offence was dealt with by a severe beating, although it did not allay fears that the clan would become ill.

One effect of missionary influence was a ban on carrying out all elements of the Gunapipi ceremony whether or not they involved ritual coitus. Nevertheless, the ban on this practice has meant that it has become more eroticised and is carried out surreptitiously (Berndt 1976: 95). In some places, such as Galiwin'ku, Yolngu themselves have banned the ritual but, in other places, elements are still performed and people travel from across the region to participate. The purpose of ritual sexuality is not simply for the release of sexual frustration or desire, rather it is a social instrument of power providing a source of collective and individual control over others (Merlan 1988: 52).

Incest and marital taboos

As in all cultures, very rigid rules exist around the incest taboo and sexual intercourse is not allowed between members of the same moiety. In Arnhem Land, sisters are taboo to brothers, and brothers refer to them as 'worthless', 'rubbish' and 'without kin' (*wakinngu*). Sexual distance is inscribed in senses of touch, sight, smell and hearing. Older brothers and sisters should not touch each other or be seen to go into the forest to relieve themselves. If husbands and wives fight, the brother of a wife should never be in earshot of the argument, as he cannot hear his sister swear or hear obscene language used against her. If the brother is privy to this offence, the sister is held to be in the wrong as having incited her husband's anger. Consequently, she and all her sisters will be the recipients of her brother's indignation at hearing offensive remarks. In the past, brothers would have thrown spears at their sisters. Warner (1937: 54) tells how Balli, an adolescent girl, called her own mother *dalardumaru* ('big vagina') and Natjurili, a near-clan brother of the mother, heard the girl use this term, and he then threw spears at all his classificatory and actual sisters. His action suggests symbolic retaliation for breach of the incest taboo by penetrating the sisters as a result of their indiscretion, since in the past transgression had to be rectified by avenging the transgressor through payback.

As sexual taboos are generally oriented around the prohibition of particular desires or erotic encounters, the taboo gives value to the desire and its erotic potential. So taboos need to be managed as much as the transgressions that may occur in relation to them. In the 1930s, Warner (1937: 75) identified five tabooed sexual relations, although the majority of them still resulted in permanent union between couples, as outlined in this paraphrase:

1. Relations when the legal spouse of either spouse or both spouses are carrying on an affair without the mate's full knowledge.
2. Runaway (love) matches when the man and woman go to a distant clan to live although neither partner's family approves.
3. A union when a man steals a woman from her husband and takes her to his own clan. (The man's family will often support him, especially if the theft is between rival clans).
4. A union when warring clansmen kill off the husbands of the women and keep the women for themselves (no longer practised).

5. The union of a daughter whose father has given her to a relative who does not have a legal claim to her within the kinship system.

The promise system of north-east Arnhem Land serves to contain the threat of social disorder, spiritual harm and bodily pollution that could result from these kinds of transgressions. It establishes how a man may take a woman's daughter in marriage when he comes of age through the mother-in-law rite. This rite takes place between a mother-in-law and the future son-in-law, although it is only in ritual that these two relatives may be in contact with one another. The wife's mother (*mukul rumaru*) and daughter's husband (*gurung*) stand in an avoidance relationship to one another as both are in the same moiety and he receives his future wife from her. Shapiro reports (1981: 48):

> The girl is made to sit in public view. Her father holds her, beckoning to the boy or man who would be her son-in-law and who waits in the wings: 'Come forth ZDC and perform the mother-in-law rite'. The son-in-law approaches the girl and sits nearby facing her. With his thumb he removes some facial oil from the side of his nose, places it directly upon the girl's abdomen a few inches above her navel and proceeds to move it downwards to the navel itself.

One word for penis is 'nose for working' (*ngurru-djamawurru*) and '"working" a woman', as Berndt (1976: 6) puts it, is to have coitus, the child being a result of this. The son-in-law will make payments to the mother-in-law over a number of years until he is able to claim her daughter in marriage. At a formal kinship level, 'straight' (*dhunupa*) skin marriages control sexual transgression. Nevertheless, ideals are not always adhered to and crooked (*djarrpi'*) relations do occur between people of the wrong 'skin'. These are not just strongly frowned upon; they are not recognised as proper unions even though the partnerships may persist for a lifetime and, in very rare circumstances, a couple may have been married in church. Where offenders in crooked marriages were once speared to death, nowadays parents and grandparents speak strongly to young couples, but it often does not result in breaking up their relationship. Consequently, the concept of a de facto relationship does not parallel its Western counterpart. Rather, the de facto relationship is seen to be a state of cohabitation prior to the families' recognition of 'straight marriage' occurring between couples who are the right skin for one another (Margaret Miller personal communication). If unions between people of the wrong skin are not socially recognised, this brings into question whether the concept of adultery is perceived to be the same in Yolngu relationships as in the West.

Marital jealousy

In the 1930s, Warner (1937) reported that mutual fidelity was demanded by husband and wife; a woman was expected to stay away from all other men and the husband could not cohabit with any woman except his wives. Thus, the concept of adultery was not relevant to a husband's liaisons with his promised wives, only to those women who stood in a distant/crooked relationship to him. Nevertheless, sexual jealousy would occur between actual and potential wives who would protest about their husband's choice to take another wife, and husbands would punish wives who showed an interest in other men. Today, women will assert their rights over their husband, rebuking him by not feeding him, staying away from the family home, and leaving to stay with other relatives in another community for a time to get away 'from the humbug'. If emotions are running high, a wife has the choice of either attacking her husband's mistress or publicly reprimanding her husband in order to shame him.

Yolngu marriage used to be entirely polygynous and so, where adultery with women of the wrong skin did occur, sanctions included warnings about causing infertility in a wife and removing protection from spiritual harm for the husband. Since a man's status relies on the bestowal of women and the clan reputation is carried on through the political and ritual strength of sons, the threat of infertility was effectively a threat of loss of clan status and reputation and ultimately social isolation by a depletion of sons to work for his mother's clan and lack of daughters to bestow on men of other clans. With the arrival of missions monogamy became the ideal. Nevertheless, as recently as thirty years ago, 90 per cent of men had polygynous marriages, while today roughly half the population has multiple wives, often determined by love marriages rather than by arrangement (Sexton and Wilson 2006).

By the 1970s, in north-east Arnhem Land, young women were vigorously opposing polygynous marriage and claiming a greater degree of choice in the selection of a partner through 'white love marriage', as they saw that Australian marriage was based on mutual attraction. In doing so, 'they implicitly placed themselves within Australian legal jurisdiction and availed themselves of legal procedures if needed by initiating intervention, by prompting interested whites to intervene or inviting Australian legal representatives to do so' (Williams 1986: 147–48). The response by male leaders was to classify these challenges as 'family problems' or 'private', thereby allowing customary law to form the basis for their mediation (Williams 1986: 148). However, as violence between spouses in the Northern Territory averages 6000 incidents of assault on Indigenous women per year, i.e. about one-third of the Northern Territory's Indigenous female population (Bolger 1991: 11, cited in Memmott et al. 2001: 37), Aboriginal women have sought assistance outside the remit of customary law as they are predominantly at the receiving end of sexual abuse. Not all of these attacks involve sexual assault but in 50 to 60 per cent of cases, weapons such as sticks, rocks, iron bars, knives, spears, guns, firesticks, bottles and ropes were used, causing bruising, burns, broken bones, internal injuries and stab or shotgun wounds (Memmott et al. 2001: 37).[3]

Some Yolngu women have been beaten by their husbands in order to regain a sense of ownership over the wife as property, express hostility indirectly towards other men and re-establish male control. In the 1930s Warner (1937: 71) reported that 'ordinarily a husband would feel it his duty to beat his wife when she conducted herself in an unlawful way with another man'. However, the idea that women are customarily beaten has been adopted in some parts of Australia to validate beatings where customary laws either no longer exist or traditional knowledge has changed. The distortion around essentialising punishment has been recognised by Behrendt who, citing Bolger, notes that 'young Aboriginal women now believe it *is* traditional for men to beat their wives and it is older Aboriginal women who have rejected this distortion as a myth' (Bolger 1991: 51, cited in Behrendt 2004: 7). In a summation of sexual offences reported by the Aboriginal and Torres Strait Islander Women's Task Force (1999: 98) on Violence in Queensland, it was noted that 'judges and the police used cultural distortions of rape to legitimise men's behaviours … and excused the offence as the cultural right of men'. Behrendt (2004: 7, 8) has also shown how there is a lack of understanding of the severity of sexual assault against Aboriginal women, because some judges have taken the evidence of men over women and come to the conclusion that rape is not considered as serious an offence in Aboriginal society as in white society. In a 1982 case in the Northern Territory, an offender was sentenced to four years' imprisonment for killing his wife after beating her with a piece of piping arguing in his defence that 'it is not unusual for women to be beaten if they do not obey their husbands' (Law Courts of Australia 2006: 10). However, the court did not accept that this behaviour was an 'established or accepted part of Aboriginal society' (Law Courts of Australia 2006: 10). A 2003 submission by the Human Rights and Equal Opportunity Commission (HREOC) Sex Discrimination Commissioner found that there is a gender imbalance in 'the law of provocation that has been developed from a male perspective which has failed to take account of the fact that women's experiences of violence differ from men's' (Sex Discrimination Commissioner of the HREOC 2003: section 2.4). In addition, the legal process has exacerbated women's suffering further through methods of taking evidence, which require women to repeat the story a number of times, often in different proceedings, which appears as a further transgression rather than delivery of justice (Sex Discrimination Commissioner of the HREOC 2003: section 2.3). In such judgments little heed has been paid to the emotional and personal harm experienced by women.

Discourses of rape and domestic violence

An increasing number of reports on domestic violence and customary law has been commissioned across Australia since 1998, and detailed submissions from women's task forces have begun to document the views and concerns of female victims of domestic violence. Yet recent figures show that the number of children supported by Crisis Accommodation in the mining town of Gove in north-east Arnhem Land more than doubled over a year, with sixty in care in 2003 and 144 in care in 2004 (O'Meally and Barr 2005: 1). As Australian cultural values have impacted Yolngu, resulting in 'high mortality rates, excessive alcohol and substance abuse, overcrowded housing, language barriers, poor educational outcomes, limited employment opportunities, severe domestic and family violence, health conditions, gambling and welfare mentality', domestic violence has become more visible (O'Meally and Barr 2005: 1). Marriage bestowal patterns have broken down and families have found it increasingly difficult to apply injunctions to those who transgress them, especially when young people flout the authority of elders (see Burbank 1985).

In 1989, the Royal Commission into Aboriginal Deaths in Custody in Queensland found that 32 per cent of the ninety-nine deaths in custody were of inmates held for sexual assault (Aboriginal and Torres Strait Islander Women's Task Force 1999). With the introduction of mandatory sentencing to the Northern Territory in 1997, 'prison numbers almost doubled as adults were jailed for their first offence and juveniles for their second' (Munro and Bandjalan n.d.). An increase in Aboriginal deaths in custody has meant that Aboriginal leaders have been keen to have customary law and punishment recognised as being on a par with court sentences. Justice Toohey (2004: 180) has observed that courts regularly assess the extent to which there is customary acceptance of particular conduct involving violence in communities, although he further notes that what constitutes 'conduct involving violence' has sometimes been difficult to determine. Women increasingly want protection from violence, especially in places where customary laws do not operate effectively or at all, but, in order to determine how to rule on violence, courts must determine whether the sexual violation has entailed consent. As the law generally assumes that a woman has consented to sex until she forcefully states or acts to the contrary, women are expected to be sexually reactive rather than being proactive sexual agents (Townsend 1995 cited in Charlesworth et al. n.d. 11). Yet sexual consent or rejection is seldom witnessed by others and thus it is difficult to access the range of emotions entailed and the rights involved. For instance, 'the offender may argue that he believed the victim could not refuse if she was his wife' (Law Courts of Australia 2006: 15). The prosecution may opt for a finding where consent is not a relevant consideration, but this presents a double bind as consent is necessary for 'an ultimate finding of guilt or innocence' (Law Courts of Australia 2006: 15).

In some cases it has been judged that sexual violence is rape; in others it has been judged as consensual, or 'traditional' in cases where 'it has been argued that there was a sort of consent to sexual intercourse, required as a way of expiation for an offence against a customary law' (Toohey 2004: 181) or as payment for a woman. In the case of the fifteen-year-old girl in Maningrida with which I started this chapter, the Maningrida man was guilty of statutory rape on grounds of non-consensual sex. What was not tried was the emotional assault against the girl, as recourse to customary law meant that the assault fell within the remit of kinship rights and obligations. Thus, when the appeal judge took into account customary law that endorses the payment of goods for a wife, the sentence was reduced. In July 2006, the Law Council of Australia produced a report on customary law determinations to refute allegations of leniency in sentencing, as in the outcome of this case. Nevertheless, where Australian law allows customary law to intervene in sexual violence, it has been argued that harm to women may be muted and there may be a 'failure to protect human rights' (Behrendt 2004: 9).

In 1986 the Australian Law Reform Commission (ALRC 1986) considered whether customary law should be recognised as part of the State legal system and found arguments both for and against its implementation. In a summary of the report produced by the Northern Territory Law Reform Committee (NTLRC), it was suggested that 'traditional authority may be more efficient in maintaining order within Aboriginal communities, and thus be more cost-effective' (Toohey 2004: 175). In 2004 Justice Toohey further summarised the issues outlined earlier in the ALRC and NTLRC reports against recognising customary law because it:

- may incorporate rules and punishments that are unacceptable to the wider Australian society;
- may not adequately protect Aboriginal women;
- may no longer be relevant to some Aboriginal people, and some may prefer the present legal system (Toohey 2004: 175)

In a 2003 report women on Groote Eylandt in Arnhem Land felt that it would be appropriate to involve the police or courts when a traditional approach to speaking with the violent man did not help (Sex Discrimination Commissioner of the HREOC 2003: section 3.2). One woman commented, 'When a crime [such as rape] is committed, it should be dealt with by white man's law because customary law says that women are not equal. They are beneath men' (Sex Discrimination Commissioner of the HREOC 2003: Principle 7). Most Groote Eylandt women said that they wanted stronger responses to domestic violence, with mainstream law as a 'safety net' behind customary law, although some women did express concerns about whether mainstream law could adequately protect them (Sex Discrimination Commissioner of the HREOC 2003: section 3.3). Earlier that year, the report of the Committee of Inquiry into Aboriginal Customary Law (2003: 22) had noted that, in some communities, customary law can and does fully represent women because they have fought hard to preserve their rights, but it also recognised that their rights can be violated when customary law breaks down through alcohol abuse and other factors.

In response to the need to look after family matters properly and avoid young people being further marginalised by the court system, Yolngu elders invited judges, lawyers and senior government officials to a Ngärra ceremony held on Galiwin'ku in November 2005, in which they were told about the ancestral law (*madayin*), its sacred objects (*rangga*), and the system of order that governs harmonious social interaction *(mägaya)*. The Yolngu presented a document containing thirty-eight laws of discipline (*Raypirri Rom*) dealing with a range of transgressions including murder, stealing of property, theft of natural resources, swearing, assault, deceit, acts of ancestral desecration, trespass, burning, making unlawful contracts over territory, sorcery, failure to fulfil responsibilities as holders of the law, not keeping restrictions around revealing ancestral knowledge, failure to ensure correct behaviour in the ceremonial parliament, allowing women in the parliament, not seeking permission to enter another clan's estate, and causing disputes at a funeral.

Contrary to the Berndts' assertion that there was no formally constituted court of law, comprising special persons vested with authority and power to deal with cases, pass judgment and impose punishment (Berndt and Berndt 1964: 348), the Yolngu have demonstrated to the Law Council of Australia that such arenas and persons do exist. In the Yolngu system of discipline, the term transgressor means someone who breaks the law (*rom bakmaram*) and within this category there are several levels of wrongdoing and punishment. These range from a disobedient person (*wurrngatja*) to someone who is critical or rebellious of the laws of the land (*rom nyamir'yunmirr*) to a wicked person who is guilty of extreme wrongdoing (*yätjkurr yolngu*). The laws are written in a tone akin to that of the Ten Commandments which reflects the Christian backgrounds of the leaders who composed them. Three of the thirty-eight laws refer to sexual transgression. They are:

  (i).   Prohibitions against incestual [sic] relationships
  (ii). Prohibitions against sexual relations with a juvenile
  (iii). Prohibitions against sexual advances from a woman in
         a sister relationship to you (Anon. 2005)

While the first and third laws have been reported in the past as part of Yolngu transgressive practices, the second one, 'sexual relations with a juvenile', has been specifically included to deal with incongruities between Australian law and customary law. Debates ranged around whether the prohibition should specify sex with a person under sixteen but this was dropped as it had the potential to undermine the legitimacy of customary practices and require policing around current promised marriage arrangements.

Where wrong relationships once resulted in ritual spearing (*makarrata*) in the thigh, the only recourse to spearing stated in *Raypirri Rom* is for murder. Dr Djiniyini Gondarra, who coordinated the writing of these laws with colleagues in ARDS (the Aboriginal Resource Development Services), has noted that domestic violence in traditional marriages is not tolerated by the family or community and violence results either in spearing or social exclusion (Sexton and Wilson 2006), although, in reality, spearing has not occurred for many years. Where violence occurs to a teenage promised woman, the mother's clan would have the right to intervene in reprimanding her husband. Sexual offences are dealt with by judicial punishment in which elders take responsibility for the transgressor, speak to him harshly, oversee his behaviour and in some cases impose a fine. During meetings at a homeland, Gangan, to discuss Aboriginal customary law in 2003, Dr Djiniyini Gondarra and Richard Trudgen, director of ARDS, said that 'many young people could see they were bound by traditional law, but owing to a lack of similar rules operating in towns felt that they could do anything' (Committee of Inquiry into Aboriginal Customary Law 2003: 16). The authority of elders has gradually been undermined by conflicting systems of law and the challenges presented to ritual control by modernisation and technology. As elders may have little physical control over rebellious youth, threats of sorcery are sometimes employed to make the offender listen but this is not the norm. Instead, offenders should pass through a 'traditional chamber of law' that will teach them to behave properly (Law Courts of Australia 2006). This system was employed in 2005 when a man set fire to his house on Galiwin'ku after an argument with his wife. He was further subjected to 'Territorial asylum in which he was prohibited from drinking and smoking and required to spend time on his clan's homeland, Barrkira, to reflect on his country and the seriousness of his offending' (Law Courts of Australia 2006: 11, 12). Justice Southwood convicted the man to three years' imprisonment suspended on condition of the year's homeland supervision and instruction in the third level of the 'chamber of law'.

Since 1992, the Galiwin'ku Community Justice Programme has been in place in which the community dialogues with the court about offenders, but formal recognition of customary law is a new initiative designed to empower the community to take control of its own affairs and determine appropriate sentencing procedures. Since 2004, a Community Court has also been operating in the predominantly white mining town of Nhulunbuy, situated on the coast of north-east Arnhem Land, for matters deemed appropriate by the magistrate. The disputing families may provide the magistrate with a more informed picture of the circumstances in which defendants may find themselves in court (O'Meally and Barr 2005: 25). Although these efforts may be viewed as early days for direct convergences between community courts, families and the 'chamber of law', it is hoped that they will provide maximum benefit for families in rehabilitating perpetrators and protecting victims.

Conclusion

By exploring the rules that constitute sexual transgression under customary law, I have tried to demonstrate that 'normative' and 'transgressive' sexual practices in contemporary Aboriginal society are 'culturally embedded concepts which do not necessarily have commensurable salience cross-culturally' (Harvey and Gow 1994: 12). Sexual transgressions highlight internal struggles to keep control of kinship through regulating the social and sexual body by surveillance and public shaming. However, with the breakdown in kinship structures, women are experiencing an increase in sexual abuse associated with alcohol- and drug-related violence. These incidents differ in scale and intensity in different parts of Australia according to the extent of unstable social conditions, poverty, housing, lack of protection and shelters available, type of policing and whether courts are located within the community and are able to intervene in 'family matters'.

The emphasis on transgressive acts in customary law does not address the personal and emotional abuse that women and children in particular suffer as a result of violence. Transgressive acts have no sanction on the emotive violations they generate and may give rise to a new wave of transgressive practices. Children growing up in these conditions and against whom sexual abuses are carried out may suffer from and learn to be the next generation of perpetrators of transgressive sexual acts. Thus, the emotions that transgressive sexual acts entail further become part of the 'feeling rules' of young people's lives, shaping their emotional reactions to different kinds of social behaviours and responses to others (Hochschild 1983). It is pertinent to reflect upon how times have changed. Warner's (1937: 118) observation that young people used to be 'afraid of the old people' and men would kill other men if a woman's virginity was lost contrasts with a case recorded in the 1999 Queensland report on violence, which documents how a seventeen-year-old mother was tied to a bed and repeatedly raped by three men. It notes, 'fear has immobilised many people from taking action, while others have accepted it as normal behaviour because they have not been able to get help when they have tried' (Aboriginal and Torres Strait Islander Women's Task Force 1999).[4]

Courts have been partially responsible for propounding the problem as the court environment is 'alienating, frightening and stifling' and it is recognised that many Indigenous women are disadvantaged when appearing in court as they feel intimidated and unwilling to report the details of their case (Aboriginal and Torres Strait Islander Women's Task Force 1999). Implementing customary law in contemporary Aboriginal societies requires attention to the 'profound incompatibility between modernisation and cultural traditionalism in a situation where tradition was, originally at least, as far from modernism as it was possible to be' (Sutton 2001: 132). In north-east Arnhem Land, communities are trying to bridge that gap through taking control of customary law in a contemporary context by confronting the potential for sexual transgression and making offenders accountable to families and the courts. This means that community partnerships require input and coordination from many sectors to stem domestic violence, but they need not be contrary to Yolngu principles of authority and kinship. The 'chamber of law' has been recognised as an alternative sentence to court punishment where appropriate, thereby avoiding double jeopardy where an offender might receive a sentence from the courts as well as punishment through the law. In Arnhem Land, the application of customary sentences involves both senior men and women liaising with the families of the perpetrator and victim. Given the lack of government resources available to support men through anger management programmes, it is hoped that these measures will empower the community to support offenders in their own way, although questions about overseeing offenders remain. Nevertheless, further understanding of the catalysts for male aggression is needed alongside appropriate strategies of counselling and helping young men before they become offenders. If these measures were implemented from family perspectives through Yolngu systems of attention to the emotional states and needs of young men and women, they might not only assist teenage relationships at an early stage but might also identify other social and emotional needs that contribute to various forms of abuse later in life. More still needs to be done in making men accountable to their families and negotiating autonomy, integrity and safety for women in relationships as they tread the thorny paths of love and marriage between two laws.

Notes

1. On appeal, the judge in this case found that such marriages were common and morally correct under Aboriginal law (Shah 2002).
2. Yolngu give fictive kin relationships to outsiders in order to locate them appropriately within their familial networks. The term 'skin' (*mälk*) is a relationship classification according to the division of Yolngu society into sixteen paired names, eight for females and eight for males. These pairs are ideal kin relationships that order correct marriage partnerships.
3. In Victoria 46.9 per cent of Aboriginal females who reported abuse had crimes committed against their person (Mackay and Smallacombe 1986: 17–23).
4. When the Maningrida case was brought to court, it caused much furore around the country, on the one hand, from feminists and some anthropologists, who argued that appeals to Aboriginal 'tradition' have concealed systemic abuses by Aboriginal men and the white legal system – itself an intrinsic expression of male hegemonic authority – and, on the other hand, from lawyers and other anthropologists who conversely argued that it is important to recognise the overriding significance of Aboriginal customary law as holding ultimate authority on its own terms.

References

Aboriginal and Torres Strait Islander Women's Task Force. 1999. *The Aboriginal and Torres Strait Islander Women's Task Force on Violence Report*. Brisbane, Queensland: The State of Queensland. URL accessed on 6 March 2006 at http://www.women.qld.gov.au/Docs/ATSI/ATSI_Violence.pdf.

Allan, G. 1989. *Friendship: Developing a Sociological Perspective*. London: Harvester Wheatsheaf.

ALRC. 1986. *The Recognition of Aboriginal Customary Law*, Vol. 1, Report 31 AGPS, para. 499: 360. New South Wales: Law Reform Commission.

Anon 2004. 'Apology "Will Not End" Topless Dance Dispute'. ABC News Online. URL accessed at http://www.abc.net.au/news/ newsitems/ s1054894.htm 27 February.

———. 2005. 'Melngur Gapu Dhularrpa Gawiya: Raypirri Ngärra'ngu Romgur Mägayakurr'. URL accessed at http://www.ards.com.au/ yolngu_law.htm.

ARDS 2006 'Traditional Aboriginal Law Outlaws Sexual Abuse', 19 May. URL accessed at http://www.ards.com.au/media/Media19.pdf.

Barcan, R. 2004 *Nudity: a Cultural Anatomy*. Oxford: Berg.

Barker, A. 2005. 'Sentence increased for sex abuse' URL accessed at http://www.abc.net.au/pm/content/2005/s1536768.htm.

Bataille, G. 1986. *Eroticism: Death and Sensuality*, trans. Mary Dalwood. San Francisco: City Lights.

Behrendt, L. 2004 'Law Stories and Life Stories: Aboriginal Women, the Law and Australian Society'. Clare Burton Memorial Lecture. URL accessed on 2 March 2006 at http://lsn.curtin.edu.au/leadership/ clareburton/L_Behrendt_Lecture04.pdf.

Berndt, R.M. 1976. *Love Songs of Arnhem Land.* Chicago: University of Chicago Press.

Berndt, R.M. and C.H. Berndt. 1946. 'The Eternal Ones of the Dream', *Oceania,* XVII (1): 67–78.

Berndt, R.M. and C.H. Berndt. 1964 [1996]. *The World of the First Australians.* Sydney: Ure Smith. Second, revised edition 1976. Canberra: Aboriginal Studies Press.

Bolger, A. 1991. *Aboriginal Women and Violence: a Report for the Criminology Research Council and the Northern Territory Commissioner of Police.* Darwin: Australian National University, North Australian Research Unit.

Burbank, V. 1985. 'The Mirriri as Ritualized Aggression', *Oceania* 56: 47–55.

Charlesworth, S., S. Farrow, A. Goodwin and M. Neave 2001. *Sexual Offences: Law and Procedure Discussion Paper.* Melbourne: Victoria Law Reform Commission. URL accessed at http://64.233.183.104/search? q=cache:6yDIOoSGH9YJ:www.lawreform.vic.gov.au/CA256902000F E154/Lookup/Sexual_Offences/%24file/Discussion_Paper_chapters_1– 5.pdf+Townsend,+K.+1995+National+Conference+on+Sexual+Assa ult+and+the+Law,+Conference+Proceedings,+Melbourne&hl=en&ct =clnk&cd=33&gl=uk.

Committee of Inquiry into Aboriginal Customary Law. 2003. *Report on Aboriginal Customary Law.* Darwin: Northern Territory Law Reform Committee. URL accessed at http://www.nt.gov.au/justice/docs/ lawmake/ntlrc_final_report.pdf.

De Heer, R. 2006. Ten Canoes. URL accessed at http://www.tencanoes .com.au/tencanoes/video_editor/default.htm.

Foucault, M. 1977. 'A Preface to Transgression', in D.F. Bouchard (ed.) *Language, Counter-memory, Practice: Selected Essays and Interviews by Michel Foucault.* Ithaca: Cornell University Press, pp. 29–52.

Harvey, P. and P. Gow (eds). 1994. *Sex and Violence: Issues in Representation and Experience.* London: Routledge.

Hess, B.B. 1979. 'Sex Roles, Friendship and the Life Course', *Research on Ageing* 1: 494–515.

Hochschild, A. 1983. *The Managed Heart: Commercialization of Human Feeling.* Berkeley: University of California Press.

Lashgari, D. 1995. 'Introduction', in D. Lashgari (ed.) *Violence, Silence, and Anger: Women's Writing as Transgression.* Charlottesville: University Press of Virginia, pp. 1–21.

Law Council of Australia. 2006. *Recognition of Cultural Factors in Sentencing.* Canberra: Council of Australian Governments, Braddon. URL accessed at http://www.lawcouncil.asn.au/sublist.html?section= LCA&year=2006.

Mackay, M. and S. Smallacombe. 1986. 'Aboriginal Women as Offenders and Victims: the Case of Victoria', *Indigenous Law Bulletin.* 3 (80): 17–23.

Malinowksi, B. 1913. *The Family among the Australian Aborigines.* London: University of London Press.

Matthews, S.H. 1986. *Friendships Through the Life Course.* Beverley Hills: Sage.

Memmott, P., R.Stacy, C.Chambers and C.Keys. 2001. *Violence in Indigenous Communities: Report to Crime Prevention Branch of the Attorney-*

General's Department. Canberra: Commonwealth Attorney-General's Department.

Merlan, F. 1988. 'Gender in Aboriginal Social Life: a Review', in R.M. Berndt and R. Tonkinson (eds) *Social Anthropology and Australian Aboriginal Studies: a Contemporary Overview*. Canberra: Aboriginal Studies Press, 17–75.

Munro, K. and K.M. Bandjalan. n.d. 'Lonely Boy Richard: Film Australia Study Guide'. URL accessed at http://www.filmaust.com.au/programs/teachers_notes/8533lonelyboyrichardnotes.pdf.

O'Meally, S. and A. Barr. 2005. 'Families in Crisis: Implications of Change for Yolngu Living in Remote Arnhem Land'. URL accessed at http://www.engagingcommunities2005.org/abstracts/OMeally-Simone-final.pdf.

Sex Discrimination Commissioner of the Human Rights and Equal Opportunity Commission (HREOC). 2003. 'Submission to the Northern Territory Law Reform Committee: Inquiry into Aboriginal Customary Law in the Northern Territory'. URL accessed at http://www.hreoc.gov.au/sex_discrimination/customary_law/submission.html.

Sexton, J. and A. Wilson. 2006. 'Fallout Over Four Wives', *The Australian*, 12 July. URL accessed at http://www.theaustralian.news.com.au/story/0,20867,19760405-28737,00.html.

Shah, S. 2002. 'Judge Rules Rape of Aboriginal Girl "Traditional"', *Women's E-News*, 29 November 2002. http://www.womensenews.org/article.cfm/dyn/aid/1126. Accessed 21 March 2004.

Shapiro, W. 1981. *Miwuyt Marriage: the Cultural Anthropology of Affinity in Northeast Arnhem Land*. Philadelphia: Institute for the Study of Human Issues.

Sutton, P. 2001. 'The Politics of Suffering: Indigenous Policy in Australia since the 1970s', *Anthropological Forum* 11 (2 November): 125–73.

Thomas, N. 1994. *Colonialism's Culture: Anthropology, Travel and Government*. Cambridge: Polity.

Toohey, J.J. 2004. 'Aboriginal Customary Laws Reference – an Overview'. Background paper no. 5, September. Perth: State Solicitor's Office. Pp. 173–212. URL accessed at http://www.lrc.justice.wa.gov.au/2publications/reports/ACL/BP/BP-05.pdf.

Townsend, K. 1995. 'National Conference on Sexual Assault and the Law', Project for Legal Action against Sexual Assault', in M. Heenan (ed.) *Legalising Justice for All Women: National Conference on Sexual Assault and the Law*. Conference proceedings, 28–30 November, Melbourne: PLAASA. Pp.1–15.

Warner, W.L. 1937. *A Black Civilisation. A Study of an Australian Tribe*. New York: Harper.

Watson, I. 1998. 'Naked Peoples: Rules and Regulations', *Law/Text/Culture* 4 (1): 1–17.

Williams, N. 1986. *Two Laws: Managing Disputes in a Contemporary Aboriginal Community*. Canberra: Australian Institute of Aboriginal Studies.

————. 2001. 'Overview of Customary Law', Garma Festival Ngaarra Legal Forum, Thursday, 23 August, Session 4 – Workshops – The Interaction of Criminal Justice and Customary Law. URL accessed at http://www.garma.telstra.com/pdfs/ngaarra/Ngaarra_session04.pdf#search=%22Garma%20Thursday%20August%2023%2C%20Session%204%20%22

CHAPTER 12

MANAGING SEXUAL ADVANCES
IN VANUATU

Ingvill Kristiansen

This chapter considers disparities in sexual and erotic understandings and encounters between the fieldworker and those with whom she works. Few anthropologists have written about sexual transgression in the field, and published material on such issues is scant, offering only limited insight into how sexual assault and reactions to it are culturally shaped and understood when they involve the fieldworker. Nor has much been written in anthropology about the relationship between fieldwork, sex, identity and erotic subjectivism (though for an important exception see Kulick and Willson 1995). During fieldwork on Tanna (1998–99), I received a number of hazardous lessons about Tannese male and female attitudes towards gender and sexuality and I begin with an example that is typical of the kind of situation in which such attitudes were made clear to me.

One day, while walking alone along a main road, I became aware of a young man following briskly behind. As he overtook me, he greeted me politely with the west Tannese vernacular 'Raud?' ('Good?'), and engaged me in conversation. We spoke in Bislama (the pidgin English of Vanuatu). We were both heading in the same direction, to a menuk ceremony, when pigs given in the much larger *nekowiar* ceremony are reciprocated.[1] The young man was friendly and asked me the usual questions about who I was and what I was doing on Tanna. We came to a small path which the young man said was a short cut. I felt I should be cautious, but since it was daylight and I had a large umbrella for defence if necessary, I decided that it was probably safe enough. Suddenly the man stopped and asked me if I wanted to have sex with him, using the Bislama phrase *'Bae yumi fak?'* ('Shall we fuck?'). I carefully rejected his request, anxious not to insult him. He accepted my negative reply, although not without argument. On returning to the main road, he asked why I did not just say 'Yes'. I replied that I already had a boyfriend. The young man argued that I should never refuse such a request. He argued that I should have accepted his proposal simply because he had asked, implying that women are automatically expected to accept male requests for sex. Luckily we were able to discuss the issue in a calm and joking manner, and we continued walking, while I gradually managed to change the topic and defuse the tension between us.

When we came to another short cut, I refused to take it, anxious that the young man might not respect my unwillingness to have sex with him. There was also a chance that, if I agreed to take this second short cut, he would misinterpret it as accepting his sexual advances. There was no doubt that he understood my reasons for wishing to remain on the main road. Nevertheless, it was with relief that I accepted a lift from a pickup truck that drew alongside moments later. The occupants were also going to the ceremony. It was, however, embarrassingly obvious to me that they thought they knew what a young man and woman had been doing alone together. The young men in the pickup laughed, smiled and nodded at the young man, who did nothing to clarify their misconception.

Upon arriving back that evening in Ianupun, a pseudonym for the village in which I was based, I told some friends what had happened. Some said that I had been lucky that the young man had not forced me to have sex him. When I mentioned his name, one of the villagers said that he was distantly related to him, and that he knew that he was 'good', meaning that he would accept a woman's refusal to have sex with him. These responses made me realise that I had not understood the seriousness of my decision to go to the ceremony alone. It was evident from the villagers' reactions that my experience was less a consequence of my being a foreigner, and had more to do with being in a particular place. It was harder to understand why the villagers had not warned me about going to the ceremony unaccompanied when they knew the risks for women travelling alone. Part of the aim of this chapter is to explain their reticence in this regard.

This example highlights three important aspects to understanding sexual encounters on Tanna: what I refer to as 'positioning', 'degrees of persuasion' and the local understanding of the 'giving of physical hurt', which is how I define 'violence' (see Kristiansen 2007). 'Positioning' has to do with being (made) accessible and male opportunism. As my fieldwork on Tanna progressed, I realised that the problems which I sometimes had with men were directly related to how I ended up in situations where it was safe for men to ask me for sex, and where the chance of getting help was limited were my refusal to be ignored. The remainder of this chapter focuses mainly on the importance of positioning in understanding sexual transgression on Tanna.

To some extent these situations arose because of the fieldworker's position 'in between' the norms of 'two cultures'. As others have pointed out, a fieldworker is often at the mercy of the people around her, as she is forced to negotiate her identities and her values (see Briggs 1970; Blackwood 1995). In my case, this 'in-betweenness' resulted not only in occasional requests for sex but in attempted rape. My aim here is not to impugn the morality of Tannese men, or to elicit the reader's sympathy, but rather to explore how and why I learned about Tannese sexual etiquette and how this conflicted or overlapped with my own views on proper sexual behaviour derived from my upbringing in Norway.[2] The case also raises an ethical dilemma in relation to sexual harassment in the field. As well as having to deal with the physical and psychological affects of such harassment, the anthropologist must also decide how to react, and assess the implications which any reaction may have for fieldwork. The ethical guidelines of anthropological fieldwork are of little help when confronted with the decision of how to deal with sexual harassment or whether to report an attempted rape to the police. Reporting the incident to the police would have serious consequences for both the anthropologist and the perpetrator, as well as for the perpetrator's family, and could well destroy any chances of continuing the fieldwork.

Throughout fieldwork, the extent to which I had to follow the rules of conduct appropriate to an unmarried Tannese woman varied according to different settings, and I continually had to negotiate the terms of my behaviour. At first I was expected to become involved in female activities such as cooking, carrying firewood and weeding, and was given a *kastom* name. My different statuses as a young, unmarried woman, an anthropologist and a student from Europe were made relevant in different contexts, at different times and with different people.

Young, unmarried men initially kept me at a respectful distance, but later began to address me as 'tawi' (Bislama for 'affine'), in a playful, flirtatious way.

Altork (1995) has pointed out the difficulty of balancing the rational teachings of how to collect data with the messy business of fieldwork, which, as Hastrup puts it, 'implies that the well-established opposition between subject and object dissolves' (1990: 46). The result is that one is often left bewildered and disoriented. In hindsight, my fieldwork clearly mapped the passage from childhood to female adulthood in terms of the knowledge I slowly acquired about how to relate to Tannese men, and, given the many mistakes I made in this regard, I now share similar concerns about returning to the field to those expressed by Morton (1995) following her Tongan fieldwork and eventual divorce from a Tongan man. Fieldwork can be dangerous, perhaps especially for female anthropologists, as Hastrup (1990: 46) notes when she admitted to experiencing loneliness, sexual assaults and loss of identity.

Like Hastrup (1989), I wanted to retain some of my usual independence while on fieldwork, and during the first six months I had my own bamboo house built. When a Tannese girl moves to another house before she marries, she is expected to share it with other young women whose presence deters young men from visiting at night, a precaution I endeavoured to follow. Hastrup (1989), by contrast, was perceived as being sexually available because of her housing arrangements, which led to men breaking into her apartment one night. Because I was unmarried, some villagers suspected that I had come to Tanna in search of a husband, and my initial Tannese contact went as far as to 'set me up' with one young villager, whom I refer to here as Bruce. He even told Bruce that he would have married me himself had he not already been married. In the end, Bruce and I did form a relationship which lasted almost five years, beyond the fieldwork itself, thereby no doubt confirming people's suspicions. My initial Tannese contact also told me that when I first arrived he had introduced me to the villagers as his wife, although I believe that he did so in a joking manner, since he never approached me sexually and I remained a close friend of his wife throughout. When I was asked for sex by men, I was told that this had nothing to do with my appearance or personality, was because I was 'different' and, according to Tannese women (and some men), most men ask for sex if they think they can get away with it.

On Tanna, married men and women should not talk to members of the opposite sex without a legitimate reason. This may lead to jealousy and accusations of adulterous behaviour, as I learned first-hand following a night of *kava* drinking with some male villagers at a bar in the nearby town of Lenakel. A man from another village had engaged me in conversation, and since there were other people present I had thought nothing of the event until a villager rebuked me the next day, saying that the man's wife had heard of the encounter and was very angry with me, suspecting her husband of infidelity. I continued to talk to men as well as women throughout my fieldwork, while gradually learning to be more cautious about insulting jealous wives.

Positioning and opportunism

I turn now to the notions of 'positioning' and 'opportunism' and examine how these are related to sexual attitudes on Tanna. I begin with the story of Kava, in which Kava and Water feature as mythical figures.[3] The myth was related to me by Jonathan, a married man from Ianupun, and refers to the origin of the sexual taboo connected to women and the ceremonial ground (*yimwayim*).[4]

> In the past the men stayed at the *yimwayim*. Before Kava came to the *yimwayim*, Kava stayed at the houses with the women. Kava had a body like a woman. The men decided that they should bring Kava to the *yimwayim*. The men sent a man who went and asked for Kava, but Kava refused, because she was afraid of all the men at the *yimwayim*. Then the men sent Water to ask for Kava. Water said to Kava, 'Now I have come to take you, come and let us go to the *yimwayim*.' Then the men had sex with Kava. Because Kava went to the *yimwayim*, she felt ashamed. She went to the women and said to them, 'Now I am too ashamed to come back to you at the houses. You must stay at the houses and I will stay at the *yimwayim*.' It was Kava and not the men who made the laws that govern the restrictions on women when the men drink kava. After Kava let the men have her body, she brought all the food that the people of Tanna now eat, like manioc, yam, taro and banana. She went and got all this food, and then she told all the men that they should go and plant it. She also told the men to use stones to control the growth of the food. The use of special stones makes sure that all the food is not ready at the same time. Because of the stones, there is a separate

time when each kind of food is ready to eat. After all this,
Kava went and hid her body.

In this story Kava was ashamed because she had agreed to go to
the *yimwayim*, thus giving the men the chance to have sex with
her. She had been coerced into joining the men and, in accepting,
she 'positioned' herself in a situation where the men could take
advantage of her. In the story Kava stops the women from coming
to the *yimwayim* when Kava 'is there', i.e. when the men drink
kava every afternoon. The story could also be taken to show that
Tannese women, like *kava*, have the power to attract men, and
make men dependent on their skills and knowledge for food and
social order. In other Tannese origin myths about making food
and *kava*, women are always described as the agents who provide
men with what they need in order to live a good life (see
Lindstrom 1987; Bonnemaison 1994).

Numerous little episodes throughout fieldwork made me
realise that one's positioning in certain contexts had sexual
undertones. Strathern's (1988) account of how Melanesians
move each other to act is relevant here. In sexual encounters, the
term 'move' encompasses all kinds of actions and intentions from
seduction and persuasion to rape. Once, when sailing between
Vila and Tanna on the rusty old ship Killian, whose deck was
packed with Tannese passengers, many of them asleep or seasick,
the Captain invited me for a chat in his cabin next to the
wheelhouse. While I sat there on a chair talking to him, he tried
to persuade me to use his bed to get some sleep while he worked,
an offer I understood as tantamount to agreeing to sleep with
him, and I politely declined. Late at night, on this rusty
overcrowded ship I was very tired and vulnerable and perhaps
more easily 'moved' than usual. Declining the Captain's offer
meant sleeping on the wheelhouse floor, as the deck was already
full. This was one of my first encounters with the opportunistic
strategies that Tannese may use in an attempt to 'move' people in
the direction they desire.

On another occasion I was chatting to some married men in
the village when one of them, who always seemed to like to put
me in my place, asked me to hold the sheath of a knife I had lent
him, so that he could replace the blade. At the time I saw no
reason to refuse. But as he very slowly replaced the knife in the
sheath, the sexual symbolism became obvious to me, as it already
was to the other men present. I felt awkward and embarrassed,
naively caught again in a situation where I was the butt of male
sexual advance and innuendo.

A young American woman, Mona, who had been visiting another part of Tanna, described to me her experience of Tannese sexual opportunism. Mona was staying with a family in a small village, and, stepping outside one night to smoke, was spotted by the household head, a man much older than her, who immediately asked her for sex. She was shocked by the boldness of the request and by the fact that she had been propositioned so close to the man's family. Like me, Mona had unwittingly made herself sexually available according to Tannese male and female perception.

The few men who asked me for sex did not seem to understand that I found it an offensive question, as had Mona. They also confirmed that they did not ask me because they had any special feelings for me. One man even offered money when I refused. I once asked the men about the attempted rape of a young Australian woman, an incident which they seemed to find amusing. They commented: 'It's not good; one may ask for sex, but it is no good to use force.' They emphasised that rape is bad, but added that they had little understanding of how a woman might feel about such an experience since they themselves were men, other than that they assumed she would feel bruised and angry afterwards. A 'good man' despises those who lower themselves to commit acts of rape, and *kastom* laws demand that if found guilty such men pay a fine to the woman and her family. What the men had found amusing about the story was not the assailant's immoral and criminal intent but his clumsiness.

Discos and *kastom* dances

I was told that if a young woman put herself in situations where she risked being sexually harassed, for instance, by going to a disco or by drinking alcohol in mixed company, she would receive little sympathy if assaulted. This attitude is also found in Papua New Guinea (Banks 2000). As in other cases where somebody was seen to have done something stupid, people would remark: 'That's good, that will teach them.'

Gell (1995) has explained that, for the Umeda and elsewhere in Papua New Guinea, direct sustained eye contact between men and women old enough to be sexually active implies sexual solicitation or complicity. Like the Tannese, Umeda men strive to catch a woman's eye, whether this is at a dance or just walking through the village. While married men and women are thought to attend dances for the music and to chat, young people are thought to be looking for a sexual partner, even though their motives for participating may be varied. Mere presence at a disco is considered morally wrong by some churches on Tanna such as the Assemblies of God.

Two very different types of dancing take place on Tanna; modern-style discos and *kastom* dances held on the *yimwayim*. Both men and women go to see and be seen at discos. Discos are held irregularly, usually on a Friday, and usually on the outskirts of a given village near a main road. They are organised by villagers whose aim is to make some extra money. A permanent disco near Lenakel, where some of the men in Ianupun first met their wives, was shut down after a drunken man died in an accident on his way home. The three discos I attended during fieldwork had some common characteristics. As in Papua New Guinea, all were 'six-to-six' (i.e. from 6 p.m. to 6 a.m.), though how long a disco lasts depends on the number of people who turn up and on the number of fights between drunken men. The entry charge was often half-price for women, at 100 vatu (approximately 50p). Everyday clothes are worn, with women in T-shirts and skirts and the men in T-shirts and shorts. Sometimes local bands perform live, and at other times tapes are played.

Discos are not the only opportunity a boy has to meet a girl from another village, since there are occasionally other inter-village gatherings, such as the *kaor* or *nekowiar* ceremonies.[5] Any such meetings must be clandestine, and, when couples wish to meet (which always implies having sex), arrangements are usually made through a friend. At *kastom* dances, a taboo restricts men and women from touching each other, and, at the women's *napen-napen* dance during the *nekowiar*, when women dress in their finery and paint their faces, women are chaperoned to ensure that the performance goes well and that no man tries to 'steal' them. When attending a *nekowiar*, I was told that there had been one rape and two attempted rapes of women who were in the audience. Two of these incidents had occurred when the women had gone to relieve themselves in the bushes behind the dancing-ground. I was warned by the Ianupun villagers that I was not to go anywhere alone. I had received similar advice when attending a musical performance earlier in my fieldwork, and had naively asked a young man from the village to be my chaperone. When returning from the performance, I realised we were walking in the wrong direction. The young man grabbed me and tried to kiss me. I resisted and, following a short discussion, he released me, accepting my refusal. On another occasion, I planned to attend a disco with some male and female friends from the village. Alerted to possible dangers by earlier experiences such as those described above, I decided to wear overalls rather than a dress or a skirt, and to carry a personal alarm. While we were walking along the road, my friends disappeared in pairs, without warning, leaving me alone in total darkness with one young man who suddenly pushed me to the ground and tried to remove my clothes. While I struggled with him and demanded he stop, he would not listen and only the sound of the alarm prevented him from going further. I got up and swore at the young man who seemed to have come to his senses again, saying, 'Sorry, sorry.' I caught up with one of the other young women in the group and we walked back to the village together.

I decided to tell my closest friends in the village that somebody had attempted to assault me, aware that this meant that the whole village would soon know about it. I needed to talk to somebody about what had happened in order to understand my own feelings. Barely containing my anger, I told my Tannese female friends, naively expecting them to be outraged. Instead, some laughed and joked, suggesting that perhaps I had not been entirely unwilling since I had wanted to go to the disco, though no one had criticised me for going at the time. Others expressed concern at the attack, perhaps in a gesture of support to calm me down, though most seemed to agree that the attacker had been wrong. However, I had not anticipated some of the laughs and shrugs that greeted my account, even from my closest friends. I had also not anticipated how my own feelings about the incident would dissipate when faced with such reactions. Given the very real risks for women who attend discos, I now realise that I had a lucky escape.

The anthropologist writing under the pseudonym of Moreno (1995) was not so lucky. Like me, she seems to have thought that men would respect her wishes and accept a refusal to have sex. The nature of her fieldwork also meant she positioned herself so that she seemed available to her male informants. The fieldworker's dependency on good relations with 'the locals' leaves her (or him) in a vulnerable position which automatically fosters a much greater tolerance towards others' behaviour. Considering that sexual harassment is a potential risk of fieldwork, it is easier to understand why some female fieldworkers like myself develop an intimate relationship with a local male friend who is attractive and morally 'good' (see Gearing 1995; Morton 1995). In hindsight I realise that developing a relationship with Bruce helped me to restore belief in the decency and good morals of Tannese men, and made me less afraid of being assaulted.

Like roads outside the village, discos are considered particularly dangerous for women. Most of those who go to discos know the hazards, and how to work around them. Lisa, a young woman from the village, told me how she and two friends had been on their way home from a disco when they were chased by some boys. She said that they had been lucky and had escaped, and that she would never go to a disco again. If something had happened on that occasion, she and her friends would have been particularly shamed because they belonged to one of the churches in the area that disapproved of discos.

Two other young women from Ianupun told me how they had gone to a dance, and had passed the time watching young couples enter and leave the disco to have sex in the bushes nearby. They also laughed at how, the next day, they could see where the long grass had been flattened by the activities of the night before. When I asked an older woman about the dance, she suggested that the two girls knew what was going on because they themselves had participated. Once, when visiting Tannese friends in Vila, I went to a second-hand shop and bought some clothes. When I complained about my shrinking funds, the jovial young woman behind the counter smiled and remarked: 'Why don't you join me and we'll go to a disco tonight and make some money?' I was shocked, but did not take offence at the invitation. I believe that she was simply pointing out a way of making quick money. These attitudes are not just part of contemporary Tannese life; they reflect a history of modes of sexual encounter and enticement.

Gender and sexual attitudes, past and present

Captain Cook and his company were the first Europeans known to have visited Tanna. During a week's stay in 1774, Cook observed how on several occasions Tannese men had attempted to 'entice' some of his men into the bush, especially those who carried Forster's plant bag (Cook 1777: 66).[6] (Carrying anything except weapons, especially in those days, was exclusively a female task.) Cook wondered whether the Tannese had 'an unnatural passion', until he realised that his men were performing tasks that the Tannese associate with women. Tannese men had thus mistaken the carriers for women. Cook noted the ease with which wrong conclusions may be drawn of such people (and perhaps also by them), of whose language and manner they knew so little. 'Had it not been for this discovery, I make no doubt that these people would have been charged with this vile custom' (Cook 1777: 67).

Tannese men are understood by Tannese themselves to 'need sex', an attitude which, in the past, was manifest in the service provided by the *iohnanen*, the name given to a girl or young woman who provided sexual favours for men whose wives were pregnant, breastfeeding or menstruating, and who often provided young men with their first experience of sex. This practice no longer exists, and in some marriages the period of sexual abstinence in relation to pregnancy and after childbirth has been reduced.

It is difficult to determine exactly what people today think of the institution of *iohnanen*. Two 'big women' (*pranasul*) I asked about the practice burst into shy giggles as soon as I mentioned it, and would only say that this was the way it used to be, adding that today in the eyes of the Church it is morally wrong. They told me that in the past the period of sexual abstinence following delivery lasted for two or three years, and that when this was observed babies became ill less frequently than they do today. Spouses slept separately, but carried out their daily chores as usual. Although these two women told me that there should be no sex as long as the child was breastfed, there were cases in which mothers became pregnant before a baby was weaned. Other villagers confirmed this, saying that they knew of many couples in Ianupun who have sex when breastfeeding, despite the taboo.

Based on her own observations in the nineteenth century, the missionary Agnes Watt records that: 'Polygamy is prevalent. I know of no case of five wives; but some have four, three or two. One is a rare exception. Such crimes as adultery... are very frequent' (Watt 1896). Lindstrom (1981: 123–24) explains that the introduction of Christianity led to the demise of polygamy, just as it did for the *iohnanen*:

> Although Tannese once accepted polygyny as a legitimate form of marriage, Christian ideology during the present century has established the rule of monogamy ... The necessity of returning ... an equal number of sisters or daughters in exchange must have worked to keep down the number of polygynists and the number of women each one of these married ... The extent and significance of traditional polygyny, however, are unclear.

Watt describes an adulterous man whom the Tannese said had acquired a 'hot temper' after a long jail sentence in Fiji for murder. The man had been pursuing a woman who lived with Watt at the time. The woman declined his advances, refusing to have sex with him on the grounds that she was a good Christian, at which point the man 'ran for a club and struck her two severe blows on the forehead, breaking her skull, and ran off leaving her for dead' (Watt 1896: 160). During fieldwork, I was told of one case where a furious husband grabbed his bush knife and in one movement severed his wife's forehead and killed her. The point of the story was to stress to me how quickly some Tannese men incline to anger when their desires are frustrated. From my visits in Vila, the capital of Vanuatu, I learned that there Tannese men have a reputation for being notoriously hot-tempered.

The discussion above does not give an impression of leniency towards adultery in the past. In the case cited by Watt, the chief (*ieremera*) had wanted the perpetrator punished, even if it meant war, though Watt does not explain whether this was because of the injury he caused the woman or because he had insulted the husband. According to Humphreys (1926), long before the end of the nineteenth century adultery was not punished by the village *ieremera*. However, a man who had been wronged was allowed to fight his wife's accomplice using clubs (Humphreys 1926: 44). If adultery is less tolerated on Tanna today, this may in part be a result of the missionary influence that led to the end of the *iohnanen*.

Rape and sexual transgression on Tanna and beyond

From the examples outlined here, it may seem that Tannese men have an opportunistic view of sex. All the men I talked to agreed that it is acceptable to ask a woman for sex if the situation allows it. I shall also show that, when refused sex, some men today still resort to physical force as they did in the past. Such behaviour is hardly unique to Tanna or Melanesia. But what, to a 'Westerner', is striking about rape and attempted rape on Tanna is that it is a woman's physical injuries and her anger that are emphasised afterwards, rather than the psychological trauma that is commonly associated with sexual assaults in the West.

I learned about attitudes towards male and female sexuality through my own encounters, by hearing stories about rape, jealousy and adultery told mostly by married middle-aged men and women, and by attending several meetings in Ianupun that aimed to solve disputes between spouses over accusations of adultery and, on one occasion, a meeting dealing with an accusation of attempted rape. Women rarely initiated conversations with me about sex, though men sometimes did in a joking manner. Overall I found it a difficult topic to try to talk about with both women and men. There was also very little opportunity to discuss women's views and experiences of rape (but see below), and I worried that by raising such issues I would embarrass them and jeopardise our friendship. I generally had to learn to 'go with the flow' on these matters, and wait until another person raised the topic before I could address it.

For young unmarried men, talking to me about sex seemed a way of flirting, bragging and confirming their masculinity. One man volunteered a story of how he had attempted to abduct a young woman from a dance with the intent of forcing her to have sex with him. The abduction was mentioned only in passing, as the point of his story was to describe their car accident on their way back. To the young man the abduction seemed incidental. I did not get a chance to talk to the young woman herself, and so cannot confirm whether she had been taken against her will. The responses of my village friends to my own experiences offered a serendipitous insight into sexual transgression and attitudes that I would not otherwise have been able to obtain. When discussing these incidents with married and unmarried women, they sometimes told me about other similar incidents, almost always concerning a woman other than themselves. One was about how a gang of men repeatedly tried to separate a young woman from her mother and grandmother as they walked along the road together with the intention of raping her. I was also told how one young man from Ianupun had fled the capital by jumping on board a ship bound for Tanna after a woman had reported him to the police for having raped her.

Lindstrom (1987) describes Tannese women as having no say in their participation in sexual activities. He understands Tannese female sexuality as passive and subject to male control. He further reasons that in cases of (sexual) abuse the female is in no way blamed because, 'Women cannot give it; men can only take it. Thus, men expect women, as totally mastered beings, to follow any male pulling them off into some bush arbor' (1987: 109). This view of female sexuality differs from that which I recorded nearly twenty years later. My material suggests that Tannese do recognise the notion of consent in relation to sexual activities. On Tanna consent is communicated non-verbally through positioning, so that it makes little sense to a Tannese to say 'No' if one has already signalled one's willingness. Thus, Tannese women who are serious about not wanting this kind of attention from men simply avoid situations in which they may be propositioned. Young women are careful where they go, with whom and when. Some wear bicycle shorts under skirts or dresses for 'safety', to limit the risk of being raped if, for example, they want to go to a disco only to dance and look at other people.

On Tanna, as elsewhere in Melanesia, the Bislama term *'fos'* ('force') encompasses almost all forms of sexual activity except that between spouses. Since marriage is understood to imply consent, it is impossible on Tanna for a man to rape his wife. *'Fos'* is used to describe cases where it is assumed that the woman had no intention of having sex. This would include cases of seduction, persuasion, attempted rape, rape or even adultery. When a woman signals availability through positioning, the question of consent becomes superfluous, because to a Tannese she has already shown her intent. However, if a woman who has not signalled her consent through her positioning is raped, this is strongly condemned by the Tannese. The stories collected by Lindstrom and Gwero (1998) from ni-Vanuatu men about sexual encounters between ni-Vanuatu women and American soldiers stationed in Vanuatu during the Second World War show a lack of clarity on the issue of consent versus forced sexual intercourse.

According to Strathern (1975: 35, cited in Banks 2000: 94), Melanesians are less concerned with the issue of consent than with the 'correctness of the social relationship between the couple'. This was also the case on Tanna, where I was told that forcible sex between a man and his daughter and between a young man and his classificatory sister were not wrong because of the force that was used, but because the protagonists were kin. Strathern (1975: 37, cited in Banks 2000: 94) also points out that in Melanesia 'no moral or physical damage is held to result from the simple act of intercourse even if the act is done against their will (except in special circumstances, e.g. the woman is sexually immature)'.

Banks (2000: 100) refers to three main types of rape on the basis of her research in Papua New Guinea: rape 'as punishment against the victim or others; rape as a response to spurning; and opportunistic rape'. On Tanna, I recorded only incidents of opportunistic rape.

Helliwell (2000) argues that the Gerai of Indonesia do not believe that rape is possible, at least not in the sense of inflicting hurt upon someone. As one Gerai woman explained: 'it's only a penis … How can a penis hurt anyone?' Helliwell (2000) uses this understanding to challenge the notion that rape is universal, and suggests that the reason Western feminists universalise rape is because 'the intermeshing of sexuality and personal identity in contemporary Western societies … imbues the practice of rape with particular horror for most victims from those societies, since there it involves a violation of personhood itself' (Helliwell 2000: 791–92). Rape, she continues, 'is not everywhere experienced by women victims in the deeply traumatic terms taken for granted by most western feminist writers on the topic' (Helliwell 2000: 792; see also Day 1994). Feminist writers like Sanday (1981a, b), Anderson (1997) and Dobash et al. (2000) have linked rape to a general tendency of male violence against women, whereby 'violence [is] used to override a woman's sexual choices, rendering her completely degraded and powerless even over her own body' (Archer 1994: 16).

In the Gerai case 'rape' does not seem to exist because Gerai believe that a woman cannot be forced to have sexual intercourse. On Tanna, and elsewhere in Melanesia, a different logic prevails, one based on a perceived lack of harm associated with the sexual act. On Tanna, some men believe that *'fos'* is allowed if the man desires sex, even if the woman refuses, for by being in a situation of no witnesses, where the man is able to ask her, she has already signalled her availability. One young, unmarried *'strong head'* (Bislama for a young person who is obstinate, stubborn and not always law-abiding) whom others had accused of several rapes, told me: *'Samting blong woman hemi blong man'* (i.e. 'What is the woman's belongs to the man'). According to state law in Vanuatu, which is modelled on the British and French legal system, rape is a serious offence which should be reported to and dealt with by the police. However, in cases where local views do not correspond with state law, the former take precedence and disputes are settled according to *kastom*.

Conclusion

I have tried to show how female positioning may encourage men to seek opportunistic sexual encounters. A male right to ask for sex and the expectation that women will accept circumscribe these encounters. Since the conditions under which women may be asked are seen to imply intent and thus consent, men do not perceive the use of *'fos'* as illegitimate in this context. In fact, rather than being transgressive for Tannese, women endorse illicit sexual encounters if they place themselves in potentially precarious positions such as being seen alone, flirting at a disco or allowing a man to accompany them on a deserted track, even if they refuse a man's sexual advances. Thus, the concept of *'fos'* blurs the boundaries between rape and sex, as men's understanding of a woman's refusal is not a sufficient barrier to the male desire for sex. This leads to women's experiences of forcible and consensual sex as being broadly similar. It thus makes sense for Tannese not to view *'fos'* negatively, as something that affects a woman psychologically.

This blurring of boundaries is brought sharply into focus in the cross-cultural context between the fieldworker's rules of sexual negotiation and Tannese male expectations. Male sexual expectations of non-Tannese women are transgressive for the fieldworker. The right to negotiate sex as well as notions of consent, positioning and opportunism, conflicts with the fieldworker's need to participate in cultural activities. The method of participant observation thus places the female fieldworker in a potentially ambiguous and ambivalent position with regard to sexual availability. Fieldwork entails constant consideration of what is safe and unsafe to do. The different variables, such as the problem of knowing whose advice to listen to, the particular Tannese understanding of sexuality and the false assumption that any sexual advances could be averted simply through refusal, make it almost impossible for a female anthropologist not to experience incidents of sexual transgression during fieldwork on Tanna. Consequently, continual reflection upon the possibilities and potential impacts of sexual transgression is necessary whilst negotiating social relationships between female researchers and male informants in the field.

Notes
1. The *nekowiar* ceremony is the largest on Tanna, and many villages take part. The complex process of negotiating the quantity of pigs and *kava* to be exchanged and rehearsing the songs and dances can last a year, and culminates in the grand finale of the three-day *nekowiar* itself. Andrew, a man of *kastom*, explained to me that the group of villages that first gives pigs and *kava* are seen as 'male', while the receiving groups are seen as 'female'. He compared the initial stages of negotiation to a wife who asks something of her husband, and nags him until he finally agrees (see Kristiansen 2007). The *nekowiar* symbolises peace and erases all past disputes between the villages.
2. My account may risk distorting the reader's perception of everyday life on Tanna and a few words are needed to restore the balance. Women do not live in constant fear of rape on Tanna. They grow up learning about the relationship between positioning and sexuality, and are careful to avoid situations that might lead to unwanted sexual encounters. Had I not attended discos or *kastom* dances, I would have learned little about sexual transgression and the contexts in which it is likely to occur.
3. *Kava* is the name of the root *Piper methysticum*, which is ground and mixed with water and drunk every day at dusk by most adult men.

4. *Yimwayim* is the vernacular for the area where all ceremonies are held, and where men meet and drink *kava*. Every Tannese village has one or more *yimwayims* depending on the size of the settlement.
5. *Kaor* is the vernacular for male circumcision, which usually takes place when a boy is between three and ten years old.
6. The naturalist, Forster, collected plants on Cook's second journey, which took place between 1772 and 1775.

References

Altork, K. 1995. 'Walking the Fire Line: the Erotic Dimension of the Fieldwork Experience', in D. Kulick and M. Willson (eds) *Taboo: Sex, Identity and Erotic Subjectivity in Anthropological Fieldwork*. London: Routledge, pp. 107–39.

Anderson, K.L. 1997. 'Gender, Status and Domestic Violence: an Integration of Feminist and Family Violence Approaches', *Journal of Marriage and the Family* 59 (3): 655–69.

Archer, J. 1994. 'Power and Male Violence', in J. Archer (ed.) *Male Violence*. London: Routledge, pp. 310–31.

Banks, C. 2000. 'Contextualising Sexual Violence: Rape and Carnal Knowledge in Papua New Guinea', in S. Dinnen and A. Ley (eds) *Reflections on Violence in Melanesia*. Canberra: Asia Pacific Press, pp. 83–104.

Blackwood, E. 1995. 'Falling in Love with An-Other Lesbian: Reflections on Identity in Fieldwork', in D. Kulick and M. Willson (eds) *Taboo: Sex, Identity and Erotic Subjectivity in Anthropological Fieldwork*. London: Routledge, pp. 51–75.

Bonnemaison, J. 1994. *The Tree and the Canoe: History and Ethnogeography of Tanna*. Honolulu: University of Hawaii Press.

Briggs, J.L. 1970. 'Kapluna Daughter', in P. Golde (ed.) *Women in the Field. Anthropological Experiences*. Chicago: Adeline Publishing, pp. 19–44.

Cook, J. 1777. 'An Intercourse Established with the Natives: Some Account of the Island, and a Variety of Incidents that Happened during Our Stay at it', in *A Voyage towards the South Pole and Round the World*. London: W. Strahan and T. Cadell, pp. 53–74.

Day, S. 1994. 'What Counts as Rape? Physical Assault and Broken Contracts: Contrasting Views of Rape among London Sex Workers', in P. Harvey and P. Gow (eds) *Sex and Violence: Issues in Representation and Experience,* London: Routledge.

Dobash, R.P., R.E. Dobash, M. Wilson and M. Daly. 2000. 'The Myth of Sexual Symmetry in Marital Violence', in M.S. Kimmel and A.Aronson (eds) *The Gendered Society Reader.* Oxford: Oxford University Press, pp.410–26.

Gearing, J. 1995. 'Fear and Loving in the West Indies. Research from the Heart (as well as the Head)', in D. Kulick and M. Willson (eds) *Taboo: Sex, Identity and Erotic Subjectivity in Anthropological Fieldwork*. London: Routledge, pp. 186–218.

Gell, A. 1995. 'The Language of the Forest', in E. Hirsch and M. O'Hanlon (eds) *The Anthropology of Landscape: Perspectives on Place and Space*. Oxford: Clarendon Press, pp. 232–54.

Hastrup, K. 1989. 'Den tredie person. Køn og tid i det islandske landskab', in K. Hastrup and K. Ramløv (eds) *Feltarbejde. Opplevelse og metode i etnografien*. Denmark: Akademisk forlag, pp. 199–213.

————. 1990. 'The Ethnographic Present: a Reinvention', *Cultural Anthropology* 5 (1): 45–61.

Helliwell, C. 2000. '"It's only a penis": Rape, Feminism and Difference', *Signs* 25 (3): 789–816.

Humphreys, C.B. 1926. *The Southern New Hebrides: an Ethnological Record*. Cambridge: Cambridge University Press.

Kristiansen I. 2007. 'Gender and Conflict: The Relationship between Women and Men on Tanna'. Harstad: Harstad University College.

Kulick, D. and M. Willson. (eds) 1995. *Taboo: Sex, Identity and Erotic Subjectivity in Anthropological Fieldwork*. London: Routledge.

Lindstrom, L. 1981. 'Achieving Wisdom: Knowledge and Politics on Tanna (Vanuatu)'. Doctoral dissertation, University of California, Berkeley.

Lindstrom, L. 1987. 'Drunkenness and Gender on Tanna, Vanuatu', in L. Lindstrom (ed.) *Drugs in Western Pacific Societies: Relations of Substance*. Association for Social Anthropology in Oceania Monograph No.11. Lanham, MD: University Press of America, pp. 99–119.

Lindstrom, L. and J. Gwero. (eds) 1998. *Big wok: Storian blong Wol Wo Tu long Vanuatu*. Suva: Institute of Pacific Studies. University of the South Pacific.

Moreno, E. 1995. 'Rape in the Field. Reflections from a Survivor', in D. Kulick and M. Willson (eds) *Taboo: Sex, Identity and Erotic Subjectivity in Anthropological Fieldwork*. London: Routledge, pp. 219–50.

Morton, H. 1995. 'My "chastity belt". Avoiding Seduction in Tonga', in D. Kulick and M. Willson (eds) *Taboo: Sex, Identity and Erotic Subjectivity in Anthropological Fieldwork*. London: Routledge, pp. 168–85.

Sanday, P.R. 1981a. 'The Socio-Cultural Context of Rape: a Cross-Cultural Study', *Journal of Social Issues* 37 (4): 5–27.

————. 1981b. *Female Power and Male Dominance. On the Origins of Sexual Inequality*. Cambridge: Cambridge University Press.

Strathern, M. 1975. *Report on Questionnaire Relating to Sexual Offences as Defined in the Criminal Code*. Report for the Department of Law. Boroko: New Guinea Research Unit.

————. 1988. *The Gender of the Gift*. Berkeley: University of California Press.

Watt A.C.P. 1896. *Twenty Five Years' Mission Life on Tanna, New Hebrides*. London: Houlston and Sons.

NOTES ON CONTRIBUTORS

Kalissa Alexeyeff is a research fellow at the University of Melbourne Department of Anthropology, seconded from her position as Lecturer in the Gender Studies Programme. She has a doctorate from the Australian National University, with a PhD thesis entitled 'Dancing from the Heart: Gender, Movement and Sociality in the Cook Islands'. Her research interests include gender, sexuality, dance, expressive culture, globalisation and development.

Monika Baer, PhD, is Assistant Professor of Ethnology and Cultural Anthropology, Wrocław University, Wrocław, Poland. Her research interests include the anthropology of gender/sexuality, the anthropology of post-socialism and the anthropology of knowledge. She published a book entitled *Women's Spaces: Class, Gender and the Club. An Anthropological Study of the Transitional Process in Poland* (Wydawnictwo Uniwersytetu Wrocławskiego, Wrocław, 2003) and is co-editor of two collections, *Spaces of Women's Cultures in Sex/Gender Research* (*Obszary kultur kobiecych w badaniach płci/rodzaju*, Wydawnictwo Fundacji Humaniora, Poznań, 2003) and *From a Different Perspective. Queer Studies in Poland* (*Z odmiennej perspektywy. Studia Queer w Polsce*) (Oficyna Wydawnicza Arboretum, Wrocław, 2007).

Rebecca Cassidy is Senior Lecturer in the Anthropology Department, Goldsmiths, University of London. Her research interests include gender, class and heredity, human–animal relationships and gambling. Her first book, *Sport of Kings: Kinship, Gender and Thoroughbred Breeding in Newmarket*, was published by Cambridge University Press in 2002. A second book based on fieldwork in Kentucky, *Horse People: Thoroughbred Culture in Lexington and Newmarket*, was published by Johns Hopkins

University Press in 2007. She is currently conducting research in betting shops in south-east London.

Suzanne Clisby is Lecturer in Gender Studies at the University of Hull. Her primary research interest is in the gendered analyses of development issues and she has extensive field experience in Latin America and Britain. Among her most recent publications are 'Both "One" and "Other": Environmental Cosmopolitanism and the Politics in Costa Rica' (with Mark Johnson, 2008), 'Popular Participation in Bolivia: Gender Mainstreaming or Just More Male-Streaming?' (2005), and a number of consultancy reports, including *Living on the Edge: Sexual Behaviour and Young Parenthood in Rural and Seaside Areas* (with B. Bell et al., 2004) and *Beyond the Bus Shelter: Young Women's Choices and Challenges in Rural Areas* (with R. Alsop et al., 2002).

Hastings Donnan is Professor of Social Anthropology at the Queen's University of Belfast and a Member of the Royal Irish Academy. He has published widely on issues of border crossing, including *Borders: Frontiers of Identity, Nation and State* (with T.M. Wilson, Berg, 1999) and *Border Identities* (with T.M. Wilson, Cambridge University Press, 1998). He is currently working with Fiona Magowan on an ESRC-funded project that explores the relationship between the senses and risk as people walk and drive the streets of Belfast.

Laurent Gaissad obtained his PhD in sociology and social sciences from the University of Toulouse le Mirail, France, in 2006, and presently holds a two-year postdoctoral fellowship at the Fonds de la Recherche Scientifique (FNRS/Université Libre de Bruxelles, Belgium) in a comparative history research programme on 'Norms, Gender and Sexuality' (nineteenth to twentieth century). His surveys on sex in public space (men-to-men sex and sex work) have identified gaps between identities and practices and generated his current research interest in the dialectics of exposure/secrecy in urban and rural contexts. He has published on these topics in social anthropology, public health, urban history and geography. Formerly a teaching assistant in sociology and anthropology in Toulouse, he is also a member of the CIRUS (urban sociology) and FRAMESPA (Mediterranean history) local CNRS research units.

Ann-Karina Henriksen is an anthropologist from the University of Copenhagen. She has conducted fieldwork on young women and sexuality in South Africa and is currently working on a project for girls at risk in the municipality of Copenhagen, Denmark.

Mark Johnson has research interests in gender/sexuality, environment, landscape and material culture, movement and transnationalism. Publications include *Beauty and Power* (1997, Berg), 'Critical Regionalities and the Study of Gender and Sexual Diversity in East and South East Asia' (2000, *Culture, Health and Sexuality*) and 'Living Like Men, Loving Like Women: *Tombois* in the Southern Philippines' (2005, in A. Shaw and S. Ardener, *Changing Sex and Bending Gender*). Current research includes projects on the social relations of environmentalism in Costa Rica (with Suzanne Clisby), and the place of religion in the experiences of Filipino migrant workers in the Middle East (with Pnina Werbner and others) as well as ongoing work in queer anthropology.

Ingvill Kristiansen has a PhD in Social Anthropology from the Queen's University of Belfast. She is a Lecturer in the Department of Child Welfare Work at the Institute of Health and Social Work at Harstad University College in northern Norway. Her doctoral thesis, published by Harstad University College (2007), addresses issues of violence and gender on Tanna, Vanuatu. Her research interests include gender, violence, non-verbal communication and trauma.

Marie Rosenkrantz Lindegaard is an anthropologist from the University of Copenhagen. She has carried out fieldwork in South Africa on the following themes: living with violence as a part of everyday life; strategies of safety among youth; practices of masculinity; intersubjectivity and perpetrators; youth as a risk and at risk. She is currently working on her PhD dissertation on youth, violence and perpetrators in South Africa at the University of Amsterdam. She is also affiliated with the Leiden University Medical Centre.

Fiona Magowan is Senior Lecturer in Social Anthropology at Queen's University, Belfast. She is Chair of the Anthropological Association of Ireland and Associate Editor of the *Irish Journal of Anthropology*. Her book *Melodies of Mourning: Music and Emotion in Northern Australia* (2007) examines the role of the environment in Australian Aboriginal ritual music and Christian song and sentiment. Among her other publications are two co-edited books

Landscapes of Indigenous Performance: Music and Dance of the Torres Strait and Arnhem Land (Aboriginal Studies Press, 2005) and *Telling Stories: Indigenous Life Narratives, Memory and History: Aotearoa/New Zealand and Australia* (Allen and Unwin, 2001).

Heather Montgomery is Senior Lecturer in Childhood Studies at the Open University. She completed a PhD at Cambridge in Social Anthropology, focusing on the issue of child prostitution in Thailand, which she published in a monograph called *Modern Babylon: Prostituting Children in Thailand* (Berghahn, 2001). She also writes more generally on anthropology and childhood and her book entitled *An Introduction to Childhood: Anthropological Perspectives on Children's Lives*, which will be published by Blackwell in 2008.

Rosellen Roche received her PhD in Anthropology from the University of Cambridge in 2004 and is Lecturer in Social Anthropology in the School of History and Anthropology at Queen's University Belfast. She is currently the Head of Project for 'Facts, Fears and Feelings: the Impact and Role of Sectarianism in Everyday Life', funded by the Special European Union Programmes Body for Peace and Reconciliation, which is administered by the Northern Ireland Community Relations Council. Rosellen also acts as an adviser in the area of 'Young People' for Northern Ireland's comprehensive anti-sectarian legislation, *A Shared Future*.

INDEX